FACTFILE

SCOTLAND

The Printer's Devil

additional research by Brian Glancey

HarperCollins*Publishers*

HarperCollins Publishers
Westerhill Rd, Bishopbriggs, Glasgow G64 2QT

www.**fire**and**water**.com

First published 2000

Reprint 10 9 8 7 6 5 4 3 2 1 0

© The Printer's Devil 2000

ISBN 0 00 472499 2

A catalogue record for this book is available from The British Library

Printed in Great Britain by
Caledonian International Book Manufacturing Ltd, Glasgow

CONTENTS

ACKNOWLEDGMENTS

THE LAND AND THE PEOPLE

The Land   9
  Physical Characteristics   9
  Islands   9
  Rivers and Lochs   10
  Mountains   10
  Earthquakes: 25 biggest since 1970   11
  Earthquakes: 25 biggest ever   11
  Shipping areas around Scotland   12
  Climate   13
The People   14
  Population statistics   14
  Population of the Highlands   15
  Population of the Unitary Authorities   15
  Most popular children's names in Scotland   15
  Most popular children's names by Scottish council area   16

PLACES

Cities and Towns   20
  Settlements over 5000 population   20
Royal Burghs   22
The Old Counties of Scotland   24
The Scottish Regions 1974-1997   25
Scotland's Unitary Councils 1997-   26
Linguistic roots of place names   27
New Towns   29
Major Visitor Attractions   29

POLITICS

The 1999 Scottish Parliamentary Elections   31
  Numbers of MSPs Elected by Party   31
  Votes by Party   31
  Constituency Results   32

CONTENTS

General Election Results in Scotland 1974–97   34
    28th February 1974   34
    10th October 1974   34
    3rd May 1979   35
    9th June 1983   35
    11th June 1987   35
    9th April 1992   35
    1st May 1997   35
By-election Results in Scotland 1960-2000   36
European Parliamentary Elections 1979-1999   37
    7th June 1979   37
    14th June 1984   37
    15th June 1989   37
    9th June 1994   37
    10th June 1999   38
Party Composition of the Scottish Unitary Councils   38
Devolution Referenda   41
    1st March 1979   41
    11th September 1997   42
Secretaries of State for Scotland   44
Deputy Secretaries of State for Scotland   44
First Ministers   44
Presiding Officers of the Scottish Parliament   45
    Presiding Officer   45
    Deputy Presiding Officers   45
Members of the Scottish Parliament (MSPs)   45
Westminster MPs for Scottish Seats   48
MSP and MP Superlatives   50
    Youngest MPs   50
    Oldest MPs   50
    Most Votes in a General Election   50
    Least Votes in a General Election   50
    Highest Percentage of Votes in a General Election   50
    Lowest Percentage of Votes in a General Election   50
    Largest Majority in a General Election   50
    Smallest Majority in a General Election   51

HISTORY

Timeline   52
    A Political Chronology   52
Kings and Queens of Scots   59
    The House of Macalpin 834-1034   59
    The House of Dunkeld 1034-1290   60
    The House of Balliol 1292-1296   61
    The House of Bruce 1306-1371   61

CONTENTS

The House of Stewart 1371-1649   62
The House of Stewart 1660-1707   63

MILITARY

The Army   64
    The Scottish Regiments   64
    Territorial Regiments   70
The Royal Navy   71
    Principal Scottish Bases   71
    Royal Navy Reserves   71
The Royal Air Force   72
    Principal Scottish RAF Bases   72
    Royal Auxiliary Air Force   72
Scottish Victoria Cross Winners   72
Scottish Battles   78

CLANS AND FAMILIES

Clan Heraldry   86
Heraldic Terms   100
The Septs   102
Clan Chiefs   112

ARISTOCRACY

The Royal Household in Scotland   121
Her Majesty's Officers of Arms in Scotland   122
    The Court of the Lord Lyon   122
    Pursuivants of Earls   123
Order of Precedence in Scotland   123
Scottish Peers   125
The Most Ancient and Most Noble Order of the Thistle   129
Lords Lieutenant   130
Lord High Commissioners   131
Royal Salutes in Scotland   131
Territorial Titles   131

FAMOUS SCOTS

By Profession   133
By Personality   137

RELIGION

Churches in Scotland   162
    Membership   162

CONTENTS

Christian Churches in Scotland   162
   Archbishops and Bishops of the Catholic Church since 1878   162
   Moderators of the General Assembly of the Church of Scotland   164
   Holders of the office of Primus of the Scottish Episcopal Church   165
   Bishops of the Scottish Episcopal Church: 1900-Present   166
Christian Martyrs in Scotland   168
   Early Martyrs   168
   Reformed Martyrs   168
   Post-Reformation Catholic Martyrs   168
Religious Houses in Scotland Before the Reformation   170
Feast Days of Scottish Saints   171
Secessions from and Disruption of the Church of Scotland   173

HIGHER EDUCATION

Universities   174
Term Days   174
University Rectors   175
   Glasgow   175
   Edinburgh   175
   Aberdeen   175
   Dundee   175
   St Andrews   176

SPORT

Football   177
   Scottish League Champions   177
   Scottish Cup Winners   178
   Senior Clubs   179
World Cup Campaigns   184
   1958 Sweden   184
   1974 West Germany   184
   1978 Argentina   185
   1982 Spain   185
   1986 Mexico   186
   1990 Italy   186
   1998 France   187
Golf   187
   British Open Championship Courses in Scotland   187
Horse Racing   188
   Scottish Grand National Winners and Venues   188
Rugby   189
   Scotland vs England 1871-2000   189
   includes Five Nations Champions and Grand Slam winners   189

CONTENTS

Shinty   196
Commonwealth Games   197
    Scottish Gold Medal Winners   197

EVENTS AND FESTIVALS

Traditional Scottish Festivals   200
    Calendar   200
Highland Games and Celtic Festivals   204
    Scotland   204
    Australia   206
    Barbados   207
    Canada   207
    Finland   208
    France   208
    Japan   209
    New Zealand   209
    South Africa   209
    United States   209

FOOD AND DRINK

Traditional Scots Food   213
Malt Whisky   214
    A Regional Guide   214
    A Pronunciation Guide   216
Whisky Distilleries   216
    A Visitor's Guide   216

SCOTS MEASURES, WEIGHTS AND MONEY

Scots Measures   219
Scottish Banks   220
Scots Weights   222
Scots Money   222

Acknowledgements

Many individuals and organisations have contributed the information contained in this book but The Printer's Devil wishes to thank particularly the following for their help in sourcing material and/or for their permission to reproduce it: George Way of Plean; Davie Galloway of the British Geological Survey; Dr David M. Bertie; the Met Office, the Lowland and Highland TAVR; the RAF; the Royal Navy; The General Register Office for Scotland; the House of Lords Information Service; the Scottish Conservative Party; the Scottish Labour Party; the Scottish Liberal Democrats; the Scottish National Party; the Church of Scotland; the Roman Catholic Church; the Mitchell Library, Glasgow; the Imperial War Museum; Alan Cameron of the Bank of Scotland; Dr Christopher Munn of the Chartered Institute of Bankers in Scotland, The Royal Bank of Scotland; Longman Publishers; HarperCollins Publishers; the Universities of Aberdeen, Dundee, Edinburgh, Glasgow and St Andrews; the Scottish Tourist Board; Sport Scotland.

THE LAND AND THE PEOPLE

• THE LAND •

PHYSICAL CHARACTERISTICS

Geographic Position
Latitude between 60° 51′ 30″ and 54° 38′ N; Longtitude between 1° 45′ 32″ and 6° 14′ W

Area
78,789 km^2 ; 30,420 ml^2

Maximum length of the mainland
440 km; 274 ml (Cape Wrath – Mull of Galloway)

Maximum width
248 km; 154 ml (Buchan Ness – Applecross)

Minimum width
41 km; 25 ml (between Firths of Forth and Clyde)

Northermost point
Dunnet Head

Westermost point
Ardnamurchan Point

Easternmost point
Budian Ness

Length of Coastline
10,000 km; 6214 ml

Land Cover (1996)

Arable and ley pasture	25.0%
Heather moorlands	22.2%
Grasslands	13.4%
Peatlands	13.1%
Plantation woodlands	12.5%
Montane	4.4%
Built-up area	3.0%
Inland water	2.3%
Native woodlands	1.8%
Rock	0.5%

Topographic Altitudes

Land above 600 m/2000 ft	6.0%
Land above 120 m/400 ft	65.0%
Land above 60 m/200 ft	20.0%

ISLANDS

Scotland has 790 islands, of which 130 are inhabited. The main island groupings are listed below. Island population statistics are from the 1991 census.

Orkney
Comprises 90 islands and islets, with approximately 30 inhabited.
Principal town: Kirkwall (pop. 6,469).
Populations of main islands: Mainland (15,128); Burray (363); Eday (166); Flotta & Farra (126); Graemsay & Hoy (477); North Ronaldsay (92); Papa Westray (85); Rousay (291); Sanday (533); Shapinsay (322); South Ronaldsay (943); Stronsay (382); Westray (704).

Shetland

Comprises over 100 islands, with 16 inhabited.

Principal town: Lerwick (pop. 7,280)

Population of inhabited islands: Mainland (17,596); Bressay (352); East Burra (72), Fair Isle (67); Fetlar (90); Housay (85); Muckle Roe (115); Tondra (117); Unst (1,055); West Burra (857); Whalsay (1,041); Yell (1,075)

The Hebrides

Comprises over 500 islands and islets, of which approximately 100 are inhabited in two major groupings

The Inner Hebrides

Skye (8,868; principal town: Portree); Arran (4,474); Coll & Tiree (940); Colonsay & Oronsay (106); Islay (3,538); Jura (196); Mull (2,708; principal town: Tobermory); Raasay (163); Rum; Eigg; Muck.

The Outer Hebrides

Lewis with Harris (21,377; principal town: Stornoway); Baleshare (55); Barra (1,244); Benbecula (1,803); Bernera (262); Berneray (141); Eriskay (179); Grimsay (215); North Uist (1,404); Scalpay (382); South Uist (2,106); Vatersay (72).

RIVERS AND LOCHS

Longest Rivers		Largest Freshwater Lochs	
Tay	193 km; 120 ml	Lomond	71.1 km^2; 27.5 ml^2
Spey	172 km; 107 ml	Ness	56.4 km^2; 21.8 ml^2
Clyde	171 km; 106 ml	Awe/Etive	38.5 km^2; 14.9 ml^2
Tweed	156 km; 97 ml	Maree	28.6 km^2; 11.0 ml^2
Dee	137 km; 85 ml	Morar	26.7 km^2; 10.3 ml^2
Don	132 km; 82 ml	Tay	26.4 km^2; 10.2 ml^2
Forth	105 km; 65 ml	Shin	22.5 km^2; 8.7 ml^2
Findhorn	101 km; 63 ml	Shiel	19.6 km^2; 7.6 ml^2
Deveron	98 km; 61 ml	Rannoch	19.1 km^2; 7.4 ml^2
Annan	79 km; 49 ml	Ericht	18.7 km^2; 7.2 ml^2

MOUNTAINS

Highest Munros (peaks over 914 m/3000 ft; currently 284 in total)

Ben Nevis	1,344 m	Carn Eige	1,183 m
Ben Macdui	1,309 m	Beinn Mheadhoin	1,182 m
Braeriach	1,296 m	Mam Sodhail	1,181 m
Cairn Toul	1,291 m	Stob Choire Claurigh	1,177 m
Cairn Gorm	1,245 m	Ben More	1,174 m
Aonach Beag	1,234 m	Ben Avon	1,171 m
Aonach Mor	1,221 m	Stob Binnein	1,165 m
Carn Mor Dearg	1,220 m	Beinn Bhrotain	1,157 m
Ben Lawers	1,214 m	Lochnagar	1,155 m
Beinn a'Bhuird	1,197 m	Derry Cairngorm	1,155 m

Highest Corbetts (peaks over 770 m/2,500 ft)		*Highest Grahams (peaks over 615 m/2,000 ft)*	
Foinaven	914 m	Beinn Talaidh	761 m
Lealhad an Taobhain	912 m	Cnoc Coinnich	761 m
Beinn Bhreac	912 m	Sgurr a'Chaorainn	761 m
The Farer	911 m	Beinn a'Chapuill	759 m
Meall Buidhe	910 m	Carn an Tionail	759 m
Beinn Dearg Mor	910 m	Shee of Ardtalnaig	759 m
Streap	909 m	Beinn Shiantaidh	757 m
Beinn nan Oighneag	909 m	Creag Dhubh	756 m
Leum Uilleim	909 m	Cook's Cairn	755 m
Beinn Maol Chaluinn	907 m	The Stob	753 m

EARTHQUAKES: 25 BIGGEST SINCE 1970
(START OF INSTRUMENTAL MONITORING IN THE UK)

Date	*Location*	*Magnitude*	*Date*	*Location*	*Magnitude*
29.8.72	Lochgilphead	3.5	27.11.75	Kintail	3.4
13.11.72	Fort William	3.4	27.11.75	Kintail	3.4
4.8.74	Kintail	3.7	5.12.75	Colonsay	3.4
6.8.74	Kintail	4.0	17.1.78	Kintail Area	3.4
6.8.74	Kintail	3.4	16.3.78	Kintail Area	3.4
6.8.74	Kintail	3.4	11.6.78	Kinlochewe	3.4
6.8.74	Kintail	3.4	9.9.78	Kintail Area	3.6
10.8.74	Kintail	4.4	16.9.85	Ardentinny	3.3
22.1.75	Kinlochleven	3.4	1.12.85	Nr Mallaig	3.7
23.7.75	Fort William	3.4	29.9.86	Oban	4.1
11.10.75	Fort William	4.0	3.5.98	Off Jura	3.5
21.11.75	Kintail	3.4	4.3.99	Arran	4.0
27.11.75	Kintail	4.1			

EARTHQUAKES: 25 BIGGEST EVER

Date	*Location*	*Magnitude*	*Date*	*Location*	*Magnitude*
28.11.1880	Argyll	5.2	17.1.1907	Oban	4.4
13.8.1816	Inverness	5.1	31.5.1948	Ullapool	4.4
18.9.1901	Inverness	5.0	10.8.1974	Kintail	4.4
23.10.1839	Comrie	4.8	23.12.1925	Oban	4.3
2.2.1888	Invergarry	4.8	1.3.1728	Galashiels	4.2
13.8.1816	Inverness	4.7	28.1.1912	Inverary	4.1
7.9.1801	Comrie	4.6	27.1.1927	Colintraive	4.1
8.11.1608	Comrie	4.6	16.8.1934	Torridon	4.1
23.7.1597	Scotland	4.6	25.12.1946	Lochaber	4.1
15.11.1890	Inverness	4.5	23.10.1839	Comrie	4.1
23.4.1817	Western Scotland	4.5	27.11.1975	Kintail	4.1
24.11.1846	Comrie	4.4	29.9.1986	Oban	4.1
18.9.1901	Inverness	4.4			

SHIPPING AREAS AROUND SCOTLAND

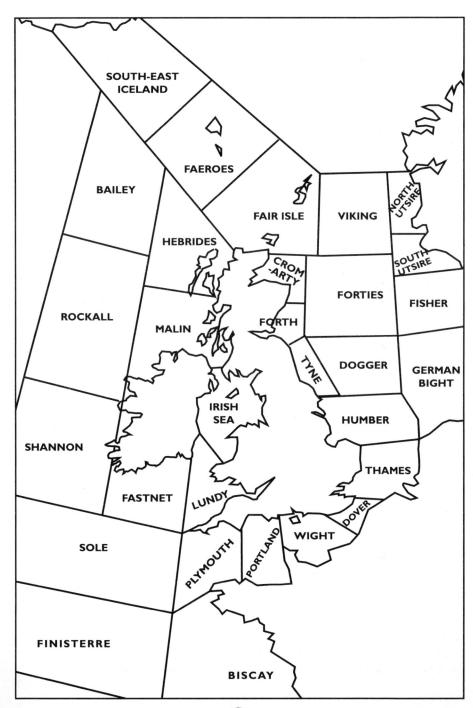

CLIMATE

Sunshine
Brightest parts of Scotland:
Angus, Fife. the Lothians, Ayrshire, and Dumfries and Galloway with an average of 1400 hours of sunshine per year

Dullest parts of Scotland:
The mountain regions of the Highlands with an average of less than 1,100 hours of sunshine per year

Sunniest months on record:
May 1946 and May 1975 with 329 hours recorded at Tiree

Dullest month on record:
January 1983 with 0.6 hours recorded at Cape Wrath

Rainfall
Wettest parts of Scotland:
The western Highlands with over 3000 mm of rain per year (falling on an average of over 250 days per annum)

Driest parts of Scotland:
The east coast with less than 800 mm of rain per year (falling on an average of 175 days per annum)

Wettest day on record:
17th January 1974 with 283 mm of rain recorded at Sloy Main Adit , Loch Lomond

Winds
Windiest parts of Scotland:
The Western Isles, the northwest coast, Orkney and Shetland with over 30 days of gales per year

Strongest gust recorded at low level:
142 mph at Fraserburgh on 13th February 1989

Strongest gust recorded at high level:
173 mph at Cairngorm Automatic Weather Station on 20th March 1986

Temperature
Mean annual air temperatures at low level:
Ramges from around 7 °C in Shetland to 9 °C on the Ayrshire coast

Coldest months:
January and February with daytime maximum temperatures over low groundaveraging betwen 5 – 7 °C

Hottest day in Scotland:
2nd July 1908 with a recorded temperature of 32.8 °C at Dumfries

Coldest day in Scotland:
11th February 1985 and 10th January 1982 with a recorded temperature of -27.2 °C at Braemar

Snow
Average number of days with sleet or snow falling:
Ranges from less than 10 days near the west coast and in the Western Isles to over 100 days in the Cairngorm mountains

• THE PEOPLE •

POPULATION STATISTICS

Census Statistics for Scotland

Year	Population	Pop. per m^2/km^{2*}	Year	Population	Pop. per m^2/km^{2*}
1811	1,805,864	60	1911	4,760,904	160
1821	2,091,521	70	1921	4,882,497	164
1831	2,364,386	79	1931	4,842,980	163
1841	2,620,184	88	1951	5,096,415	171
1851	2,888,742	97	1961	5,179,344	174
1861	3,062,294	100	1971	5,228,963	68*
1871	3,360,018	113	1981	5,130,735	66*
1881	3,735,573	125	1991	5,102,400	66*
1891	4,025,647	125			
1901	4,472,103	150			

General Registrar Population Estimates

Year	Population	Year	Population
1992	5,111,200	1996	5,128,000
1993	5,120,200	1997	5,122,500
1994	5,132,400	1998	5,120,000
1995	5,136,600		

POPULATION OF THE HIGHLANDS

Statistics given are for the seven Crofting Counties (Argyll, Caithness, Inverness, Ross & Cromarty, Sutherland, Orkney and Zetland)

Year	Population	Year	Population	Year	Population
1811	318,266	1861	380,442	1911	341,535
1821	361,184	1871	371,356	1921	325,853
1831	388,876	1881	369,453	1931	293,139
1841	396,045	1891	360,367	1951	285,786
1851	395,540	1901	352,371	1961	277,948

POPULATION OF THE UNITARY AUTHORITIES (JUNE 1995)

Authority	Population	Area (ha)	Authority	Population	Area (ha)
Aberdeen	218,220	18,216	Highland	206,900	2,611,906
Aberdeenshire	223,630	631,735	Inverclyde	89,900	16,724
Angus	111,020	218,396	Midlothian	79,910	34,966
Argyll & Bute	90,550	702,300	Moray	86,250	223,694
Clackmannan	48,660	15,809	N. Ayrshire	139,020	88,755
Dumbarton/			N. Lanarkshire	326,750	47,648
Clydebank	97,790	17,573	Orkney	19,760	102,498
Dumfries/G'way	147,900	644,567	Perthshire/		
Dundee	153,710	5,500	Kinross	130,470	539,479
E. Ayrshire	123,820	127,527	Renfrewshire	176,970	26,250
E. Dunbarton	110,220	17,551	Scottish Borders	105,300	472,749
E. Lothian	85,640	66,558	Shetland	22,830	147,097
E. Renfrew	86,670	16,802	S. Ayrshire	113,960	123,021
Edinburgh	441,620	26,001	S. Lanarkshire	307,100	117,789
alkirk	142,610	29,300	Stirling	81,630	224,230
Fife	351,200	134,045	W. Lothian	146,730	42,664
Glasgow	623,850	17,472	Western Isles	29,410	307,005

TOP 10 MOST POPULAR CHILDREN'S NAMES IN SCOTLAND, 1999

Girls	Boys
1 Chloe	1 Jack
2 Rebecca	2 Lewis
3 Laurne	3 Ryan
4 Emma	4 Cameron
5 Amy	5 Ross
6 Megan	6 James
7 Caitlin	7 Andrew
8 Rachel	8 Liam
9 Erin	9 Scott
10 Sophie	10 Connor

TOP 3 CHILDREN'S NAMES BY SCOTTISH COUNCIL AREA, 1999

<u>Girls</u>	<u>Boys</u>
* indicates a tie	

Aberdeen City

Girls	Boys
1 Chloe	1 Lewis
2 Rebecca	2 Cameron
3 Emma	3 Ryan

Aberdeenshire

Girls	Boys
1 Chloe	1 Cameron, Lewis*
2 Amy	3 Matthew
3 Megan	

Angus

Girls	Boys
1 Chloe	1 Cameron
2 Rebecca	2 Ryan
3 Emily, Kirsty, Sarah, Sophie*	3 Adam, Fraser, Jamie, Kieran, Lewis, Liam*

Argyll & Bute

Girls	Boys
1 Chloe	1 Jack
2 Emma	2 Ross
3 Megan	3 Callum, James, Scott*

Clackmannanshire

Girls	Boys
1 Chloe	1 Ross
2 Rachel, Sophie*	2 Lewis, Robert*

Dumfries & Galloway

Girls	Boys
1 Chloe	1 Lewis
2 Megan	2 Connor, Jordan, Ryan*
3 Caitlin	

Dundee City

Girls	Boys
1 Chloe	1 Ryan
2 Caitlin	2 Connor, Lewis*
3 Megan	

E. Ayrshire

Girls	Boys
1 Chloe	1 Ryan
2 Rebecca	2 Jack
3 Amy	3 Callum, Cameron, Connor, Scott*

E. Lothian

Girls	Boys
1 Chloe	1 Jack
2 Lauren	2 Cameron
3 Amy	3 Lewis

E. Renfrewshire

1 Rebecca	1 Jack
2 Rachel	2 Andrew
3 Lauren	3 Cameron, David, Lewis, Scott*

City of Edinburgh

1 Chloe	1 Jack
2 Emma, Rebecca*	2 Cameron
	3 Lewis

E. Dunbartonshire

1 Emma	1 Jack
2 Chloe, Rachel*	2 Cameron
	3 Andrew

Falkirk

1 Rebecca	1 Ryan
2 Chloe	2 Cameron
3 Amy	3 Lewis, Ross*

Fife

1 Chloe	1 Cameron, Liam*
2 Megan	3 Lewis
3 Amy	

Glasgow City

1 Chloe	1 Jack
2 Caitlin	2 Ryan
3 Megan, Rebecca*	3 Liam

Highland

1 Chloe	1 Ryan
2 Lauren	2 Lewis
3 Emma, Rebecca, Sophie*	3 Liam

Inverclyde

1 Chloe	1 Jack
2 Amy	2 Lewis
3 Erin, Rebecca*	3 Andrew

Midlothian

1 Chloe	1 Lewis
2 Lauren, Rebecca*	2 Jack
	3 Cameron

Moray

1 Lauren	1 James
2 Chloe	2 Kieran, Lewis, Ross*
3 Kirsty	

N. Ayrshire

1 Chloe	1 Jack
2 Lauren	2 James
3 Caitlin, Rebecca*	3 David

N. Lanarkshire

1 Chloe	1 Jack
2 Caitlin	2 Ryan
3 Emma	3 Lewis

Orkney

1 Abigail, Amber, Charlotte, Chloe, Emily, Katie, Kayla, Kelsey, Molly, Neve, Rachel, Sarah, Shannon, Zoe*	1 Aaron, Aidan, Liam, Owen*

Perth & Kinross

1 Chloe	1 Cameron
2 Megan, Rebecca*	2 Lewis
	3 David, Jack*

Renfrewshire

1 Amy, Chloe*	1 Andrew
3 Rebecca	2 Jack, Ross*

S. Ayrshire

1 Chloe	1 Jack
2 Rebecca	2 Lewis
3 Lauren	3 Cameron

Scottish Borders

1 Rachel	1 Jack
2 Chloe	2 Lewis, Ryan*
3 Emily	

Shetland

1 Chloe	1 James, Ross*
2 Caitlin, Catherine, Rachel*	2 Scott, Thomas*

S. Lanarkshire

1 Chloe	1 Jack
2 Rebecca	2 Lewis
3 Emma	3 Ross

Stirling

1 Rebecca	1 Jack
2 Amy, Erin*	2 James, Lewis*

W. Dunbartonshire

1 Rebecca	1 Cameron, Ryan*
2 Lauren	3 Andrew, Matthew*
3 Megan	

W. Lothian

1 Chloe	1 Lewis
2 Rebecca	2 Cameron
3 Emma	3 Ryan

Western Isles

1 Eilidh	1 Andrew
2 Caitlin, Christina, Sarah*	2 Cameron, Connor, David*

PLACES

• CITIES AND TOWNS •

SETTLEMENTS OVER 5,000 POPULATION

Cities over 100,000

Glasgow *(653,713)*
Edinburgh *(404,316)*

Aberdeen *(189,707)*
Dundee *(148,920)*

Towns over 50,000

Paisley *(73,627)*

East Kilbride *(69,376)*

Towns 40,000–50,000

Greenock *(49,135)*
Hamilton *(49,029)*
Cumbernauld *(48,427)*
Kirkcaldy *(47,930)*

Ayr *(47,399)*
Dunfermline *(43,670)*
Coatbridge *(43,617)*
Kilmarnock *(43,354)*

Perth *(41,512)*
Livingston *(41,065)*
Inverness *(41,234)*

Towns 30,000–40,000

Glenrothes *(39,440)*
Airdrie *(36,998)*

Irvine *(32,767)*
Dumfries *(32,072)*

Falkirk *(31,860)*
Motherwell *(30,717)*

Towns 20,000–30,000

Wishaw *(29,936)*
Stirling *(29,120)*
Clydebank *(28,541)*
Bearsden *(27,234)*

Arbroath *(23,680)*
Bishopbriggs *(23,615)*
Bridge of Don *(21,880)*
Bellshill *(21,624)*

Dumbarton *(21,555)*
Musselburgh *(20,630)*
Renfrew *(20,345)*
Kirkintilloch *(20,291)*

Towns 10,000–20,000

Elgin *(19,325)*
Port Glasgow *(19,311)*
Newton Mearns *(18,798)*

Peterhead *(18,780)*
Clarkston *(18,571)*
Grangemouth *(18,517)*

Johnstone *(18,276)*
Buckhaven *(17,069)*
Penicuik *(16,896)*

Barrhead (16,876)
Methil (15,850)
Helensburgh (15,852)
Buckhaven (15,850)
Giffnock (15,771)
Hawick (15,506)
Larkhall (15,493)
Kilwinning (15,285)
Viewpark (14,872)
Troon (14,800)
Boness (14,410)
St Andrews (14,050)
Alexandria (14,041)
Galashiels (13,782)

Bathgate (13,522)
Bonnyrigg (13,499)
Prestwick (13,451)
Rosyth (13,100)
Forfar (13,047)
Alloa (12,970)
Erskine (12,944)
Fraserburgh (12,890)
Carluke (12,697)
Milngavie (12,233)
Mayfield (12,103)
Linlithgow (11,623)
Saltcoats (11,623)
Montrose (11,440)

Dalkeith (11,340)
Gourock (11,325)
Broxburn (11,309)
Stranraer (11,298)
Whitburn (11,165)
Largs (10,645)
Ardrossan (10,597)
Stenhousemuir (10,500)
Carnoustie (10,488)
Fort William (10,391)
Cowdenbeath (10,360)
Larbert (10,070)

Towns 5,000–10,000

Stevenston (9,948)
Kilsyth (9,918)
Bonhill (9,836)
Inverurie (9,620)
Stonehaven (9,475)
Cumnock (9,475)
Dunoon (9,038)
Haddington (8,844)
Armadale (8,823)
Annan (8,772)
Shotts (8,756)
Lanark (8,754)
Ellon (8,670)
Forres (8,590)
Thurso (8,488)
East Calder (8,458)
Leven (8,440)
Tranent (8,313)
Buckie (8,210)
Oban (8,203)
Dalgety Bay (8,070)
Blairgowrie (8,001)
Denny (7,930)
Nairn (7,892)
Kilbirnie (7,876)
Cupar (7,780)
Duntocher (7,727)
Wick (7,681)

Brechin (7,655)
Dunblane (7,368)
Girvan (7,361)
Lossiemouth (7,295)
Lerwick (7,280)
Lochgelly (7,260)
Monifieth (7,198)
Peebles (7,068)
Prestonpans (7,014)
Tullibody (6,700)
Bothwell (6,542)
Dunbar (6,518)
Kirkwall (6,469)
Bannockburn (6,419)
Ballingry (6,393)
Dyce (6,360)
Stewarton (6,349)
Banchory (6,320)
Strathaven (6,254)
Beith (6,244)
Inverkeithing (6,130)
Burntisland (6,040)
Crieff (6,023)
Stornoway (5,975)
Bonnybridge (5,961)
Sauchie (5,910)
Kelso (5,867)
Selkirk (5,811)

Dunipace (5,800)
Gorebridge (5,772)
Campbeltown (5,722)
Alness (5,696)
Dalry (5,650)
Kirriemuir (5,571)
Kelty (5,560)
Carron (5,547)
Loanhead (5,538)
Uddingston (5,367)
Locharbriggs (5,349)
Houston (5,347)
Stonehouse (5,328)
Auchterderran (5,300)
Bishopton (5,300)
Cardenden (5,300)
Polmont (5,270)
Tillicoultry (5,269)
Rothesay (5,264)
Cults (5,265)
Dingwall (5,228)
Elderslie (5,200)
Neilston (5,163)
Galston (5,069)
Tillicoultry (5,035)
Blackburn (5,014)
Bridge of Allan (5,012)

• ROYAL BURGHS •

Royal burghs were those who received their burghal privileges direct from the Crown and who as a consequence, enjoyed various political and economic advantages, not the least of which were considerable and exclusive trading privileges. In many cases, the exact year in which a royal charter was granted is impossible to determine from extant records; often it can be dated only to a particular monarch's reign or a date by which records show that it was operating as a royal burgh, the charter having been granted at some point prior to this.

Burgh	County	Original Grant of Charter
Aberdeen	Aberdeen City	1124–54
Annan	Dumfries	1532
Arbroath	Angus	1178–82
Auchterarder	Perth	1246
Auchtermuchty	Fife	1517
Ayr	Ayr	1203–06
Banff	Banff	1189–98
Brechin	Angus	1165–1171
Burntisland	Fife	1541
Campbeltown	Argyll	1700
Crail	Fife	1178
Cullen	Banff	1589–98
Culross	Fife	1592
Cupar	Fife	1327
Dingwall	Ross & Cromarty	1226–7
Dornoch	Sutherland	1628
Dumbarton	Dunbarton	1222
Dumfries	Dumfries	1186
Dunbar	E. Lothian	1445
Dundee	Dundee City	1191–95
Dunfermline	Fife	1124–27
Edinburgh	Edinburgh City	1124–27
Elgin	Moray	1130–53
*Elie[1] & Earlsferry[2]	Fife	1599[1], 1589[2]
Falkland	Fife	1458
Forfar	Angus	1153–62
Forres	Moray	1130–53
Fortrose	Ross & Cromarty	1590
Glasgow	Glasgow City	1611
Haddington	E. Lothian	1124–53
Inveraray	Argyll	1648
Inverbervie	Kincardine	1341
Inverkeithing	Fife	1153–62

Burgh	County	Original Grant of Charter
Inverness	Inverness	1130–53
Inverurie	Aberdeen	1195
Irvine	Ayr	1372
Jedburgh	Roxburgh	1159–65
*Kilrenny[1], Anstruther Easter[2] & Anstruther Wester[3]	Fife	1578[1], 1583[2], 1587[3]
Kinghorn	Fife	1165–72
Kintore	Aberdeen	1187–1200
Kirkcaldy	Fife	1644
Kirkcudbright	Kirkcudbright	c. 1330
Kirkwall	Orkney	1486
Lanark	Lanark	1153–59
Lauder	Berwick	1502
Linlithgow	W. Lothian	c. 1138
Lochmaben	Dumfries	c. 1447
Montrose	Angus	1124–53
Nairn	Nairn	c. 1190
New Galloway	Kirkcudbright	1630
Newburgh	Fife	1631
North Berwick	E. Lothian	c. 1425
Peebles	Peebles	1153
Perth	Perth	1124–27
Pittenweem	Fife	1541
Queensferry	W. Lothian	1636
Renfrew	Renfrew	1124–47
Rothesay	Bute	1400–01
Rutherglen	Lanark	1124–53
Sanquhar	Dumfries	1598
Selkirk	Selkirk	1328
St Andrews	Fife	1620
Stirling	Stirling	1124–27
Stranraer	Wigtown	1617
Tain	Ross & Cromarty	1439
Whithorn	Wigtown	1511
Wick	Caithness	1589
Wigtown	Wigtown	c. 1292

* These burghs united in 1929.

• THE OLD COUNTIES OF SCOTLAND •

County Towns •

ORKNEY
Kirkwall

CAITHNESS
Wick

SUTHERLAND

SHETLAND
Lerwick

ROSS
AND
CROMARTY
Dingwall
Dornoch

NAIRN
Nairn
Inverness
Elgin
MORAY
BANFF
Banff

ABERDEEN
Aberdeen

INVERNESS
KINCARDINE
Stonehaven

ANGUS
Forfar

PERTH
Perth
Cupar

ARGYLL
CLACKMANNAN
KINROSS
Kinross
FIFE

DUNBARTON
Stirling
Alloa
Linlithgow
STIRLING
Haddington

Dumbarton
W. LOTHIAN
EAST
LOTHIAN

Rothesay
RENFREW
Renfrew
MIDLOTHIAN
Edinburgh
Duns

BUTE
LANARK
Peebles
BERWICK

Ayr
AYR
Lanark
PEEBLES
Selkirk
SELKIRK
Jedburgh
ROXBURGH

DUMFRIES
KIRKCUDBRIGHT
Dumfries

WIGTOWN
Kirkcudbright
Wigtown

• THE SCOTTISH REGIONS 1974–1997 •

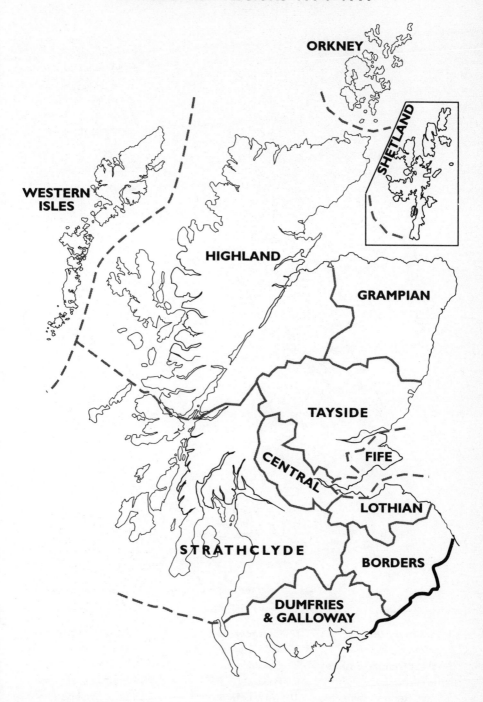

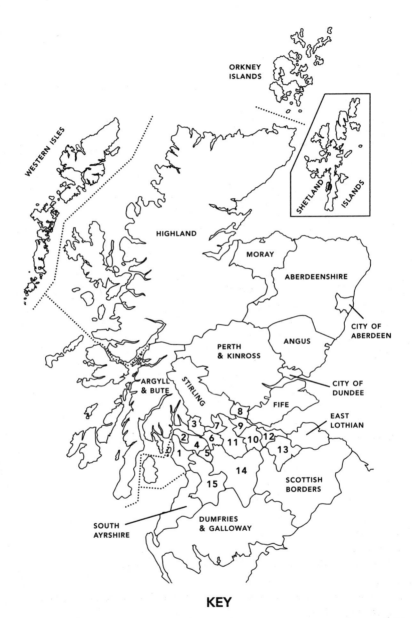

• SCOTLAND'S UNITARY COUNCILS 1997– •

KEY

1	North Ayrshire	6	Glasgow	11	North Lanarkshire
2	Inverclyde	7	East Dunbartonshire	12	Edinburgh
3	West Dunbartonshire	8	Clackmannanshire	13	Midlothian
4	Renfrewshire	9	Falkirk	14	South Lanarkshire
5	East Renfrewshire	10	West Lothian	15	East Ayrshire

• LINGUISTIC ROOTS OF PLACE NAMES •

Aber at the mouth (of a river)
    Aberdeen (mouth of the Dee)
  also at the confluence of
    Aberfoyle (confluence of the streams); Aberlour (loud confluence)
Ach from *achadh,* a field
    Achaleven (field of the elm); Achnacarry (field of the weir)
Alt, Aid, Auld from *alit,* stream, burn
    Aitnabreac (stream of the trout); Auldearn (stream of the Earn)
An little
    Lochan (little loch)
Ar a form of **Aber**
    Arbroath (at the mouth of the Brothock)
Ard high
    Ardfern (height of the alders); Ardrishaig (height of the briars); Ardrossan (height of the little cape)
Auch another form of *achadh,* like **Ach**
    Auchencairn (field with the cairn)
Auchter high field
    Auchterarder (upland of the high stream)
Bad thicket
    Badenoch (bushy place)
Bal from *bail, baile,* house, or village
    Balmoral (laird's dwelling); Bellahouston (village with the cross or crucifix)
Bar height or hill
    Bardowie (black height); Barlinnie (height with the pool)
Blair from *blar* plain
    Blairgowrie (plain of the goat); Blair Atholl (plain of Atholl)
Bon, Bun foot
    Bonawe (foot of river Awe)
Cairn pile or heap of stones
    Cairngorm (blue pile of stones)
Cal from *coile,* wood
    Calton (hazel wood)
Cambus bay, creek
    Cambuslang (creek of the boat); Cambusmore (big bay)
Car from *caru* rock
    Carfin (white rock); Carluke (rock by the hollow); Carrick (sea rock or cliff)
Clack, Cloch from *clach,* stone
    Clackmannan (stone of Mann, a mythical figure)
Cor from *coire* cauldron, circular glen
    Corrievreckan (whirlpool of Brecan, a mythical figure)
Craig from *craeg,* crag, rock
    Craigievar (pointed rock); Craignure (rock of the yew)

Cul from *cuil* nook, corner
   Cullen (little nook); Culrain (nook of ferns)
Cul from *cul* behind
   Culloden (behind the ridge)
Dal from *dail* field or meadow
   Dalbeattie (field of the birches); Dalnaspidal (field of the spittal or inn);
   Dalry (field of the king)
Doug from *dub* dark
   Douglas (dark stream)
Drum ridge, rise
   Drummore (big ridge)
Dum, Dun fort, hill
   Dumbarton (fort or hill of the Britons); Dundas (south hill); Dunmore (big hill)
Fin from *fionn*, white, clear
   Loch Fyne (clear loch); Finhaven (white or clear river)
Gair, Gir from *gearr* short
   Gairloch (short loch); Girvan (short river)
Gart enclosure
   Gartcosh (enclosure with cave); Gartness (enclosure by the waterfall)
Inch from *innis* island, pasture, links
   Inchcolm (isle of Colm or Columba); Inchinnan (isle of Finnan)
Inner from *inver*
   Innerleithen (confluence of the Leithen)
Inver mouth of the river, confluence
   Inveraray (mouth of the Aray); Inverness (mouth of the Ness)
Ken, Kin from *ceanin*, head
   Kenmore (big head); Kinbuck (buck's head); Kinloch (head of the loch)
Kil from *cill*, church
   Kilbarchan (church of St Barchan); Kilbride (church of St Bride or Bridget);
   Kilmacolm (church of Colm or Columba)
Kill from *coill*, wood
   Killiecrankie (wood of the aspens)
Knock from *cnoc*, hillock
   Knockando (hill of business)
Kyle from *caol*, strait (of water)
   Kyles of Bute
Lag hollow, cave
   Laggan (little hollow)
Linnhe pool, sheltered loch
   Loch Linnhe
Lis from *lios*, garden, enclosure
   Lismore (big garden)
Loch lake
   Lochaber (still, stagnant lake); Lochgelly (clear lake)
Mon from *moine*, moss, moor
   Monifieth (peaty moor); Montrose (moor on the hill)

Mor big
>Ben More (big ben, or hill); Morven (big glen)

Pit croft
>Pitcairn (croft with the barrow, or cairn); Pittenweem (croft by the cave)

Poll burn, stream
>Polmont (stream on the hilly moor); Poltalloch (stream at the smithy)

Sguir, Scurr, Sgòrr steep or precipitous hill
>Sguir Alastair, Scurr Ouran

Strath broad or wide valley
>Strathavon (valley of the Avon); Strathclyde (valley of the Clyde)

Uisge water
>Eskdale (valley of water)

• NEW TOWNS •

In 1946, the Clyde Valley Plan proposed to solve the problems of overcrowding in Glasgow and urban sprawl across the Central Belt by surrounding existing settlements with 'green belts' in which no development was permitted and by decanting Glasgow's populations to a series of new towns.

East Kibride (designated 1947)   Irvine (designated 1965)
Glenrothes (designated 1948)   Livingstone (designated 1962)
Cumbernauld (designated 1956)

• MAJOR VISITOR ATTRACTIONS •

Attractions with free admission

	Visitors '97	Visitors '98
Kelvingrove Art Gallery & Museum	1,053,745	1,128,455
Royal Botanic Garden, Edinburgh	899,316	812,574
Royal Scots Regimental Museum, Edinburgh	300,000*	550,000*
Museum of Transport, Glasgow	438,429	497,874
Gallery of Modern Art, Glasgow	410,332	452,678
National Gallery of Scotland, Edinburgh	404,841	442,322*
People's Palace, Glasgow	47,717**	442,153
The Botanic Gardens, Glasgow	400,000*	400,000*
The Burrell Collection	331,285	343,325
New Lanark Village, New Lanark	400,000*	304, 500*

Attractions with paid admission

	Visitors '97	Visitors '98
Edinburgh Castle	1,238,140	1,219,055
The Old Blacksmith's Shop Centre, Gretna Green	500,000*	711,480*

	Visitors '97	Visitors '98
Edinburgh Zoo	548,426	525,000*
Museum of Scotland, Edinburgh	591,152	424,320
Stirling Castle	422,615	398,828
Burns National Heritage Park, Ayr	300,000*	345,000*
The Palace of Holyroodhouse, Edinburgh	272,428	288,000
The Official Loch Ness Monster Exhibition Centre	180,000*	280,000*
Urquhart Castle	244,786	235,745
Blair Drummond Safari Park	205,821	203,195

* Estimated
** Closed for part of the year to allow upgrading

POLITICS

• THE 1999 SCOTTISH PARLIAMENTARY ELECTIONS •

RESULTS

NUMBERS OF MSPs ELECTED BY PARTY

Labour	56	Scottish Green Party	1
SNP	35	Scottish Socialist Party	1
Conservative	18	Independent	1
Liberal Democrat	17		

VOTES BY PARTY

	Total Votes	% of Votes	MSPs Elected
Labour			
Constituency Vote	908,392	38.81	53
Regional Vote	786,818	33.64	3
'97 General Election Vote	1,283,353	45.63	56
Scottish Natonal Party			
Constituency Vote	672,757	28.74	7
Regional Vote	638,644	27.26	28
'97 General Election Vote	617,260	21.94	6
Conservative			
Constituency Vote	364,225	15.56	0
Regional Vote	359,109	15.35	18
'97 General Election Vote	493,059	17.53	0
Liberal Democrat			
Constituency Vote	331,279	14.15	12
Regional Vote	290,760	12.4	5
'97 General Election Vote	365,359	12.99	10
Scottish Green Party			
Constituency Vote	0	0	0
Regional Vote	84,024	3.59	1
'97 General Election Vote	1,721	0.06	0

(contd)

	Total Votes	% of Votes	MSPs Elected
Scottish Socialist Party			
Constituency Vote	23,654	1.01	0
Regional Vote	46,635	1.99	1
'97 General Election Vote	9,740	0.35	0
Independent (MSP for Falkirk West)			
Constituency Vote	18,511	0.79	1
Regional Vote	27,700	1.18	0
'97 General Election Vote	0	0	0
Others			
Constituency Vote	21,662	0.93	0
Regional Vote	105,221	4.50	0
'97 General Election Vote	41,947	1.49	0

CONSTITUENCY RESULTS

Highlands & Islands Region (8 constituency and 7 regional seats)

Constituency	*Elected Party*
Argyll & Bute	Liberal Democrat (SNP majority in regional vote)
Caithness, Sutherland & Easter Ross	Liberal Democrat
Inverness, East Nairn & Lochaber	SNP
Moray	SNP
Orkney	Liberal Democrat
Ross, Skye & Inverness West	Liberal Democrat (SNP majority in regional vote)
Shetland	Liberal Democrat
Western Isles	Labour

North East Scotland Region (9 constituency and 7 regional seats)

Constituency	*Elected Party*
Aberdeen Central	Labour
Aberdeen North	Labour (SNP majority in regional list vote)
Aberdeen South	Liberal Democrat (Labour majority in regional list vote)
Aberdeenshire West & Kincardine	Liberal Democrat (Conservative majority in regional list vote)
Angus	SNP
Banff & Buchan	SNP
Dundee East	Labour (SNP majority in regional list vote)
Dundee West	Labour
Gordon	Liberal Democrat

Mid Scotland & Fife Region (9 constituency and 7 regional seats)

Constituency	Elected Party
Dunfermline East	Labour
Dunfermline West	Labour
Fife Central	Labour
Fife North East	Liberal Democrat
Kirkcaldy	Labour
Ochil	Labour
Perth	SNP
Stirling	Labour
Tayside	North SNP

West of Scotland Region (9 constituency and 7 regional seats)

Constituency	Elected Party
Clydebank & Milngavie	Labour
Cunninghamc North	Labour
Dumbarton	Labour
Eastwood	Labour
Greenock & Inverclyde	Labour
Paisley North	Labour
Paisley South	Labour
Renfrewshire West	Labour
Strathkelvin & Bearsden	Labour

Glasgow Region (10 constituency and 7 regional seats)

Constituency	Elected Party
Anniesland	Labour
Baillieston	Labour
Cathcart	Labour
Govan	Labour
Kelvin	Labour
Maryhill	Labour
Pollok	Labour
Rutherglen	Labour
Shettleston	Labour
Springburn	Labour

Central Scotland Region (10 constituency and 7 regional seats)

Constituency	Elected Party
Airdrie & Shotts	Labour
Coatbridge & Chryston	Labour
Cumbernauld & Kilsyth	Labour
East Kilbride	Labour
Falkirk East	Labour
Falkirk West	Independent
Hamilton North & Bellshill	Labour
Hamilton South	Labour

Constituency	Elected Party
Kilmarnock & Loudoun	Labour
Motherwell & Wishaw	Labour

Lothians Region (9 constituency and 7 regional seats)

Constituency	Elected Party
Edinburgh Central	Labour
Edinburgh East & Musselburgh	Labour
Edinburgh North & Leith	Labour
Edinburgh Pentlands	Labour
Edinurgh South	Labour
Edinburgh West	Liberal Democrat
Linlithgow	Labour
Livingston	Labour
Midlothian	Labour

South of Scotland Region (9 constituency and 7 regional seats)

Constituency	Elected Party
Ayr	Labour
Carrick, Cumnock & Doon Valley	Labour
Clydesdale	Labour
Cunninghame South	Labour
Dumfries	Labour
East Lothian	Labour
Galloway & Upper Nithsdale	SNP (Conservative majority in regional list vote)
Roxburgh & Berwickshire	Liberal Democrat
Tweeddale, Ettrick & Lauderdale	Liberal Democrat

• GENERAL ELECTION RESULTS IN SCOTLAND 1974–97•

28TH FEBRUARY 1974

Party	Total Votes	% of Votes	% change	MPs Elected
Labour	1,057,601	36.63		40
Conservative	950,668	32.93		21
SNP	633,180	21 93		7
Liberal	229,162	7.94		3
Others	16,464	0.57		0

10TH OCTOBER 1974

Party	Total Votes	% of Votes	% change	MPs Elected
Labour	1,000,581	36.28	-0.35	41
Conservative	681,327	24. 70	-8.23	16
SNP	839,617	30.44	+8.51	11

Party	Total Votes	% of Votes	% change	MPs Elected
Liberal	228,855	8.30	+0.36	3
Others	7,721	0.28	-0.29	0

3RD MAY 1979

Party	Total Votes	% of Votes	% change	MPs Elected
Labour	1,211,445	41.54	+5.26	44
Conservative	916,155	31.41	+6.71	22
SNP	504,259	17.29	-13.15	2
Liberal	262,224	8.99	+0.69	3
Others	22,554	0.77	+0.49	0

9TH JUNE 1983

Party	Total Votes	% of Votes	% change	MPs Elected
Labour	990,654	35.07	-6.47	41
Conservative	801,485	28.37	-3.04	21
SNP	331,975	11.75	-5.54	2
SDP/Liberal	693,034	24.53	+15.44	8
Others	7,830	0.28	-0.49	0

11TH JUNE 1987

Party	Total Votes	% of Votes	% change	MPs Elected
Labour	1,258,132	42.39	+7.32	50
Conservative	713,099	24.02	-4.35	10
SNP	416,873	14.04	+2.29	3
SDP/Liberal	570,053	19.21	-5.32	9
Others	10,069	0.34	+0.06	0

9TH APRIL 1992

Party	Total Votes	% of Votes	% change	MPs Elected
Labour	1,131,078	39.04	-3.35	49
Conservative	746,695	25.77	+1.75	11
SNP	621,290	2I 45	+7.17	3
Liberal Democrats	373,729	12.90	-6.31	9
Others	24,182	0.84	+0.50	0

1ST MAY 1997

Party	Total Votes	% of Votes	% change	MPs Elected
Labour	1,283,353	45.63	+6.59	56
Conservative	493,059	17.53	-8.24	0
SNP	617,260	21.94	+0.49	6
Liberal Democrats	365,359	12.99	+0.09	10
Others	53,408	1.91	+1.07	0

• BY-ELECTION RESULTS IN SCOTLAND 1960–2000•

Date	Constituency	Result	MP elected
19th May 1960	Edinburgh North	Con hold	Walter Scott, Earl of Dalkeith
20th April 1961	Paisley	Lab hold	John Robertson
8th November 1961	Fife East	Con hold	Sir John Gilmour
16th November 1961	Glasgow Bridgeton	Lab hold	James Bennet
14th June 1962	West Lothian	Lab hold	Tam Dalyell
22nd November 1962	Glasgow Woodside	Lab gain	Neil Carmichael
7th November 1963	Kinrosshire & West Perthshire	Con hold	Sir Alec Douglas Home
21st November 1963	Dundee West	Lab hold	Peter Doig
12th December 1963	Dunfriesshire	Con hold	D. Anderson
14th May 1964	Rutherglen	Lab gain	J. Gregor MacKenzie
24th March 1965	Roxburgh, Selkirk & Peebles	Lib gain	David Steel
9th March 1967	Glasgow Pollock	Con gain	Esmond Wright
2nd November 1967	Hamilton	SNP gain	Winnie Ewing
30th October 1969	Glasgow Gorbals	Lab hold	Frank McElhone
19th March 1970	South Ayrshire	Lab hold	Jim Sillars
16th September 1971	Stirling & Falkirk	Lab hold	Harry Ewing
1st March 1973	Dundee East	Lab hold	George Machan
8th September 1973	Edinburgh North	Con hold	Alex Fletcher
8th September 1973	Glasgow Govan	SNP gain	Margo MacDonald
13th April 1978	Glasgow Garscadden	Lab hold	Donald Dewar
31st May 1978	Hamilton	Lab hold	George Robertson
26th October 1978	Berwick & E. Lothian	Lab hold	John Home Robertson
26th June 1980	Glasgow Central	Lab hold	Robert McTaggert
25th March 1982	Glasgow Hillhead	SDP/Lib gain	Roy Jenkins
24th June 1982	Coatbridge & Airdrie	Lab hold	Tom Clarke
2nd December 1982	Glasgow Queen's Park	Lab hold	Helen McElhone
10th November 1988	Glasgow Govan	SNP gain	Jim Sillars
16th June 1989	Glasgow Central	Lab hold	Mike Watson
29th November 1990	Paisley North	Lab hold	Irene Adams
29th November 1990	Paisley South	Lab hold	Gordon McMaster
7th November 1991	Kincardine & Deeside	Lib Dem gain	Nicol Stephen
30th June 1994	Monklands East	Lab hold	Helen Liddell
25th May 1995	Perth & Kinross	SNP gain	Roseanna Cunningham
6th November 1997	Paisley South	Lab hold	Douglas Alexander
23rd September 1999	Hamilton South	Lab hold	Bill Tynan
16th March 2000	Ayr	Con gain	John Scott

• EUROPEAN PARLIAMENTARY ELECTIONS 1979–99 •

7TH JUNE 1979

Party	Total Votes	% of Vote	Candidates	Seats
Conservative	430,772	33.7	8	5
Labour	421,968	33.0	8	2
SNP	247,836	19.4	8	1
Liberal	178,433	13.9	8	0
Total	1,279,009	100.0	32	8

14TH JUNE 1984

Party	Total Votes	% of Vote	Candidates	Seats
Labour	526,026	40.7	8	5
Conservative	332,771	25.8	8	2
SNP	230,590	17.9	8	1
SDP/Liberal	201,782	15.6	8	0
Ecology	2,560	0.2	1	0
Total	1,293,759	100.0	33	8

15TH JUNE 1989

Party	Total Votes	% of Vote	Candidates	Seats
Labour	664,263	41.9	8	7
SNP	406,686	25.6	8	1
Conservative	331,495	20.9	8	0
Green	115,028	7.2	8	0
Liberal Democrats	68,056	4.3	8	0
Communist	1,164	0.07	1	0
I. Communist	193	0.01	1	0
Total	1,586,885	100.0	42	8

9TH JUNE 1994

Party	Total Votes	% of Vote	Candidates	Seats
Labour	635,955	42.5	8	6
SNP	487,239	32.6	8	2
Conservative	216,669	14.5	8	0
Liberal Democrats	107,811	7.2	8	0
Green	23,304	1.6	8	0
Militant Labour	12,113	0.8	1	0
Natural Law	5,037	0.3	8	0
Liberal	3,249	0.2	1	0
Socialist	1,832	0.1	2	0
UK Independence	1,096	0.1	1	0
Communist (GB)	689	0.05	1	0

N-E Ethnic	584	0.04	1	0
I. Communist	381	0.03	1	0
Total	1,495,9595	100.0	56	8

For the 1999 election, the eight MEPs were elected using the D'Hondt system from party lists

10TH JUNE 1999

Party	Total Votes	% of Vote	Seats
Labour	283,490	28.69	3
SNP	268,582	27.17	2
Conservative	195,296	19.76	2
Liberal Democrats	96,971	9.81	1
Scottish Green	57,142	5.78	0
Scottish Socialist	39,720	4.02	0
Pro Euro Con.	17,781	1.80	0
UK Independence	12,459	1.26	0
Socialist Labour	9,385	0.95	0
BNP	3,729	0.38	0
Natural Law	2,087	0.21	0
Accountant for Lower Scottish Taxes	1,632	0.17	0

• PARTY COMPOSITION OF THE SCOTTISH UNITARY COUNCILS •

The following results show the make-up of Scotland's unitary councils following the elections on 6th May 1999. The composition at the previous elections in April 1995 (for the mainland councils) and May 1994 (for the island councils) is also included. Boundary changes for the 1999 elections increased or decreased the number of wards in some council areas, such as in Scottish Borders and Aberdeenshire. (NOC = no overall control; Indep = Independent; LD = Lib Dem)

Council	Date	Control	Lab	SNP	Con	LibDem	Indep	Others
Aberdeen	99	NOC	21	4	7	11	0	0
	95	Lab	30	1	9	10	0	0
Aberdeenshire	99	NOC	0	23	8	27	10	0
	95	LD/Ind	0	15	4	15	13	0
Angus	99	SNP	1	21	2	2	3	0
	95	SNP	0	21	2	2	1	0

Council	Date	Control	Lab	SNP	Con	LibDem	Indep	Others
Argyll & Bute	99	Indep	1	5	4	6	20	0
	95	Indep	2	4	3	3	21	0
East Ayrshire	99	Lab	17	14	1	0	0	0
	95	Lab	22	8	0	0	0	0
North Ayrshire	99	Lab	25	2	2	0	1	0
	95	Lab	27	1	1	0	1	0
South Ayrshire	99	Lab	17	0	13	0	0	0
	95	Lab	21	0	4	0	0	0
Clackmannan	99	NOC	8	9	1	0	0	0
	95	Lab	8	3	1	0	0	0
East Dunbarton	99	LD/Con	11	0	3	10	0	0
	95	Lab	15	0	2	9	0	0
West Dunbarton	99	Lab	14	7	0	0	1	0
	95	Lab	14	7	0	0	1	0
Dumfries & Galloway	99	NOC	14	5	8	6	13	1
	95	IndLab/LD	21	9	2	10	28	0
Dundee	99	NOC	14	10	4	0	0	1
	95	Lab	28	3	4	0	0	1
Edinburgh	99	Lab	31	1	13	13	0	0
	95	Lab	34	0	14	10	0	0
Falkirk	99	NOC	15	9	2	0	5	1
	95	Lab	23	8	2	0	3	0
Fife	99	Lab	43	9	1	21	2	2
	95	Lab	54	9	0	25	3	1
Glasgow	99	Lab	74	2	1	1	0	1
	95	Lab	77	1	3	1	0	1
Highland	99	Ind	10	7	0	12	48	3
	95	Lab	6	9	1	4	49	3
Inverclyde	99	NOC	10	0	1	9	0	0
	95	Lab	14	0	1	5	0	0

Council	Date	Control	Lab	SNP	Con	LibDem	Indep	Others
N. Lanarkshire	99	Lab	56	12	0	0	2	0
	95	Lab	60	7	0	0	2	0
S. Lanarkshire	99	Lab	54	10	2	1	0	0
	95	Lab	62	8	2	2	0	0
East Lothian	99	Lab	17	1	5	0	0	0
	95	Lab	15	0	3	0	0	0
Midlothian	99	Lab	17	0	0	1	0	0
	95	Lab	13	2	0	0	0	0
West Lothian	99	Lab	20	11	1	0	0	0
	95	Lab	15	11	1	0	0	0
Moray	99	NOC	6	2	1	2	13	2
	95	SNP	3	13	0	0	2	0
Orkney	99	Ind	0	0	0	0	21	0
	94	Ind	0	0	0	0	26	1
Perthshire & Kinross	99	NOC	6	16	11	6	2	0
	95	SNP	6	18	2	5	1	0
E. Renfrewshire	99	NOC	9	0	8	2	0	1
	95	Lab/LD	8	0	9	2	0	1
Renfrewshire	99	Lab	21	15	1	3	0	0
	95	Lab	22	13	2	3	0	0
Scottish Borders	99	NOC	1	4	1	14	14	0
	95	Ind/LD/SNP/Lab	2	8	3	15	30	0
Shetland	99	Lab	0	0	0	8	13	1
	94	Lab	1	0	0	2	16	7
Stirling	99	NOC	11	2	9	0	0	0
	95	Lab	13	2	7	0	0	0
Western Isles	99	Ind	6	3	0	0	22	0
	94	Ind	5	0	0	0	25	0

• DEVOLUTION REFERENDA •

1ST MARCH 1979

'Do you want the provisions of the Scotland 1978 Act to be put into effect?'

The Scottish electorate voted:
Yes 1,230,937 votes (52%)
No 1,153,502 votes (48%)

Yes majority **77,435**

At Westminster, Scottish MPs voted:
Yes 43 votes (69%)
No 19 votes (31%)

Yes majority **24**

English, Welsh and Irish MPs voted:
Yes 163 votes (37%)
No 282 votes (63%)

No majority **119**

Total MPs votes:
Yes 206 votes (41%)
No 301 votes (59%)

No majority **95**

REGIONAL BREAKDOWN OF THE VOTE

Region	Yes vote	% vote	% electorate	No vote	% vote	% electorate
Shetland	2,020	27	14	5,466	73	36
Orkney	2,104	28	15	5,439	72	39
Borders	20,746	40	27	30,780	60	40
Dumfries & Galloway	27,162	40	26	40,239	38	64
Grampian	94,944	48	28	101,485	52	30
Tayside	91,482	49	31	93,325	51	32
Lothian	187,221	50	33	186,421	50	33
Highland	44,973	51	33	43,274	49	32
Fife	86,252	54	35	74,436	46	30
Str'clyde	596,519	54	34	508,599	46	29
Central	71,296	55	36	59,105	45	30
Western Isles	6,218	56	28	4,933	44	22
Scotland	*1,230,937*	*52*	*33**	*1,153,502*	*48*	*31**

* Percentage on electoral register of 3,747,112 as adjusted by Secretary of State.

In spite of the 'yes' vote having triumphed, the Labour government implemented a clause in the Act requiring 40% of the entire Scottish electorate to vote for devolution before it could come into force. Since this had not been achieved, the government did not implement the Scotland Act and the subsequent Conservative administration of Margaret Thatcher removed it from the statute books.

11TH SEPTEMBER 1997

'I agree/do not agree that there should be a Scottish parliament'
'I agree/do not agree that a Scottish Parliament should have tax-varying powers'

RESULTS

I agree that there should be a Scottish Parliament	1,775,045
I do not agree that there should be a Scottish Parliament	614,400

For: 74.3 %   Against: 25.7 %

I agree that a Scottish Parliament should have tax-varying powers	1,512,889
I do not agree that a Scottish Parliament should have tax-varying power	870,263

For: 63.5%   Against: 36.5 %

REGIONAL BREAKDOWN OF THE VOTE

That there should be a Scottish Parliament

Authority	Yes votes	Yes %	No votes	No %
Orkney	4,749	57.3	3,541	42.7
Dumfries & Galloway	44,619	60.7	28,863	39.3
Perthshire & Kinross	40,344	61.7	24,998	38.3
E. Renfrewshire	28,253	61.7	17,573	38.3
Shetland	5,430	62.4	3,275	37.6
Scottish Borders	33,855	62.8	20,060	37.2
Aberdeenshire	61,621	63.9	34,878	36.1
Angus	33,571	64.7	18,350	35.3
South Ayrshire	40,161	66.9	19,909	33.1
Moray	24,822	67.2	12,122	32.8
Argyll & Bute	30,452	67.3	14,796	32.7
Stirling	29,190	68.5	13,440	31.5
E. Dunbartonshire	40,917	69.8	17,725	30.2
Aberdeen	65,035	71.8	25,580	28.2
Edinburgh	155,900	71.9	60,832	28.1
Highland	72,551	72.6	27,431	27.4
East Lothian	33,525	74.2	11,665	25.8
Dundee	49,252	76.0	15,553	24.0
Fife	125,668	76.1	39,517	23.9
North Ayrshire	51,304	76.3	15,931	23.7
South Lanarkshire	114,908	77.8	32,762	22.2
Inverclyde	31,680	78.0	8,945	22.0
Renfrewshire	68,711	79.0	18,213	21.0
Western Isles	9,977	79.4	2,589	20.6

Authority	Yes votes	Yes %	No votes	No %
West Lothian	56,923	79.6	14,614	20.4
Midlothian	31,681	79.9	7,979	20.1
Clackmannanshire	18,790	80.0	4,706	20.0
Falkirk	55,642	80.0	13,953	20.0
East Ayrshire	49,131	81.1	11,426	18.9
North Lanarkshire	123,063	82.6	26,010	17.4
Glasgow	204,269	83.6	40,106	16.4
W. Dunbartonshire	39,051	84.7	7,058	15.3
Scotland	**1,775,045**	**74.3**	**614,400**	**25.7**

That the Scottish Parliament should have tax-varying powers

Authority	Yes votes	Yes %	No votes	No %
Orkney	3,917	47.4	4,344	52.6
Dumfries & Galloway	35,737	48.8	37,499	51.2
Scottish Borders	27,284	50.7	6,497	49.3
Perthshire & Kinross	33,398	51.3	31,709	48.7
East Renfrewshire	23,580	51.6	22,153	48.4
Shetland	4,478	51.6	4,198	48.4
Aberdeenshire	50,295	52.3	45,929	47.7
Moray	19,326	52.7	17,344	47.3
Angus	27,641	53.4	24,089	46.6
South Ayrshire	33,679	56.2	26,217	43.8
Argyll & Bute	25,746	57.0	19,429	43.0
Stirling	25,044	58.9	17,487	41.1
E. Dunbartonshire	34,576	59.1	23,914	40.9
Aberdeen	54,320	60.3	35,709	39.7
Edinburgh	133,843	62.0	82,188	38.0
Highland	61,359	62.1	37,525	37.9
East Lothian	28,152	62.7	16,765	37.3
Renfrewshire	55,075	63.6	31,537	36.4
Fife	108,021	64.7	58,987	35.3
Dundee	42,304	65.5	22,280	34.5
North Ayrshire	43,990	65.7	22,991	34.3
Inverclyde	27,194	67.2	13,277	32.8
West Lothian	47,990	67.3	23,354	32.7
South Lanarkshire	99,587	67.6	47,708	32.4
Midlothian	26,776	67.7	12,762	32.3
Western Isles	8,557	68.4	3,947	31.6
Clackmannanshire	16,112	68.7	7,355	31.3
Falkirk	48,064	69.2	21,403	30.8
East Ayrshire	42,559	70.5	17,824	29.5

Authority	Yes votes	Yes %	No votes	No %
N. Lanarkshire	107,288	72.2	41,372	27.8
W. Dunbartonshire	34,408	74.7	11,628	25.3
Glasgow	182,589	75.0	60,842	25.0
Scotland	*1,512,889*	*63.5*	*870,263*	*36.5*

• SECRETARIES OF STATE FOR SCOTLAND •

1885	The Duke of Richmond
1886	G. O. Trevelyan
1886	The Earl of Daihousie
1886	Arthur J. Balfour
1887	The Marquis of Lothian
1892	Sir G. O. Trevelyan
1895	Alexander Bruce
1903	Andrew Murray
1905	The Marquis of Linlithgow
1905	John Sinclair
1912	T. P. Mackinnon-Wood
1916	Harold John Tennant
1916	Robert Munro
1922	Viscount Novar
1924	William Adamson
1924	Sir John Gilmour
1929	William Adamson
1931	Sir Archibald Sinclair
1932	Sir Godfrey Collins
1936	Walter Elliot
1938	D. J. Colville
1940	Ernest Brown
1941	Tom Johnston
1945	Earl of Roseberry
1945	Joseph Westwood
1947	Arthur Woodburn
1950	Hector MacNeil
1951	James Stuart
1957	John S. Maclay
1962	Michael Noble
1964	William Ross
1970	Gordon Campbell
1974	William Ross
1976	Bruce Millan
1979	George Younger
1986	Malcolm Rifkind
1990	Ian Lang
1994	Michael Foryth
1997	Donald Dewar
1999	John Reid

• DEPUTY-SECRETARIES OF STATE FOR SCOTLAND •

This new office was created on 28th July 1998

1998 Helen Liddell
1999 Office vacant

1999 Brian Wilson

• FIRST MINISTERS •

Unlike at Westminster where the leader of the largest party automatically becomes Prime Minister, the First Minister is voted in by all MSPs

1999 Donald Dewar

• PRESIDING OFFICERS OF THE SCOTTISH PARLIAMENT •

Fulfilling a role similar to the Speaker at Westminister, the Presiding Officer of the Scottish Parliament also chairs the Business Committee and represents the Parliament at external forums such as the Council of the Isles. The Presiding Officer does not vote in divisions. There are also two similarly elected Deputy Presiding Officers, each of equal status and who retain their vote in divisions.

PRESIDING OFFICER

1999 David Steel (Liberal)

DEPUTY PRESIDING OFFICERS

1999 George Reid (SNP)
      Patricia Ferguson (Labour)

• MEMBERS OF THE SCOTTISH PARLIAMENT (MSPS) •

Adam, Brian, SNP, Scotland North East region

Aitken, William, Con, Glasgow region

Alexander, Wendy, Lab, Paisley North, maj. 4,616

Baillie, Jackie, Lab, Dumbarton, maj. 4,758

Barrie, Scott, Lab, Dunfermline West, maj. 5,021

Boyack, Sarah, Lab, Edinburgh Central, maj. 4,626

Brankin, Rhona, Lab Co-op., Midlothian, maj. 5,525

Brown, Robert, Lib Dem, Glasgow region

Campbell, Colin, SNP, Scotland West region

Canavan, Dennis A., MP, Indep, Falkirk West, maj. 12,192

Chisholm, Malcolm G.R., MP, Lab, Edinburgh North and Leith, maj. 7,736

Craigie, Cathy, Lab, Cumbernauld and Kilsyth, maj. 4,259

Crawford, Bruce, SNP Scotland Mid and Fife region

Creech, Christine, SNP, Scotland South region

Cunningham, Roseanna, MP, SNP, Perth, maj. 2,027

Curran, Margaret, Lab, Glasgow Baillieston, maj. 3,072

Davidson, David, Con, Scotland North East region

Deacon, Susan, Lab, Edinburgh East and Musselburgh, maj. 6,714

Dewar, Rt. Hon. Donald, MP, Lab, Glasgow Anniesland, maj. 10,993

Douglas Hamilton, Rt. Hon. Lord James (The Lord Selkirk of Douglas), QC, Con, Lothians region

Eadie, Helen, Lab Co-op., Dunfermline East, maj. 8,699

Elder, Dorothy, SNP, Glasgow region

Ewing, Fergus, SNP, Inverness East, Nairn and Lochaber, maj. 441

Ewing, Margaret A., MP, SNP, Moray, maj. 4,129

Ewing, Winifred, SNP, Highlands and Islands region

Fabiani, Linda, SNP, Scotland Central region

Farquhar-Munro, John, Lib Dem, Ross, Skye and Inverness West, maj. 1,539

Ferguson, Patricia, Lab, Glasgow Maryhill, maj. 4,326

Fergusson, Alex, Con, Scotland South region

Finnie, Ross, Lib Dem, Scotland West region

Gailbraith, Samuel L., MP, Lab, Strathkelvin and Bearsden, maj. 12,121

Gallie, Phil, Con, Scotland South region

Gibson, Kenneth, SNP, Glasgow region

Godman, Patricia, Lab, Renfrewshire West, maj. 2,893

Goldie, Annabel, Con, Scotland West region

Gorrie, Donald C. E., MP, Lib Dem, Scotland Central region

Grant, Rhoda, Lab, Highlands and Islands region

Gray, Iain, Lab, Edinburgh Pentlands, maj. 2,885

Hamilton, Duncan, SNP, Highlands and Islands region

Harding, Keith, Con, Scotland Mid and Fife region

Harper, Robin, Green, Lothians region

Henry, Hugh, Lab, Paisley South, maj. 4,495

Home Robertson, John D., MP, Lab, East Lothian, maj. 10,946

Hughes, Janice, Lab, Glasgow Rutherglen, maj. 7,287

Hyslop, Fiona, SNP, Lothians region

Ingram, Adam, SNP, Scotland South region

Jackson, Gordon, Lab, Glasgow Govan, maj. 1,756

Jackson, Sylvia, Lab, Stirling, maj. 3,981

Jamieson, Cathy, Lab Co-op., Carrick, Cumnock and Doon Valley, maj. 8,803

Jamieson, Margaret, Lab, Kilmarnock and Loudoun, maj. 2,760

Jenkins, Ian, Lib Dem, Tweeddale, Ettrick and Lauderdale, maj. 4,478

Johnston, Nicholas, Con, Scotland Mid and Fife region

Johnstone, Alex, Con, Scotland North East region

Kerr, Andy, Lab, East Kilbride, maj. 6,499

Lamont, Johann, Lab Co-op., Glasgow Pollock, maj. 4,642

Livingstone, Marilyn, Lab Co-op., Kirkcaldy, maj. 4,475

Lochhead, Richard, SNP, Scotland North East region

Lyon, George, Lib Dem, Argyll and Bute, maj. 2,057

McAllion, John, MP, Lab, Dundee East, maj. 2,854

MacAskill, Kenny, SNP, Lothians region

McAveety, Frank, Lab Co-op., Glasgow Shettleston, maj. 5,467

McCabe, Tom, Lab, Hamilton South, maj. 7,176

McConnell, Jack, Lab, Motherwell and Wishaw, maj. 5,076

Macdonald, Lewis, Lab, Aberdeen Central, maj. 2,696

MacDonald, Margo, SNP, Lothians region

MacGrigor, Jamie, Con, Highlands and Islands region

McGugan, Irene, SNP, Scotland North East region

Macintosh, Ken, Lab, Eastwood, maj. 2,125

Mcintosh, Lindsay, Con, Scotland Central region

MacKay, Angus, Lab, Edinburgh South, maj. 5,424

MacLean, Kate, Lab, Dundee West, maj. 121

McLeish, Henry B., MP, Lab, Fife Central, maj. 8,675

McLeod, Fiona, SNP, Scotland West region

McLetchie, David, Con, Lothians region

McMahon, Michael, Lab, Hamilton North and Bellshill, maj. 5,606

MacMillan, Maureen, Lab, Highlands and Islands region

McNeil, Duncan, Lab, Greenock and Inverclyde, maj. 4,313

McNeill, Pauline, Lab, Glasgow Kelvin, maj. 4,408

McNulty, Des, Lab, Clydebank and Milngavie, maj. 4,710

Martin, Paul, Lab, Glasgow Springburn, maj. 7,893

Marwick, Tricia, SNP, Scotland Mid and Fife region

Matheson, Michael, SNP, Scotland Central region

Monteith, Brian, Con, Scotland Mid and Fife region

Morgan, Alasdair N., MP, SNP, Galloway and Upper Nithsdale, maj. 3,201

Morrison, Alasdair, Lab, Western Isles, maj. 2,093

Muldoon, Bristow, Lab, Livingston, maj. 3,904

Mulligan, Mary, Lab, Linlithgow, maj. 2,928

Mundell, David, Con, Scotland South region

Murray, Elaine, Lab, Dumfries, maj. 3,654

Neil, Alex, SNP, Scotland Central region

Oldfather, Irene, Lab, Cunninghame South, maj. 6,541

Paterson, Gil, SNP, Scotland Central region

Peacock, Peter, Lab, Highlands and Islands region

Peattie, Cathy, Lab, Falkirk East, maj. 4,139

Quinan, Lloyd, SNP, Scotland West region

Radcliffe, Nora, Lib Dem, Gordon, maj. 4,195

Raffan, Keith, Lib Dem, Scotland Mid and Fife region

Reid, George, SNP, Scotland Mid and Fife region

Robison, Shona, SNP, Scotland North East region

Robson, Euan, Lib Dem, Roxburgh and Berwickshire, maj. 3,585

Rumbles, Mike, Lib Dem, Aberdeenshire West and Kincardine, maj. 2,289

Russell, Michael, SNP, Scotland South region

Salmond, Alex E.A., MP, SNP, Banff and Buchan, maj. 11,292

Scanlon, Mary, Con, Highlands and Islands region

Scott, John, Con, Ayr, maj. 3,344

Scott, Tavish, Lib Dem, Shetland, maj. 3,194

Sheridan, Tommy, SSP, Glasgow region

Simpson, Richard, Lab, Ochil, maj. 1,303

Smith, Elaine, Lab, Coatbridge and Chryston, maj. 10,404

Smith, Iain, Lib Dem, Fife North East, maj. 5,064

Smith, Margaret, Lib Dem, Edinburgh West, maj. 4,583

Steel, Rt. Hon. Sir David (The Lord Steel of Alkwood), KBE, QC, Lib Dem, Lothians region

Stephen, Nicol, Lib Dem, Aberdeen South, maj. 1,760

Stone, Jamie, Lib Dem, Caithness, Sutherland and Easter Ross, maj. 4,391

Sturgeon, Nicola, SNP, Glasgow region

Swinney, John R., MP, SNP, Tayside North, maj. 4,192

Thomson, Elaine, Lab, Aberdeen North, maj. 398

Tosh, Murray, Con, Scotland South region

Turnbull, Karen, Lab, Clydesdale, maj. 3,880

Ullrich, Kay, SNP, Scotland West region

Wallace, Ben, Con, Scotland North East region

Wallace, James R., MP, Lib Dem, Orkney, maj. 4,619

Watson, Mike (Lord Watson of Invergowrie), Lab, Glasgow Cathcart, maj. 5,374

Welsh, Andrew P., MP, SNP, Angus, maj. 8,901

White, Sandra, SNP, Glasgow region

Whitefield, Karen, Lab, Airdrie and Shotts, maj. 8,985

Wilson, Allan, Lab, Cunninghame North, maj. 4,796

Wilson, Andrew, SNP, Scotland Central region

Young, John, Con, Scotland West region

• WESTMINSTER MPS FOR SCOTTISH SEATS•

Adams Irene K., Lab, Paisley North, maj. 12,814

Alexander, Douglas G., Lab, Paisley South, maj. 2,731

Begg, Anne, Lab, Aberdeen South, maj. 3,365

Brown, Rt. Hon. J. Gordon, Lab, Dunfermline East, maj. 18,751

Brown, Russell L., Lab, Dumfries, maj. 9,643

Browne, Desmond, Lab, Kilmarnock and Loudoun, maj. 7,256

Bruce, Malcolm G., Lib Dem, Gordon, maj. 6,997

Campbell, Rt. Hon. W. Menzies, CBE, QC, Lib Dem, Fife North East, maj. 10,356

Canavan, Dennis A., Lab, Falkirk West, maj. 13,783

Chisholm, Malcolm G.R., Lab, Edinburgh North and Leith, maj. 10,978

Clark, Lynda M., Lab, Edinburgh Pentlands, maj. 4,862

Clarke, Eric L., Lab, Midlothian, maj. 9,870

Clarke, Rt. Hon. Thomas, CBE, Lab, Coatbridge and Chryston, maj. 19,295

Connarty, Michael, Lab, Falkirk East, maj. 13,385

Cook, Rt. Hon. R.E. (Robin), Lab, Livingston, maj. 11,747

Cunningham, Roseanna, SNP, Perth, maj. 3,141

Dalyell, Tam (Sir Thomas Dalyell of the Binns, Bt.), Lab, Linlithgow, maj. 10,838

Darling, Rt. Hon. Alistair M., Lab, Edinburgh Central, maj. 11,070

Davidson, Ian G., Lab Co-op., Glasgow Pollok, maj. 13,791

Dewar, Rt. Hon. Donald C., Lab, Glasgow Anniesland, maj. 15,154

Donohoe, Brian H., Lab, Cunninghame South, maj. 14,869

Doran, Frank, Lab, Aberdeen Central, maj. 10,801

Ewing, Margaret A., SNP, Moray, maj. 5,566

Foulkes, George, Lab Co-op., Carrick, Cumnock and Doon Valley, maj. 21,062

Fyfe, Maria, Lab, Glasgow Maryhill, maj. 14,264

Galbraith, Samuel L., Lab, Strathkelvin and Bearsden, maj. 16,292

Galloway, George, Lab, Glasgow Kelvin, maj. 9,665

Godman, Norman A., Lab, Greenock and Inverclyde, maj. 13,040

Gorrie, Donald C.E., Lib Dem, Edinburgh West, maj. 7,253

Graham, Thomas, SLI, Renfrewshire West, maj. 7,979

Griffiths Nigel, Lab, Edinburgh South, maj. 11,452

Home Robertson, John D., Lab, East Lothian, maj. 14,221

Hood, James, Lab, Clydesdale, maj. 13,809

Ingram, Rt. Hon. Adam P., Lab, East Kilbride, maj. 17,384

Kennedy, Charles P., Lib Dem, Ross, Skye and Inverness West, maj. 4,019

Kirkwood, Archibald J., Lib Dem, Roxburgh and Berwickshire, maj. 7,906

Liddell, Rt. Hon. Helen, Lab, Airdrie and Shotts, maj. 15,412

McAllion, John, Lab, Dundee East, maj. 9,961

McAvoy, Thomas M., Lab Co-op., Glasgow Rutherglen, maj. 15,007

Macdonald, Calum A., Lab, Western Isles, maj. 3,576

McFall, John, Lab Co-op., Dumbarton, maj. 10,883

McGuire, Anne, Lab, Stirling, maj. 6,411

McKenna, Rosemary, Lab, Cumbernauld and Kilsyth, maj. 11,128

McLeish, Henry B., Lab, Fife Central, maj. 13,713

Maclennan, Rt. Hon. Robert A.R., Lib Dem, Caithness, Sutherland and Easter Ross, maj. 2,259

Marshall, David, Lab, Glasgow Shettleston, maj. 15,868

Martin, Michael J., Lab, Glasgow Springburn, maj. 17,326

Maxton, John A., Lab, Glasgow Cathcart, maj. 12,245

Michie, J. Ray, Lib Dem, Argyll and Bute, maj. 6,081

Moonie, Dr Lewis G., Lab Co-op., Kirkcaldy, maj. 10,710

Moore, Michael K., Lib Dem, Tweeddale, Ettrick and Lauderdale, maj. 1,489

Morgan, Alastair N., SNP, Galloway and Upper Nithsdale, maj. 5,624

Murphy, James, Lab, Eastwood, maj. 3,236

O'Neill, Martin J., Lab, Ochil, maj. 4,652

Osborne, Sandra C., Lab, Ayr, maj. 6,543

Reid, Rt. Hon. John, Lab, Hamilton North and Bellshill, maj. 17,067

Ross, Ernest, Lab, Dundee West, maj. 11,859

Roy, Frank, Lab, Motherwell and Wishaw, maj. 12,791

Salmond, Alexander E.A, SNP, Banff and Buchan, maj. 12,845

Sarwar, Mohammad, Lab, Glasgow Govan, maj. 2,914

Savidge, Malcolm K., Lab, Aberdeen North, maj. 10,010

Smith, Sir Robert, Bt, Lib Dem, Aberdeenshire West and Kincardine, maj. 2,662

Squire, Rachel A., Lab, Dunfermline West, maj. 12,354

Stewart, David J., Lab, Inverness East, Nairn and Lochaber, maj. 2,339

Strang, Rt. Hon. Gavin S., Lab, Edinburgh East and Musselburgh, maj. 14,530

Swinney, John R., SNP, Tayside North, maj. 4,160

Tynan Bill, Lab, Hamilton South, maj. 556

Wallace, James R., Lib Dem, Orkney and Shetland, maj. 6,968

Welsh, Andrew P., SNP, Angus, maj. 10,189

Wilson, Brian D. H., Lab, Cunninghame North, maj. 11,039

Worthington, Anthony, Lab, Clydebank and Milngavie, maj. 13,320

Wray, James, Lab, Glasgow Baillieston, maj. 14,840

• MSP AND MP SUPERLATIVES •

YOUNGEST MPs

1999 SCOTTISH PARLIAMENT

Duncan Hamilton
(SNP, Highlands & Islands) b. 1974

1997 WESTMIINSTER

Douglas Alexander
(Lab, Paisley South) b. 1967
Jim Murphy
(Lab, Eastwood) b. 1967

OLDEST MPs

1999 SCOTTISH PARLIAMENT
Winnie Ewing
(SNP, Highlands & Islands) b. 1930

1997 WESTMIINSTER
Sir Thomas ('Tam') Dalyell of the Binns
(Lab, Linlithgow) b. 1932

MOST VOTES IN A GENERAL ELECTION

1999 SCOTTISH PARLIAMENT
21,505 (50.73%) Sam Gailbraith
(Lab, Strathkelvin & Bearsden)

1997 WESTMIINSTER
29,398 (59.8%) George Foulkes
(Lab, Carrick, Cumnock & Doon Valley)

LEAST VOTES IN A GENERAL ELECTION

1999 SCOTTISH PARLIAMENT
5,435 (51.94%) Tavish Scott
(Lib Dem, Shetland)

1997 WESTMIINSTER
8,955 (55.6%) Calum Macdonald
(Lab, Western Isles)

HIGHEST % OF VOTES IN A GENERAL ELECTION

1999 SCOTTISH PARLIAMENT
73.2% (19,616) David Marshall
(Lab, Glasgow Shettleston)

1997 WESTMIINSTER
67.39% (6,010) Jim Wallace
(Lib Dem, Orkney)

LOWEST % OF VOTES IN A GENERAL ELECTION

1999 SCOTTISH PARLIAMENT
32.57% (11,300) Nicol Stephen
(Lib Dem, Aberdeen South)

1997 WESTMIINSTER
31.2% (12,178) Michael Moore
(Lib Dem, Tweedale, Ettrick & Lauderdale)

LARGEST MAJORITY IN A GENERAL ELECTION

1999 SCOTTISH PARLIAMENT
12,192 (36.21%) Denis Canavan
(Indep, Falkirk West)

1997 WESTMIINSTER
21, 062 (42.8%) George Foulkes
(Lab, Carrick, Cumnock & Doon Valley)

SMALLEST MAJORITY IN A GENERAL ELECTION

1999 SCOTTISH PARLIAMENT
25 (0.07%) Ian Welsh
(former Lab MSP, Ayr)

1997 WESTMIINSTER
1,489 (3.8%) Michael Moore
(Lib Dem, Tweeddale, Ettrick &
Lauderdale)

HISTORY

POLITICAL CHRONOLOGY

9000–6000 BC   The first migrant, Stone-Age hunter settlers arrived in Scotland.

4500–3000 BC   The first Neolithic farmer settlers arrived in Scotland.

2000–500 BC   Bronze-Age Celts arrived.

80 AD Roman Governor Agricola invaded Scotland.

84 AD Battle of Mons Graupius: Agricola's army defeated a Caledonian force (Caledonia being northern Scotland).

118 AD Romans built Hadrian's Wall to mark the boundaries of their territory.

c. 150 Antonine Wall built to mark Rome's northernmost boundaries; the wall was abandoned as the Romans consolidated in the south, c. 180.

c. 400 Ninian, the first known Christian missionary to Scotland, arrived. He established a church at Whithorn among the southern Picts. Ninian went on to establish Christianity in the southern parts of Scotland.

c. 500 The Scoti, from Ireland, settled in Argyll and Kintyre, areas which were later the strongholds of the Kingdom of Dalriada.

c. 550 Angles settled in south-eastern Scotland.

563   Colm, or Columba, an Irish missionary, arrived at Iona, and established a monastery there two years later. Columba and his monks complemented Ninian's southern work in the north.

685   The Picts defeated the Angles in the Battle of Nechtansmere, near Forfar.

794   Viking invasions of Scotland began.

843   Kenneth Macalpin united the Picts and the Scots in the kingdom of Alba, setting his capital at Scone.

1130 Moray, the northern Pictish province, was finally subdued when David I defeated Angus, grandson of King Lulach.

1138 David I's attempts to invade England came to grief at the Battle of the Standard, when his undisciplined Scots army was heavily defeated.

1158   The Norse recognised the authority of Somerled, Lord of the Isles and leader of the Western Isles. He had inflicted a series of defeats on them over several years.

1263   The near-500-year Viking threat to Scotland was finally ended when Alexander III defeated Haakon IV of Norway at the Battle of Largs. The victory won the Hebrides and the Isle of Man for Scotland.

1290–92   The First Interregnum: with no obvious candidate to succeed Alexander III's successor, Margaret, the seven-year-old 'Maid of Norway', civil war threatened. To avoid this, Edward I of England was invited to choose the new king. He agreed on condition that all nobles recognise his overlordship of Scotland; only two refused.

1292   From the 12 contestants (who included Robert Bruce, The Bruce's grandfather), Edward chose John Balliol.

1296   After intolerable and humiliating treatment by Edward, King John rebelled against his overlordship. Edward's retaliation was swift and vicious, with invasion, the capture of Berwick and a crushing defeat at Dunbar. To undermine his overlordship, he removed the Stone of Scone to Westminster and forced 2000 nobles, churchmen, burgesses and freeholders to swear fealty to him. The submissions were recorded on what became known as the 'Ragman Rolls'. Balliol left for exile.

1297   A minor noble, William Wallace, rebelled against Edward and defeated his forces at the Battle of Stirling Bridge. Wallace was an inspirational leader, but his relatively low social status prevented many higher-ranking nobles joining or helping him.

1298   Wallace was defeated by Edward at the Battle of Falkirk, after which he faded into obscurity.

1305   Wallace was betrayed near Glasgow and handed over to the English. Tried for treason, he was dragged in chains through the streets of London behind a cart, before being publicly hung, drawn and quartered.

1306   Years of personal enmity erupted in Greyfriars Church, Dumfries, when John Balliol's nephew, John Comyn, was stabbed to death by Robert Bruce, grandson of one of the contestants for the throne in 1292. Bruce was crowned Robert I later that year but was declared outlaw by Edward I and was excommunicated by the Church for the murder. With no more than a handful of supporters, Robert began his gruelling eight-year guerilla campaign which succeeded in driving the English almost completely out of Scotland.

1307   Edward I died at Burgh-by-Sands in Cumbria, on his way north to subdue this latest revolt.

1314   The Battle of Bannockburn. Robert I won an utterly crushing victory in open battle over superior English forces, effectively securing Scotland's independence.

1320 The Declaration of Arbroath. A noble and inspiring letter sent by the nobles of Scotland to Pope John XXII, asserting the independence of Scotland and their support for Robert as their king.

1328 The Treaty of Northampton was signed between the now-ailing Robert I and Edward II of England, ending the Wars of Independence and finally recognising Scotland's independence.

1333 The Battle of Halidon Hill saw Edward Balliol, son of King John, and his exiled followers, defeat the Scots army. The king, David II, Robert I's son, was still a child and was sent to France for safety for eight years.

1346 The Battle of Neville's Cross saw David's attempted invasion of England go disastrously wrong when he was taken prisoner; he was held in the Tower of London for the next 10 years.

1371 Robert II, son of Marjorie Bruce and Walter, High Steward of Scotland, took the throne as the first in the new line of Stewart kings.

1427 James I emphasised his control of the country by imprisoning 50 troublesome Highland chiefs during the Inverness parliament; the chiefs had believed they held their lands of their own right, not of the king.

1488 The Battle of Sauchieburn; James III was defeated by a group of disgruntled nobles, including his own son, James. The king was killed in the battle.

1493 The Stewarts' relentless centralising continued when James IV broke up the Lordship of the Isles.

1503 James IV married Margaret Tudor, Henry VIII of England's sister. It was this marriage that gave the Stewarts their claim over the English throne a century later.

1513 The Battle of Flodden. James IV invaded England but was killed, with many of the Scots nobility, in a disastrously executed battle.

1542 The Battle of Solway Moss was yet another military defeat for the Scots at the hands of the English, with many Scots nobles surrendering. James V died a few days after the battle, leaving his infant daughter, Mary, as queen.

1547 The Battle of Pinkie. Scots forces were again defeated by the English. Henry VIII wanted Mary to be contracted to marry his son, the future Edward VI, and harried the Scots to force the match. But Mary was betrothed to the French Dauphin, and left for France the following year. She married him in 1558.

1560 The Reformation was officially recognised in Scotland with the passing of the Confession of Faith by Parliament. As well as being supporters, many Scots lords resented the influence of the Catholic French under the Queen Mother, Mary of Guise. Papal supremacy and the Mass were abolished. A zealous and fundamentalist discipline, complete with courts, would be established by the new church.

1561 Queen Mary was invited to return to Scotland after the death of her husband.

After her return she continued to use the French spelling of her name, Stuart, and it became common practice for the royal house to be so styled thereafter. Mary was allowed to practice her Catholic religion and, for the first few years of her reign and with the help of her half-brother, James Stewart, the Earl of Moray, negotiated her way well through Scotland's complicated religious and poliitical landscape.

1566 James VI was born after Queen Mary's marriage to her cousin, Henry Stewart, Lord Darnley. Darnley was a vain and weak man and he and Mary soon separated.

1567 Darnley was murdered and Mary married the chief suspect, James Hepburn, the Earl of Bothwell, just three months later. She was forced to abdicate in favour of her son, with the Earl of Moray as Regent.

1568 Queen Mary fled to England after her defeat at the Battle of Langside. She was imprisoned by her cousin, Elizabeth I, for 19 years before being executed in 1587. (When Mary's son became king in England, he razed to the ground Fotheringay Castle, her final prison.)

1582 James VI was kidnapped by a group of extremist Protestant nobles and imprisoned in Ruthven Castle in a raid approved by the highly politicised new Church of Scotland. After his escape, James set about a counter-offensive against the Church to ensure it could never again threaten the monarch.

1597 The clans were brought under yet more centralised control, with new laws requiring chiefs to guarantee clansmen's good conduct and produce titles to prove their right to own their lands.

1603 After Elizabeth I of England died, James travelled south to take possession of his new kingdom. Both countries were united under one monarch, but they were still independent, each with their own systems of government.

1609 The Statutes of Iona, a further measure of pacification for the Highlands.

1610 The successful culmination of James VI's campaign against the Church of Scotland in the introduction of an episcopal system of church government.

1612 Henry, Prince of Wales, James VI's brilliant and popular eldest son, died of typhoid. The grieving king's successor was now his less talented and more distant younger son, Charles.

1638 The signing of the National Covenant. Charles I had introduced changes in religious practice to the Church of England, and in the late 1630s was attempting to change the liturgy in the Scottish Church. The symbol of this was the new prayer book, introduced the previous year. Scottish Protestants signed the National Covenant to consolidate opposition to the changes.

1643 The signing of the Solemn League and Covenant. Scottish supporters of the National Covenant agreed to help the English Parliament fight the king in return for an overthrow of the system of episcopacy in the Church of Scotland.

1644–45 Campaign of Marquis of Montrose in support of Charles I. Montrose, originally a supporter of the Solemn League and Covenant, was persuaded by the king to become his captain general in Scotland. He conducted a superb campaign against the Army of the Covenant, winning battles at Tippermuir, Aberdeen, Inverlochy, Auldearn, Alford and Kilsyth. His forces were finally surprised and defeated at Philiphaugh in the Borders by Covenant cavalry.

1648 Charles I surrendered to the Scots, who handed him over to the English Parliament in 1647 in return for £400,000, about one third of the money owed to the Scots army. But the king continued to negotiate with the Covenanters, and agreed to a limited restoration of presbyterianism in return for armed support. The Scots consequently re-entered the war, this time on the royalist side.

1650–51 Charles II was crowned at Scone following the execution of his father the previous year. He was forced to accept the Solemn League and Covenant. At the Battle of Dunbar in 1651, a numerically superior Scottish force was routed by Parliament's New Model Army, led by Oliver Cromwell. Cromwell's subsequent campaign against the Covenanter army was concluded at Worcester in 1651, when the Scots were crushed. Scotland became part of the Commonwealth, and later the Protectorate. Charles fled to the Continent.

1660 Charles II returned from exile and the monarchy was restored.

1666 The Pentland Rising. Extremist elements among the Covenanters, in protest against the restoration of episcopal government in 1661, marched on Edinburgh. But at Rullion Green in the Pentland Hills they were crushed by Government forces under Sir Thomas Dalyell.

1678 To suppress the extreme Covenanters in the south-west of Scotland, the Government ordered a 5,000-strong Highland army to march to Renfrew and Ayrshire with orders to disarm the dissidents and live off the land. The plundering of the south-west by this 'Highland Host' left the inhabitants with a lasting hatred of the Highlanders.

1679 Continuing attempts by the Government to suppress Covenanting worship meetings (conventicles) by force led to violence at Drumclog in Lanarkshire when a party of royalist cavalry under John Graham of Claverhouse were routed by the worshippers. This action gathered momentum and with an army of 5,000, the Covenanters marched on Glasgow. However, their rebellion ended with the defeat of the insurgents at Bothwell Bridge.

1689 James VII, a Catholic, succeeded his brother, Charles, in 1685 and immediately undertook to remove the penalties against his co-religionists that had been in force since the early 1660s. In 1688, William of Orange, James' brother-in-law, accepted an invitation from disaffected English Anglican nobles and clergy to depose James and assume the throne. James escaped to France and this 'Glorious Revolution' established William and his wife, Mary, as joint rulers. In Scotland a Convention of the Estates in 1689 formally declared James to have forfeited his throne by vacating it and invited William to become King of Scots.

John Graham of Claverhouse, now Viscount Dundee, raised a Highland army in support of the exiled James and at the Battle of Killiecrankie defeated a larger Williamite force. Unfortunately for the Jacobite cause, he was killed during the battle. His army subsequently failed to take the cathedral town of Dunkeld from its Covenanter defenders and the rebellion effectively ceased.

1692   Massacre at Glencoe. As an example to other rebellious clans, William authorised punitive action against the Maciain MacDonalds of Glencoe, who had been slow in taking the oath of allegiance to the king. The Campbells of Glenlyon duly murdered 38 MacDonalds while acting as their guests, in direct violation of the code of Highland hospitality.

1707   The Union with England. Scotland, suffering severe economic hardship, was pressurised into abandoning its political independence in return for English assistance. Amid great popular unrest, the Scottish Parliament voted for union with its English counterpart although still retaining its own church, courts and legal system. The separate kingdoms of Scotland and England ceased to exist and were incorporated into a United Kingdom of Great Britain.

1715   The first Jacobite rising. Hoping to capitalise on disaffection with the Union and the Hanoverian George I, the supporters of the exiled son of James VII, James, 'The Old Pretender', tried to restore the Stuart dynasty by rebellion. A Jacobite army led by the inept Earl of Mar met Government forces led by the Duke of Argyll at Sheriffmuir and although the battle was inconclusive, it was a tactical defeat for the Jacobites who subsequently retreated and dispersed.

1719   A second Jacobite rising occurred when a party of 300 Spaniards landed to raise the clans who generally refused to be drawn into the scheme. At Glen Shiel, they were defeated by Government troops.

1724   Major General George Wade was appointed commander-in-chief in Scotland with the task of demilitarising the Highlands. He increased the number of garrisons in the region and linked them with an extensive chain of military roads running along the Great Glen.

1745–46   The last Jacobite rising. At Glenfinnan, 'The Young Pretender', Prince Charles Edward Stuart, raised his standard and the Highland clans, sometimes reluctantly, rose in support. The Highland army enjoyed an easy victory at Prestonpans before moving into England. It failed to capitalise on its successes and at Derby abandoned plans to seize London. In spite of a further victory at Falkirk in 1746, the campaign reached a bloody conclusion at Culloden Moor where the Jacobite army was crushed. Charles escaped to France but his supporters were subject to cruel and bloody repression. The wearing of tartan was proscribed and the clan system was effectively destroyed in the years after Culloden as the Highland chiefs were deprived of their hereditary powers.

1782   The Act proscribing Highland dress was repealed.

1790 onwards   The Highland Clearances. During the first half of the nineteenth century, the Highland estates were reorganised to allow sheep farming at the expense of arable farming. Consequently, tenants were evicted from their holdings and removed to other, less viable parts of the estate. Great hardships often resulted and gradually, emigration to the Lowlands or the colonies became the inescapable fate of the Highlander.

1886 The Crofters' Holding Act. By the 1880s, crofter discontent at the pattern of land-holding in the Highlands threatened to became violent. To forestall this agitation, the Government passed the Crofters' Holding Act which gave the crofters security of tenure, fixed rents, the right to inherit or pass on crofts and the right to compensation for land improvement if they were evicted. The act also established the Crofters' Commission to safeguard their rights and manage disputes.

1887 The Scottish Office was established at Westminster to take responsibility for all Scottish matters

1997 A referendum held in Scotland on devolution approved the creation of a new Scottish parliament with tax-raising powers. Overall power still rested with the British government in Westminster.

1999 The new Scottish Parliament sat for the first time in almost 300 years.

• KINGS AND QUEENS OF SCOTS •

THE HOUSE OF MACALPIN, 834–1034

Kenneth I (Mac Alpin) (r. 843–58)
Donald I (r. 858–62) brother of Kenneth I
Constantine I (r. 862–77) son of Kenneth I
Aed (r. 877–78) son of Kenneth I
Eochaid (r. 878–89) grandson of Kenneth I
Donald II (r. 889–900) son of Constantine I
Constantine II (r. 900–42; d. 952) son of Aed
Malcolm I (r. 942–54) son of Donald II
Indulf (r. 954–62) son of Constantine II
Dubh (r. 962–66) son of Malcolm I
Culen (r. 966–71) son of Indulf
Kenneth II (r. 971–95) son of Malcolm I
Constantine III (r. 995–97) son of Culen
Kenneth III (r. 997–10005) son of Dubh
Malcolm II (r. 1005–34) son of Kenneth II

*Note: Not all children are shown on the genealogical charts that follow.
Names of monarchs are shown in bold*

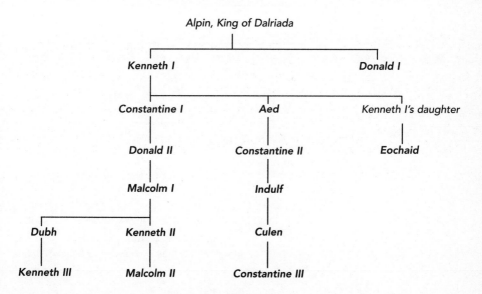

THE HOUSE OF DUNKELD 1034–1290

Duncan I (r. 1034–40) grandson of Malcolm II
Macbeth (1040–57) grandson of Malcolm II
Lulach (r. 1057–58) great-grandson of Kenneth III
Malcolm III (r. 1058–93) son of Duncan I
Donald III (r. 1093–94; deposed) son of Duncan I
Duncan II (r. 1094) son of Malcolm III
Donald III (restored r. 1094–97) son of Duncan I
Edgar (r. 1097–1107) son of Malcolm III
Alexander I (r. 1107–24) son of Malcolm III
David I (r. 1124–53) son of Malcolm III
Malcolm IV (r. 1153–65) grandson of David I
William I (r. 1165–1214) brother of Malcolm IV
Alexander II (r. 1214–49) son of William I
Alexander III (r. 1249–86) son of Alexander II
Margaret (r. 1286–90) granddaughter of Alexander III

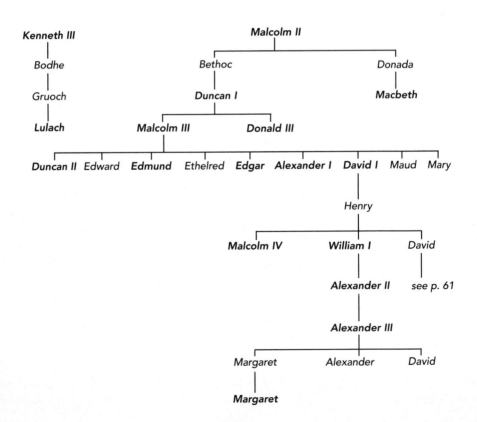

see p. 61

INTERREGNUM 1290–92

THE HOUSE OF BALLIOL 1292–96

John (r. 1292–96) great-great-great grandson of David I

INTERREGNUM 1296–1306

THE HOUSE OF BRUCE 1306–1371

Robert I (r. 1306–29) great-great-great-great grandson of David I
David II (r. 1329–71) son of Robert I

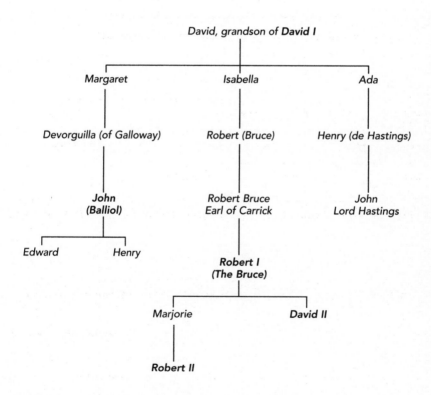

THE HOUSE OF STEWART 1371-1649

Robert II (r. 1371–90) grandson of Robert I
Robert III (r. 1390–1406) son of Robert II
James I (r. 1406–37) son of Robert III
James II (r. 1437–60) son of James I
James III (r. 1460–88) son of James II
James IV (r. 1488–1515) son of James III
James V (r. 1513–42) son of James IV
Mary I (r. 1542–67) daughter of James V
James VI (r. 1567–1625) son of Mary I
Charles I (r. 1625–49) son of James VI

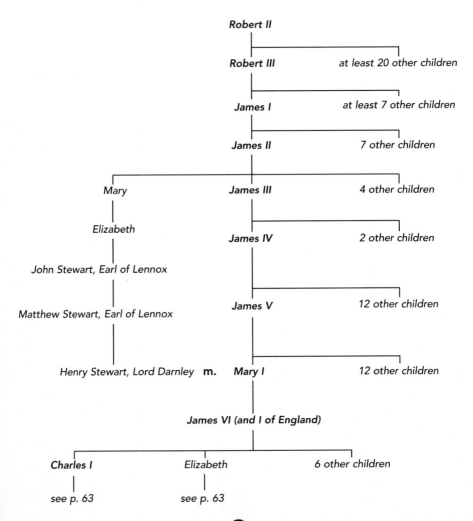

see p. 63   see p. 63

THE COMMONWEALTH (1651–53) AND PROTECTORATE (1653–60)

Oliver Cromwell (r. 1651–58)

Richard Cromwell (r. 1658–60); son of Oliver

THE HOUSE OF STEWART 1660–1707

Charles II (r. 1660–85) son of Charles I

James VII (r. 1685–89) brother of Charles I

William II & Mary II (r. 1689–1702; 1689–1694) brother-in-law and sister of James VII

Anne (r. 1702–07) daughter of James VII

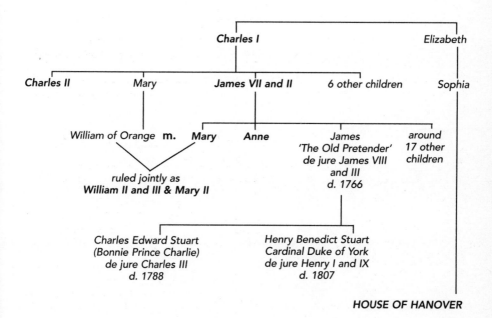

The accession of the House of Hanover in 1714 ended the line of Scots kings that stretched back almost nine hundred years to the 9th century and began the German line whose descendants still rule today. It has been calculated that in 1714 there were 57 people with a stronger claim to the throne than the Elector of Hanover who succeeded as George I; however, all were Catholic. Their descendants now run into thousands.

MILITARY

• THE ARMY•

THE SCOTTISH REGIMENTS

The Royal Scots Dragoon Guards (Carabiniers and Greys)

Home HQ: Edinburgh Castle
Colonel-in-Chief: HM The Queen
Badge: An eagle in silver upon a plaque, 'Waterloo', surmounting crossed carbines in
  gilt, with the scroll 'Royal Scots Dragoon Guards'
Tartans: Royal Stewart (regimental pipers alone wear tartan)
Regimental Music:
  Regimental Band:
    March past in quick time: *3rd Dragoon Guards*
    March past in slow time: *The Garb of the Old Gaul*
  Regimental Band & the Pipes and Drums:
    To play regiment off parade: *Scotland the Brave, The Black Bear*
  Mounted Marches:
    Walk: *Men of Harlech*
    Trot: *The Keel Row*
    Canter: *Bonnie Dundee*
  Pipe Marches:
    March past in quick time: *Highland Laddie*
    March past in slow time: *My Home*
Regimental Anniversaries: Waterloo Day (18th June); Nunshigun Day (13th April);
  Regimental birthday (2nd July)
Affiliated Regiments:
  Canada: The Windsor Regiment (RCAC)
  Australia: The 12th/16th Hunter River Lancers (RAAC)
  New Zealand: 1st & 2nd Squadrons, New Zealand and Scottish (RNZAC)
  South Africa: The Natal Caribiniers

Scots Guards

Regimental HQ: Wellington Barracks, London
Colonel-in-Chief: HM The Queen
Badge: The Star of the Order of the Thistle being the Cross of Saint Andrew, with rays in the angles, the thistle in the centre is surrounded by the words *Nemo Me Impune Lacessit* (No-one Provokes Me With Impunity)
Tartans: Royal Stewart (worn by regimental pipers and as small patches on certain headgear)
Regimental Music:
  Regimental Band & the Pipes and Drums:
    March past in quick time: *Heilan' Laddie*
    March past in slow time: *The Garb of the Old Gaul*
    Advance in Review Order: *Scotland the Brave*
  Company Marches:
  Right Flank: *Greenwood Side*
  B Company: *The Drunken Piper*
  C Company: *The Back of Benachie*
  Left Flank: *Scotland the Brave*
  Headquarter Company: *The Black Bear*
Regimental Anniversaries: St Andrew's Day (30th November)
Affiliated Regiments:
  Australia: The Royal Australian Regiment

The Royal Scots (The Royal Regiment)

Regimental HQ: Edinburgh Castle
Colonel-in-Chief: HRH The Princess Royal
Badge: The Star of the Order of the Thistle. In the centre, St Andrew and his cross, worn on a red cloth background

Tartans: Royal Stewart
Regimental Music:
  Pipe Marches:
    March in quick time: *Dumbarton's Drums*
    March in slow time: *The Garb of the Old Gaul*
    The Charge: *Monymusk*
    March on with the Band: *Scotland the Brave*
  Company Marches:
    A Company: *The Barren Rocks of Aden*
    B Company: *Marie's Wedding*
    C Company: *The Black Bear*
    D Company: *The Liberton Polka*
    Headquarter Company: *The Steamboat*
Regimental Anniversaries: Foundation Day (28th March)
Affiliated Regiments:
  The Royal Gurkha Rifles
  Canada: The Canadian Scottish Regiment (Princess Mary's); The Royal
          Newfoundland Regiment

The Royal Highland Fusiliers
(Princess Margaret's Own Glasgow and Ayrshire Regiment)

Regimental HQ: 518 Sauchiehall St, Glasgow
Colonel-in-Chief: HRH The Princess Margaret
Badge: A flaming grenade, bearing the monogram 'HLI' surmounted by a crown.
Tartans: Mackenzie and Erskine (pipers only)
Regimental Pipe Music:
  Quick marches: *Highland Laddie*
  March past in slow time: *All the Blue Bonnets are over the Border*
  Company Marches:
    A Company: *The Muckin' o' Geordie's Byre*
    B Company: *The Bugle Horn*
    C Company: *McDonald's Awa to the Wars*
    D Company: *Bonnie Dundee*
    S Company: *Orange and Blue*

Headquarter Company: *Scotland the Brave*
Funerals: *Lochaber No More*
Regimental Guest Night: *Highland Laddie; The 71st's Quick Step; The 74th's Slow March*
Regimental Anniversaries: Assaye Day (23 September)
Affiliated Regiments:
  Canada: The Highland Fusiliers of Canada
  New Zealand; 1st Bn Royal New Zealand Infantry Regiment
  Pakistan: 11th Bn The Baluch Regiment
  South Africa: Prince Alfred's Guard

The King's Own Scottish Borderers

Home HQ: The Barracks, Berwick-on-Tweed
Colonel-in-Chief: HRH Princess Alice, Duchess of Gloucester
Badge: Upon a saltire, the Castle of Edinburgh, with mottoes *In veritate religionis confido* (I trust in the truth of my belief) and *Nisi dominus frustra* (In vain without the Lord), all ensigned with the royal crest
Tartans: Leslie and Royal Stewart (regimental pipers only)
Regimental Music
  Pipe Marches:
    March in quick time: *Blue Bonnets o'er the Border*
    March in slow time: *The Borderers*
    The Charge: *The Standard on the Braes o' Mar*
  Company Marches:
    A Company: *The Bugle Horn*
    B Company: *Bonnie Dundee*
    C Company: *The Muckin' o' Geordie's Byre*
    Support Company: *The Liberton Polka*
    Headquarter Company: *Cock o' the North*
Regimental Anniversaries: Minden Day (1st August)
Affiliated Regiments:
  Canada: 1st Bn The Royal New Brunswick Regiment (Carleton & York)
  Australia: 25th Bn The Royal Queensland Regiment
  Malaysia: 5th Bn The Royal Malay Regiment

The Black Watch (Royal Highland Regiment)

Regimental HQ: Balhousie Castle, Perth
Colonel-in-Chief: HM Queen Elizabeth the Queen Mother
Badge: The Star of the Order of the Thistle, upon it the figure of St Andrew and his cross within an oval bearing the motto of the Order, *Nemo Me Impune Lacessit* (No-One Provokes Me With Impunity). Below, the Sphinx, all ensigned with the crown
Tartans: Black Watch (also known as 42nd or Government Tartan) and Royal Stewart (regimental pipers only)
Pipe Marches:
    March in quick time: *Highland Laddie*
Company Marches:
    A Company: *Atholl Highlanders*   B Company: *Lord Alexander Kennedy*
    C Company: *The Brown Haired Maiden*   D Company: *Scotland the Brave*
    Support Company: *The Steamboat*   HQ Company: *The Road to the Isles*
Regimental Anniversaries: Red Hackle Day (4th June)
Affiliated Regiments:
    Canada: The Black Watch (Royal Highland Regiment) of Canada; The Lanark and Renfrew Scottish Regiment; The Prince Edward Island Regiment
    Australia: The Royal Nw South Wales Regiment; The Royal Queensland Regiment
    New Zealand: 1st and 2nd Squadron New Zealand Scottish
    South Africa: Transvaal Scottish

The Highlanders (Seaforths, Gordons and Camerons)

Regimental HQ: Cameron Barracks, Inverness
Colonel-in-Chief: HRH The Prince Philip, Duke of Edinburgh

Badge: A stag's head caboshed, between the attires, the Thistle ensigned with the Crown with the motto *Cuidich 'n Righ* (Tribute to the King).

Tartans: Mackenzie of Seaforth, Cameron of Erracht and Gordon

Regimental Pipe Music:

    Regimental Marches: *Cock o' the North*; *Pibroch of Donuil Dubh*

    March in quick time: *The Wee Highland Laddie*

    March in slow time: *The Highlander's Slow March*

    Company Marches:

     A Company: *The Braemar Gathering*

     B Company: *Over the Chindwin*

     C/S Company: *Farewell to the Creeks*

     D Company: *Heights of Cassino*

     Headquarter Company: *The Highland Brigade at Tel-el-Kebir*

Regimental Anniversaries: None

Affiliated Regiments:

    Canada: The Cameron Highlanders of Ottawa; The 48th Highlanders of Canada; The Queen's Own Cameron Highlanders of Canada; The Seaforth Highlanders of Canada; The Toronto Scottish Regiment

    Australia: The 5th/7th Bn The Royal Australian Regiment; The Royal South Australia Regiment; The Royal Western Australia Regiment; The 5th/6th Bn The Royal Victoria Regiment; The Scotch (PGC) College, Queensland

    New Zealand: 4th Bn (Otago & Sutherland) Royal New Zealand Infantry Regiment; 7th Bn (Wellington [City of Wellington's Own] and Hawkes Bay) Royal New Zealand Infantry Regiment

    South Africa: The Capetown Highlanders

The Argyll and Sutherland Highlanders (Princess Louise's)

Regimental HQ: Stirling Castle

Colonel-in-Chief: HM The Queen

Badge: A circle inscribed 'Argyll and Sutherland' surrounded by a wreath of thistles. In the centre, the cypher of Princess Louise reversed and interlaced with the princess' coronet mounted above. The boar's head of the Duke of Argyll and the cat of the Duke of Sutherland lie within the circle.

Tartans: Black Watch

Regimental Pipe Music:

    March in quick time: *Highland Laddie; The Campbells are Coming*

The Charge: *Monymusk*
Company Marches: These change at the discretion of the Commanding Officer
Funerals: *Lochaber No More*
Regimental Anniversaries: Balaklava Day (25 October)
Affiliated Regiments:
Canada: The Argyll and Sutherland Highlanders of Canada (Princess Louise's); The Calgary Highlanders
Australia: The Royal New South Wales Regiment
Pakistan: 1st Bn (Scinde) The Frontier Force Regiment.

TERRITORIAL REGIMENTS

TA Centre	Unit
Aberdeen	205 (Scottish) Field Hospital; 51 (Highland) Signal Squadron; B (Highlanders) Coy 51st Highland Regiment; Aberdeen UOTC
Arbroath	212 (Highland) Baterry Royal Artillery
Ayr	A Sqdn, The Queen's Own Yeomanry; B (Royal Highland Fusiliers) Coy, 52nd Lowland Regiment
Bathgate	Detachment A Coy
Cumbernauld	E (Argyll & Sutherland Highlanders) Coy 51st Highland Regiment
Cupar	C (Fife Forfar Yeomanry/Scottish Horse) Sqdn, The Queen's Own Yeomanry
Dumbarton	D (Argyll & Sutherland Highlanders) Coy 51st Highland Regiment
Dumfries	Detachment D Coy
Dundee	A (Black Watch) Coy HQ 51st Highland Regiment; 225 (Highland) Field Ambulance; D Sqdn 205 (Scottish) Field Hospital; 2 (City of Dundee) Signals Sqdn; Tayforth UOTC
Dunfermline	527 HQ Sqdn, The Scottish Transport Regiment; REME
Dunoon	D (Argyll & Sutherland Highlanders) Coy 51st Highland Regiment
East Kilbride	52 Signal Sqdn (V)
Edinburgh	105th Regiment Royal Artillery (V); 61 Signal Sqdn (V); Platoon 15 Coy; A (Royal Scots) Coy; 203 Transport Sqdn, Scottish Transport Regiment Royal Logistics Corps (V); Edinburgh Sqdn 205 (Scottish) Field Hospital (V); 23 (V) Military Intelligence Coy; City of Edinburgh Universities OTC
Elgin	B (Highlanders) Coy 51st Highland Regiment
Forfar	A (Black Watch) Coy 51st Highland Regiment
Galashiels	D (King's Own Scottish Borderers) Coy
Glasgow	207th AD Battery Royal Artillery (V); 32 (Signal Corps) Signal Regiment; 52nd Lowland Regiment; C (Royal Highland Fusiliers), 52nd Lowland Regiment; 15 (SV) Coy, 4th Btn The Parachute Regiment; 125 Ration Sqdn, Scottish Transport Regiment Royal Logistics Corps (V); 221 Transport Regiment Royal Logistics Corps (V); 205 (Scottish) Field Hospital (V); 144 Parachute Sqdn Royal Army Medical Corps (V); Glasgow and Strathclyde Universities OTC

Glenrothes	231 Transport Sqdn, Scottish Tarnsport Regiment
Grangemouth	153 Workshop Coy REME
Hamilton	D Sqdn 23 SAS (V)
Invergowrie	D Sqdn 23 SAS (Volunteers)
Inverness	C (Highlanders) Coy HQ 51st Highland Regiment
Irvine	251 Transport Sqdn, Scottish Transport Regiment Royal Logistics Corps (V)
Keith	C (Highlanders) Coy 51st Highland Regiment
Kirkcaldy	212 Battery Royal Artillery
Kirkwall	C (Highlanders) Coy 51st Highland Regiment
Lerwick	C (Highlanders) Coy 51st Highland Regiment
Leuchars	HQ 71 Engineer Regiment; 117 HQ and Support Sqdn, Royal Engineers
Livingston	243 Provost Coy Royal Military Police (V)
Motherwell	C Coy King's Own Scottish Borderers Detachment
Paisley	102 Field Sqdn (Argyll & Sutherland Highlanders)
Perth	Battalion HQ 51st Highland Regiment
Peterhead	B (Highlanders) Coy HQ 51st Highland Regiment
St Andrews	Tayforth UOTC
Stirling	E (Argyll & Sutherland Highlanders) Coy HQ 51st Highland Regiment; Tayforth UOTC
Stornoway	C (Highlanders) Coy 51st Highland Regiment
Wick	C (Highlanders) Coy 51st Highland Regiment

• THE ROYAL NAVY •

PRINCIPAL SCOTTISH BASES

HM Naval Base Clyde, Helensburgh, Dunbartonshire
> HMS Neptune
> HMS Victorious (submarine sea training)
> HMS Sandown (sea training for minor war vessels and patrol craft)
> HMS Caledonia (Rosyth dockyard)

Royal Naval Air Station Prestwick
> HMS Gannet (819 Naval Air Sqdn) [Seaking helicopters]

ROYAL NAVY RESERVES

HMS Dalriada, Navy Buildings, Eldon St, Greenock
HMS Scotia, c/o HMS Caledonia, Hilton Rd, Rosyth

• THE ROYAL AIR FORCE •

PRINCIPAL SCOTTISH RAF BASES

RAF Kinloss, Kinloss Forres, Moray
        120, 201 and 206 Sqdns; 42 (Reserve Sqdn) [Nimrods]
RAF Leuchars, St Andrews, Fife
        43, 111 Sqdns [Tornados]
RAF Lossiemouth, Lossiemouth, Moray
        12, 15 (Reserve), 617 Sqdns [Tornados]; 16 (Reserve) Sqdn [Jaguars]; 202 Sqdn
        [Seaking helicopters]
RAF Macrahanish
        Presently under enhanced care and maintenance
RRAF Benbecula
        Control and Reporting post
RAF Buchan
        Control and Reporting Centre
RAF Saxa Vord, Shetland
        Control and Reporting post

ROYAL AUXILIARY AIR FORCE

No. 2 (City of Edinburgh) Maritime HQ Unit, RAuxAF, 25 Learmonth Terr. Edinburgh
No. 2622 (Highland) Squadron, RAuxAF Regiment, RAF Lossiemouth, Moray
Air Transportable Surgical Squadron, RAuxAF, RAF Leuchars, St Andrews, Fife

• SCOTTISH VICTORIA CROSS WINNERS •

The following list comprises Victoria Cross winners of Scottish birth in all the services and those won by men serving with Scottish regiments regardless of nationality. The date given is that for when the award was gazetted (usually a few months after the action) and the conflict or theatre of war in which the act of gallantry was performed.

Lt F.R. Aikman	4th Bengal Native Infantry	1858	India
Lt R.H.M. Aitken	13th Bengal Native Infantry	1863	India
Pte J. Alexander	90th Regiment (later The Cameronians)	1857	Crimea
A/Maj J.T.M. Anderson	8th Bn Argyll & Sutherland Highlanders	1943	Tunisia
Cpl W. Anderson	2nd Bn The Yorkshire Regiment	1915	France
A/Lt Col W.H. Anderson	12th Bn Highland Light Infantry	1918	France
LCpl W. Angus	8th Bn Highland Light Infantry	1915	France

Sapper A. Archibald	218 Field Coy, Royal Engineers	1919	France
Maj W. Babtie	Royal Ary Medical Corps	1900	S. Africa
Pte T. Beach	55th Regiment (later The Border Regiment)	1857	Crimea
Lt W D. Bissett	1/6th Bn Argyll & Sutherland Highlanders	1919	France
Lt R. Blair	2nd Dragoon Guards, attached 9th Lancers	1858	India
T/Maj F.G. Blaker	Highland Light Infantry, att. 3rd Bn 9th Gurhka Rifles	1944	Burma
Lt A.C. Boyle	78th Regiment (later The Seaforth Highlanders)	1859	India
2nd Lt S.H.P. Boughers	1/4th Bn Royal Scots Fusiliers	1918	Palestine
Asst Surgeon W. Bradshaw	90th Regiment (later The Cameronians)	1858	India
Cpt W. Brodie	2nd Bn Highland Light Infantry	1914	France
Lt J.A.O. Brooke	2nd Bn Gordon Highlanders	1915	Belgium
Lt W.A.M. Bruce	59th Scinde Rifles, Indian Army	1919	France
2nd Lt J.C. Buchan	7th Bn Argyll & Sutherland Highlanders	1918	France
Lt T. Cadell	2nd Bengal European Fusiliers	1862	India
Sgt T. Caldwell	12th Bn Royal Scots Fusiliers	1919	Belgium
Lt D. Cameron	Royal Naval Reserve	1944	Norway
A/Brig J.C. Campbell	Royal Horse Artillery	1942	Libya
F/O K. Campbell	22nd Sqd RAF Volunteer Reserve	1942	France
T/Col L.M. Campbell	7th Bn Argyll & Sutherland Highlanders	1943	Tunisia
Cpt N. Chavasse	Royal Army Medical Corps, att. 1/10th Bn King's Liverpool Regiment	1916 & '17	France
Cpl W. Clamp	6th Bn The Yorkshire Regiment	1917	Belgium
Lt H.S. Cochrane	86th Regiment (later The Royal Irish Rifles)	1856	India
Pte W. Coffery	34th Regiment (later The Border Regiment)	1857	Crimea
Lt R.G. Combe	27th Bn Manitoba Regiment, CEF	1917	France
Cpt J. Cook	Bengal Staff Corps and 5th Gurkha Rifles, Indian Army	1879	Afghan War
Pte W. Cook	42nd Regiment (later The Black Watch)	1859	India
Lt G.H.B. Coulson	1st Bn King's Own Scottish Borderers	1902	S. Africa
CSgt J. Craig	Scots (Fusilier) Guards	1857	Crimea
Second Lt J.M. Craig	1/4th Bn Royal Scots Fusiliers	1917	Egypt
Lt J.P.H. Crowe	78th Regiment (later The Seaforth Highlanders)	1858	India
F/O J.A. Cruikshank	RAF Volunteer Reserve	1944	
Lt W.H. Dick-Cunyngham	Gordon Highlanders	1881	Afghan War
Pte J. Davis	42nd Regiment (later The Black Watch)	1859	India
Cpl J.L. Dawson	187th Coy, Royal Engineers	1915	France
A/Sgt J.B. Daykins	2/4th Bn The York and Lancaster Regiment	1919	France
Fus. D. Donnini	4/5th Bn Royal Scots Fusiliers	1945	Holland
Sgt R. Downie	2 Bn Royal Dublin Fusiliers	1916	France
Lt J. Dundas	Bengal Engineers, Indian Army	1867	India
LCpl J. Dunlay	93rd Regiment (later The Argyll & Sutherland Highlanders)	1858	India

Pte R. Dunsire	13th Bn The Royal Scots	1915	France
Sgt A. Edwards	1/6th Bn The Seaforth Highlanders	1917	Belgium
Pte T. Edwards	1st Bn The Black Watch	1884	Sudan
Lt W M.M. Edwards	2nd Bn Highland Light Infantry	1883	Egypt
A/Cpl R.E. Elcock	11th Bn The Royal Scots	1918	France
Lt W.J. English	2nd Scottish Horse	1901	S. Africa
Sgt J. Erskine	5th Bn The Cameronians	1916	France
A/Lt L.P. Evans	The Black Watch, commanding 1st Bn Lincolnshire Regiment	1917	Belgium
Pte S. Evans	19th Regiment	1857	Crimea
Sgt D.D. Farmer	1st Bn The Queen's Own Cameron Highlanders	1901	S. Africa
Lt F.E.H. Farquharson	42nd Regiment (later The Black Watch)	1859	India
Piper G.Findlater	1st B Gordon Highlanders	1898	India
A/Maj G. deC. E. Findlay	409 (Low) Coy, Royal Engineers	1919	France
LCpl D. Finlay	2nd Bn The Black Watch	1915	France
Pte E.J. Fowler	2nd Bn The Cameronians	1882	Zulu War
LCpl S. Frickleton	3rd Bn 3rd NZ Rifle Brigade, NZEF	1917	Belgium
CSgt W. Gardner	42nd Regiment (later The Black Watch)	1858	India
Cpt W.E. Gordon	Ist Bn The Gordon Highlanders	1900	S. Africa
Lt J.R.N. Graham	9th Bn Argyll & Sutherland Highlanders	1917	Mesopotamia
Pte P.Graham	90th Regiment (later The Cameronians)	1858	India
Lt C.J.W. Grant	Indian Staff Corps	1891	Burma
Pte P. Grant	93rd Regiment (later The Argyll & Sutherland Highlanders	1858	India
Pte P. Green	75th Regiment (later The Gordon Highlanders)	1858	India
Sgt Maj J. Grieve	2nd Dragoons (Royal Scots Greys)	1857	Crimea
A/Sgt W. Grimbaldestan	1st Bn King's Own Scottish Borderers	1917	Belgium
Maj J.C. Guise	90th Regiment (later The Cameronians)	1858	India
T/Lt Col A.F.D. Hamilton	6th Bn Queen's Own Cameron Highlanders	1915	France
A/lt Col J.B. Hamilton	1st Bn Highland Light Infantry	1917	Belgium
Cpt T. deC. Hamilton	68th Regiment	1857	Crimea
Sgt J. Hannah	83 Sqdn RAF	1940	Belgium
A/Cpt A. Henderson	4th Bn Argyll & Sutherland Highlanders	1917	France
Cpt G.S. Henderson	2nd Bn The Manchester Regiment	1920	Mesopotamia
Tpr H.S. Henderson	Bulawayo Field Force	1897	Rhodesia
Sgt S. Hill	90th Regiment (later The Cameronians)	1858	India
Pte J. Hollowell	78th Regiment (later The Seaforth Highlanders)	1858	India
Surg A.B. Howe	90th Regiment (later The Cameronians)	1858	India
2nd Lt J.P. Huffam	5th Bn Duke of Wellington Regiment	1918	France
Cpl D F Hunter	1/5th Bn Highland Light Infantry	1918	France
LCpl C.A. Jarvis	57th Field Coy, Royal Engineers	1914	Belgium
Surg J. Jee	78th Regiment (later The Seaforth		

	Highlanders)	1860	India
Pte C.T. Kennedy	2nd Bn Highland Light Infantry	1901	S. Africa
Lt Col W.H.C. Kennedy	24th Bn Quebec Regiment CEF	1918	France
Drummer W. Kenny	2nd Bn Gordon Highlanders	1915	Belgium
Lt A.E. Ker	3rd Bn Gordon Highlanders	1919	France
Lt W.A. Kerr	24th Bombay Native Infantry	1858	India
T/Lt Col G.C.T. Tasker	Royal Scots Greys	1942	Libya
Pte C.J. Kinross	49th Alberta Regiment CEF	1918	Belgium
Sgt J.S. Knox	Scots (Fusilier) Guards	1857	Crimea
Piper D. Laidlaw	7th Bn King's Own Scottish Borderers	1915	France
Pte D.R. Lauder	1/4th Bn Royal Scots Fusiliers	1917	Gallipoli
Lt J. Leith	14th Light Dragoons	1858	India
Cpt J.A. Liddell	3rd Bn Argyll & Sutherland Highlanders and Royal Flying Corps	1915	Belgium
Cpt R.J. Lindsay	Scots (Fusilier) Guards	1857	Crimea
T/Cpt C.A. Lyell	1st Bn Scots Guards	1943	Tunisia
Lt H. Lysons	2nd Bn The Cameronians	1882	Zulu War
Sgt J. McAuley	1st Bn Scots Guards	1918	France
Lt W. McBean	93rd Regiment (later The Argyll & Sutherland Highlanders	1858	India
LCpl R. McBeath	I/5th Bn Seaforth Highlanders	1918	France
Pte J. McDermond	47th Regiment	1857	Crimea
CSgt H. MacDonald	Royal Engineers	1858	Crimea
Pte J. McDougall	44th Regiment	1861	China
LSgt S. McGraw	42nd Regiment (later The Black Watch)	1874	Ashanti
Lt D.S. McGregor	6th Bn Royal Scots	1918	Belgium
T/Cpt J. MacGregor	2nd Canadian Mounted Rifles CEF	1919	France
Pte R. McGregor	1st Bn Rifle Brigade	1857	Crimea
A/Sgt L. McGuffie	1/5th Bn King's Own Scottish Borderers	1918	Belgium
Gnr H. McInnes	Bengal Artillery	1858	India
Pte G.I. McIntosh	1/6th Bn Gordon Highlanders	1917	Belgium
T/Lt D.L. Macintyre	Bengal Staff Corps and 2nd Gurkha Rifles, Indian Army	1872	India
Pte H. McIver	2nd Bn Royal Scots	1918	France
Pte D. Mackay	93rd Regiment (later The Argyll & Sutherland Highlanders	1858	India
LCpl J.F. Mackay	1st Bn Gordon Highlanders	1900	S. Africa
Sgt J. McKechnie	Scots (Fusilier) Guards	1857	Crimea
Lt H. Mackenzie	7th Coy Canadian Machine Gun Corps	1918	Belgium
Pte J. Mackenzie	2nd Bn Scots Guards	1915	France
Sgt J. Mackenzie	2nd Bn Seaforth Highlanders	1901	Ashanti
Lt D. MacKintosh	3rd Bn Seaforth Highlanders	1917	France
Lt Col J.C. McNeill	107th Regiment	1864	N Zealand
LSgt F McNess	1st Bn Scots Guards	1916	France
Lt H.T. Macpherson	78th Regiment (later The Seaforth Highlanders)	1858	India

CSgt S. McPherson	78th Regiment (later The Seaforth Highlanders)	1859	India
Cpl J. McPhie	416th Field Coy, Royal Engineers	1919	France
WCmdr H.G. Malcolm	18 Sqdn RAF	1943	Tunisia
Lt J. Malcolmson	3rd Bombay Light Cavalry	1860	Persia
Pte H. May	1st Bn Cameronians	1915	France
Sgt J. Meikle	4th Bn Seaforth Highlanders	1918	France
Cpt M.F.M. Meiklejohn	2nd Bn Gordon Highlanders	1900	S. Africa
Pte C. Melvin	2nd Bn Black Watch	1917	Mesopotamia
Cmdr A.C.C. Miers	Royal Navy	1942	Corfu
Pte D. Millar	42nd Regiment (later The Black Watch)	1859	India
Conductor J. Millar	Bengal Ordnance Depot	1862	India
Pte W.J. Milne	16th Bn Manitoba Regiment CEF	1917	France
Pte G.A. Mitchell	London Scottish (Gordon Highlanders)	1944	Italy
Sgt A. Moynihan	90th Regiment (later The Cameronians)	1857	Crimea
Maj K. Muir	1st Bn Argyll & Sutherland Highlanders	1951	Korea
CSgt J. Munro	93rd Regiment (later The Argyll & Sutherland Highlanders)	1860	India
Sgt J. O'Neill	2nd Bn Prince of Wales Leinster Regiment	1918	Belgium
Gnr J. Park	Bengal Artillery	1858	India
A/Cpt G.H.T. Paton	4th Bn Grenadier Guards	1918	France
Sgt J. Paton	93rd Regiment (later The Argyll & Sutherland Highlanders)	1858	India
Sapper J. Perie	Royal Engineers	1857	Crimea
Cpt J.D. Pollock	5th Bn The Queen's Own Cameron Highlanders	1915	France
Sgt H. Ramage	2nd Dragoons (Royal Scots Greys)	1858	Crimea
Cpt H.S. Ranken	Royal Army Medical Corps, att. 1st Bn King's Royal Rifle Corps	1914	France
Pte G. Ravenhill	2nd Bn Royal Scots Fusiliers	1901	S. Africa
A/Fl Lt W. Reid	61 Sqdn RAF Volunteer Reserve	1943	Germany
Lt W. Rennie	90th Regiment (later The Cameronians)	1858	India
T/Cpt H. Reynolds	12 Bn Royal Scots	1917	Belgium
Pte W. Reynolds	Scots (Fusilier) Guards	1857	Crimea
Piper J.C. Richardson	16th Bn Manitoba Regiment CEF	1918	France
Cpt J. Ripley	1st Bn Black Watch	1915	France
Cmdr H.P. Ritchie	Royal Navy	1915	E. Africa
Drummer W.P. Ritchie	2nd Bn Seaforth Highlanders	1916	France
Sgt Maj W. Robertson	2nd Bn Gordon Highlanders	1900	S. Africa
Pte H.H. Robson	2nd Bn Royal Scots	1915	France
2nd Lt G.A.B. Rochefort	Scots Guards	1915	France
Pte G. Rodgers	71st Regiment (later The Highland Light Infantry)	1859	India
Cpl J. Ross	Royal Engineers	1857	Crimea
Cpt A.G.A.H. Ruthven	3rd Bn Highland Light Infantry	1899	Sudan

Seaman G. McK Samson	Royal Navy Reserve	1915	Gallipoli
LCpl G. Sellar	Seaforth Highlanders	1881	Afghan Wars
Lt R. Shankland	43rd Bn Manitoba Regiment CEF	1917	Belgium
Cpl J.D.F. Shaul	1st Bn Highland Light Infantry	1900	S. Africa
QM J. Simpson	42nd Regiment (later The Black Watch)	1859	India
A/CSM J. Skinner	1st Bn King's Own Scottish Borderers	1917	Belgium
T/Lt A.B. Smith	Royal Navy Reserve	1919	N. Atlantic
Pte W. Speakman	Black Watch, att. 1st Bn King's Own Scottish Borderers	1951	Korea
Sgt Maj D. Spence	9th Lancers	1858	India
Pte E. Spence	42nd Regiment (later The Black Watch)	1859	India
Sgt T. Steele	1st Bn Seaforth Highlanders	1917	Mesopotamia
Cpt W.G.D. Stewart	93rd Regiment (later The Argyll & Sutherland Highlanders	1858	India
Pte J. Stokes	2nd Bn King's Shropshire Light Infantry	1945	Germany
Lt H. Strachan	Fort Garry Horse CEF	1917	France
Lt J.E. Tait	78th Bn Manitoba Regiment CEF	1918	France
LCpl A. Thompson	42nd Regiment (later The Black Watch)	1859	India
FlSgt G. Thompson	9 Sqdn RAF Volunteer Reserve	1945	Germany
Pte R. Tollerton	1st Bn The Queen's Own Cameron Highlanders	1915	France
Pte J. Towers	2nd Bn The Cameronians	1919	France
Cpt E.B.B. Towse	1st Bn Gordon Highlanders	1900	S. Africa
Cpt W.J. Vousden	5th Punjab Cavalry 7 Bengal Staff Corps, Indian Army	1881	Afghan War
Lt R. Wadeson	75th Regiment (later The Gordon Highlanders)	1858	India
T/Lt S.T.D. Wallace	'C' Battery, 63rd Brigade, Royal Field Artillery	1918	France
Pte H. Ward	78th Regiment (later The Seaforth Highlanders)	1858	India
Cpl S.W. Ware	1st Bn Seaforth Highlanders	1916	Mesopotamia
Skipper J. Watt	Royal Naval Reserve	1917	Italy
Maj G.S. White	92nd Regiment (later The Gordon Highlanders)	1881	Afghan War
Pte G. Wilson	2nd Bn Highland Light Infantry	1914	France
Cpt H.B. Wood	2nd Bn Scots Guards	1918	France
Cpt J.A. Wood	20th Bombay Native Infantry	1860	Persia
Cpt D.R. Younger	1st Bn Gordon Highlanders	1902	S. Africa

• SCOTTISH BATTLES•

The following list features documented battles fought on Scottish soil and those in England invovling Scottish armies. The term 'battle' is used advisedly; those listed range from full-scale engagements between 'national' armies to what constituted little more than a skirmish between local rivals.

Battle Name: Battle of the Bauds (Muir of Findochty, Banffshire)
Date: 961
Opponents: The Scots of King Indulf and the Danes of Eric Blood-Axe
Outcome: The Danes were defeated

Battle Name: Battle of Carham
Date: 1077
Opponents: King Malcolm II and the Northumbrian forces of Earl Uhtred
Outcome: The Scots were victorious and Lothian returned to Scottish control
Battle Name: Battle of the Standard (Northallerton, Yorkshire)
Date: 22nd August 1138
Opponents: David I and Thurstan, Archbishop of York
Outcome: The Scots were heavily defeated

Battle Name: Battle of Largs
Date: 30th September–4th October 1263
Opponents: Alexander III and Haakon IV of Norway
Outcome: The battle was inconclusive but as a result of Haakon's failure, the Hebrides were returned to Scottish control by the Treaty of Perth, 1296

Battle Name: Battle of Dunbar
Date: 27th April 1296
Opponents: Scots forces of John Balliol and the English army of Edward I under the Earl of Surrey
Outcome: The Scots were overwhelmed and many nobles were taken hostage

Battle Name: Battle of Stirling Bridge
Date: 11th September 1297
Opponents: The Scots forces of William Wallace and the English army of Edward I led by the the Earl of Surrey and Hugh de Cressingham
Outcome: The English army was convincingly routed, suffering heavy losses

Battle Name: Battle of Falkirk
Date: 22nd July 1298

Opponents: Wallace's army and English forces under Edward I and the Earl of
              Surrey
Outcome: The Scots were comprehensively defeated

Battle Name: Battle of Methven
Date: 19th June 1306
Opponents: The army of Robert I (The Bruce) and the English under the Earl of
              Pembroke
Outcome: Robert I was defeated and forced to flee

Battle Name: Battle of Dalry
Date: 11th August 1306
Opponents: The army of Robert I and a force under John MacDougall of Lorne,
              kinsman to John Comyn, murdered by Bruce
Outcome: Robert I was defeated, became a fugitive and his army was dispersed

Battle Name: Battle of Glen Trool
Date: April 1307
Opponents: Robert I's army and an English force under the Earl of Pembroke
Outcome: The Scots were victorious

Battle Name: Battle of Inverurie
Date: 22nd May 1308
Opponents: Robert I's army and a partly English force led by John Comyn, son
              of the Earl of Buchan
Outcome: Comyn was roundly defeated and Robert subsequently ravaged
              the whole of the Buchan earldom

Battle Name: Battle of Annan
Date: 17th December 1332
Opponents: A force led by Edward Balliol and Scots led by Guardian Sir
              Archibald Douglas
Outcome: Balliol's troops were overrun and he was forced to flee to Carlisle

Battle Name: Battle of Dupplin Moor
Date: 12th August 1332
Opponents: Edward Balliol's army and the Scots led by the regent Earl of Mar
Outcome: The Scots squandered their numerical advantage and following a
              confused attack were routed with heavy losses

Battle Name: Battle of Halidon Hill
Date: 19th July 1333
Opponents: Scots under Sir Archibald Douglas and the English led by Edward
              III and Edward Balliol
Outcome: English archers devasted the Scots army and inflicted terrible
              losses including six earls, seventy barons and over 500 knights

Battle Name: Battle of Culblean (or Kilblain)
Date: 30th November 1335
Opponents: A Scottish force under Sir Andrew Murray and supporters of the English-backed Edward Balliol under the Earl of Atholl
Outcome: Murray's troops defeated Balliol's force

Battle Name: Battle of Neville's Cross
Date: 17th October 1346
Opponents: A Scottish army under David II and an English force led by the Archbishop of York
Outcome: The Scots were crushed and David was taken prisoner, spending the next 11 years in captivity at the English court

Battle Name: Battle of Nesbit
Date: August 1355
Opponents: Scottish and English armies
Outcome: The Scots were victorious, capturing Sir Thomas Gray and going on to sack Berwick

Battle Name: Battle of Invernahaven
Date: 1386
Opponents: Clan Cameron and a confederacy of the Mackintoshes, Macphersons and Davidsons
Outcome: The Macphersons withdrew from the battle having fallen out with their allies and the Camerons were the eventual victors

Battle Name: Battle of Otterburn
Date: 5th August 1388
Opponents: Scots led by the 2nd Earl of Douglas and the English led by Henry Percy ('Hotspur')
Outcome: The English were defeated and Hotspur was captured, although Douglas was killed in the battle

Battle Name: Battle of the Clans (North Inch, Perth)
Date: 28th September 1396
Opponents: 60 men chosen to represent the Clans Chattan and Mackay in a gladiatorial 'fight to the death' to resolve a long-standing feud
Outcome: In the presence of Robert III and his court, the Mackays were all but wiped out

Battle Name: Battle of Nesbit
Date: 22nd June 1402
Opponents: Scottish and English armies
Outcome: The Scots were routed and had many prominent nobles captured

Battle Name: Battle of Homildon Hill
Date: 14th September 1402
Opponents: A Scottish force under the 4th Earl of Douglas and an English army
                 led by 'Hotspur'
Outcome: The Scots were heavily defeated and Douglas was captured

Battle Name: Battle of Harlaw
Date: 24th July 1411
Opponents: A Highland force led by Douglas, Lord of the Isles and a Lowland
                 force commanded by the Earl of Mar that included some burgesses
                 of Aberdeen
Outcome: Each force inflicted considerable losses on the other but the result
                 was considered a greater victory for the Lowlanders

Battle Name: Battle of Sark
Date: 23rd October 1448
Opponents: Scots under Hugh Douglas, Earl of Ormond and the English com-
                 manded by the Earl of Northumberland
Outcome: The Scots repulsed the invading English force

Battle Name: Battle of Arkinholm
Date: 1st May 1455
Opponents: A force composed of the leading Borders families and supporters
                 of James, 9th Earl of Douglas
Outcome: The Black Douglases were routed in what marked the end of their
                 power struggle with the Stewart monarchy

Battle Name: Battle of Sauchieburn
Date: 11th June 1488
Opponents: A force led by James III and an army of disaffected Scottish nobles
                 with the king's son at their head
Outcome: James was killed during the battle and his son was proclaimed king

Battle Name: Battle of Flodden
Date: 9th September 1513
Opponents: Scots led by James IV and the English under the Earl of Surrey
Outcome: A catastrophic defeat for the Scots which saw the king, 10 earls
                 and countless other nobles slain

Battle Name: Battle of Hadden Rig
Date: 24th August 1542
Opponents: Scots under the Earl of Huntly and an English army led by Sir
                 Robert Bowes
Outcome: The English were soundly defeated and Bowes and over 600
                 nobles were captured

Battle Name: Battle of Solway Moss
Date: 24th November 1542
Opponents: A Scottish army led by Oliver Sinclair of Pitcairns and an English force under Sir Thomas Wharton
Outcome: What should have been an easy Scottish victory was turned to defeat by internal divisions amongst the Scots.

Battle Name: Battle of the Butts (Glasgow)
Date: 1544
Opponents: An army of the regent Earl of Arran and that of the Earl of Glencairn
Outcome: Arran was victorious and his force sacked Glasgow

Battle Name: Battle of the Shirts (Loch Oich, near Laggan)
Date: 3rd July 1544
Opponents: Clan Fraser and an alliance of Clans Ranald, Cameron and Donald
Outcome: The confederate clans massacred the Frasers in what was one of the bloodiest examples of clan warfare

Battle Name: Battle of Ancrum Moor
Date: 27th February 1545
Opponents: Scots led by Archibald Douglas, 6th Earl of Angus and the English led by Sir Ralph Eure and Sir Brian Layton
Outcome: Despite being heavily outnumbered, the Scots army defeated the English, killing both its commanders

Battle Name: Battle of Pinkie
Date: 10th September 1547
Opponents: An English force under the Duke of Somerset and the Scottish forces of the regent Earl of Arran
Outcome: Although the larger force, the Scots were devastated by better tactics and English cavalry

Battle Name: Battle of Langside
Date: 13th May 1568
Opponents: Supporters of Mary, Queen of Scots and a force commanded by Lord James Stewart, Regent Moray
Outcome: The queen's army was scattered and Mary withdrew to begin her flight to England

Battle Name: Battle of Glenlivet
Date: 3rd October 1594
Opponents: An advance party of James VI's army led by the 7th Earl of Argyll and disaffected nobles led by the Earls of Huntly and Errol
Outcome: The king's force was defeated but their opponents withdrew in the face of royal reinforcements

Battle Name: Battle of Glenfruin
Date: February 1603
Opponents: A Government-backed force led by Alexander Colquhoun of Luss and Clan Gregor led by Alasdair Macgregor of Glenstrae
Outcome: The Colquhouns were massacred and Government reprisals followed, including the proscription of the Macgregors

Battle Name: Battle of Tippermuir
Date: 1st September 1644
Opponents: A Royalist army under Montrose and a Covenanter army led by Lord Elcho
Outcome: This was the first of Montrose's victories

Battle Name: Battle of Inverlochy
Date: 2nd February 1645
Opponents: Montrose's Royalists and Argyll's army of Covenanters
Outcome: Montrose's troops and superior tactics routed Argyll at Inverlochy near Fort William as the earl watched from the safety of a ship

Battle Name: Battle of Auldearn
Date: 9th May 1645
Opponents: Montrose's Royalists and Hurry's Covenanters
Outcome: Montrose's forces repelled a surprise attack by the Covenanters to decimate Sir John Hurry's army

Battle Name: Battle of Alford
Date: 2nd July 1645
Opponents: Montrose's Royalists against Lieut.-Gen. Baillie
Outcome: Montrose won his fifth straight victory over the Covenanters

Battle Name: Battle of Kilsyth
Date: 15th August 1645
Opponents: Montrose and his Royalists and Lieut.-Gen. Baillie
Outcome: Almost year after his campaign began, Montrose's army routed the Covenanters, so apparently winning Scotland

Battle Name: Battle of Philiphaugh
Date: 13th September 1645
Opponents: Montrose's Royalists and David Leslie's Covenanters
Outcome: Montrose's army was surprised near Selkirk and routed; Montrose fled north. Despite Leslie's promise of quarter, religious ministers in his camp persuaded him to slaughter all his prisoners

Battle Name: Battle of Carbisdale
Date: 27th April 1650
Opponents: Montrose's Royalists and Strachan's Presbyterian extremist forces
Outcome: Strachan defeated the poorly supported Montrose, who had only

returned to fight at Charles II's request. But when the fleeing Montrose was betrayed to the authorities, the king abandoned him to his fate. Montrose was hanged in Edinburgh on 21 May

Battle Name: Battle of Dunbar
Date: 3rd September 1650
Opponents: David Leslie's Covenanters and Oliver Cromwell's New Model Army
Outcome: Cromwell's superior force defeated the now-royalist Scots Covenanters, leaving Scotland virtually his for the taking

Battle Name: Battle of Inverkeithing
Date: 20th July 1651
Opponents: Cromwellian army and Scots royalists
Outcome: A brief battle which failed to halt the northward progress of Cromwell's forces

Battle Name: Battle of Drumclog
Date: 1st June 1679
Opponents: Anti-government Covenanters and Graham of Claverhouse
Outcome: A short battle saw Claverhouse's government troops routed

Battle Name: Battle of Bothwell Brig
Date: 22nd June 1679
Opponents: Covenanters and the government forces under Monmouth and Claverhouse
Outcome: The government's regrouped and reinforced troops outclassed the zealous Covenanter rebels

Battle Name: Battle of Airds Moss
Date: 22nd July 1680
Opponents: Covenanter rebels and government troops
Outcome: The small Covenanter force was utterly crushed

Battle Name: Battle of Killiecrankie
Date: 27th July 1689
Opponents: Stuart loyalist forces of Claverhouse, now Viscount Dundee, and Williamite army under Gen. MacKay.
Outcome: Dundee won a bloody victory but was mortally wounded in the process, dealing a serious blow to James VII's hopes of regaining his throne

Battle Name: Battle of Cromdale
Date: 1st May 1690
Opponents: Stuart loyalists under Thomas Buchan against Williamite force
Outcome: Government troops surprised and routed the Jacobites, effectively ending James VII & II's attempt to regain his throne

Battle Name: Battle of Sheriffmuir
Date: 13th November 1715
Opponents: Earl of Mar's Jacobites and Duke of Argyll's government force
Outcome: An indecisive encounter which the Jacobites turned into a defeat by retreating; supporters were thereafter unwilling to commit to an unsuccessful cause

Battle Name: Battle of Glen Shiel
Date: 10th June 1719
Opponents: Spanish-inspired Jacobite force and government troops
Outcome: Defeat for the Jacobites in the only engagement of the '19 Rising

Battle Name: Battle of Prestonpans
Date: 21st September 1745
Opponents: Jacobite forces of Prince Charles Edward Stuart, 'Bonnie Prince Charlie', and the Hanoverian government army under John Cope
Outcome: The Jacobites' routing of Cope left almost all of Scotland open to the prince and was a marvellous propaganda coup for the rising

Battle Name: Battle of Falkirk
Date: 17 January 1746
Opponents: Bonnie Prince Charlie's Jacobites and Gen. Hawley's army
Outcome: Relatively minor battle saw the Jacobite forces score another victory on their retreat northwards

Battle Name: Battle of Culloden
Date: 16 April 1746
Opponents: Bonnie Prince Charlie's Jacobites against the Duke of Cumberland's army
Outcome: Charles unwisely chose to ignore the advice of his ace tactician General Murray and engaged in open battle. The resulting slaughter of the Jacobite forces spilled over into systematic repression and ethnic cleansing. The Jacobite hope of a Stuart restoration was finished, and Culloden the last pitched battle ever fought on either Scottish or British soil.

CLANS AND FAMILIES

• CLAN HERALDRY •

The clans listed below are the members of the Standing Council of Scottish Chiefs. For a short glossary of heraldic terminology used on these pages, see p. 100.

AGNEW
Crest An eagle issuant and reguardant Proper
Motto Consilio non impetu (By wisdom not by force)

ANSTRUTHER
Crest Two arms in armour holding a pole-axe with both hands gauntleted Proper
Motto Periissem ni periissem (I would have perished had I not persisted)
Plant Badge Sprig of olive

ARBUTHNOTT
Crest A peacock's head couped at the neck Proper
Motto Laus deo (Praise God)

BANNERMAN
Crest A demi man in armour holding in his right hand a sword Proper
Motto Pro patria (For my country)

BARCLAY
Crest (on a chapeau Azure doubled Ermine) A hand holding a dagger Proper
Motto Aut agere aut mori (Either to do or die)

BORTHWICK
Crest A moor's head couped Proper wreathed Argent and Sable
Motto Qui conducit (He who leads)
Plant Badge A stem of two roses Gules leaved, barbed and seeded Vert

BOYD
Crest A dexter hand erect in pale having the two outer fingers bowed inwards
Motto Confido (I trust)

BOYLE
Crest A double headed eagle displayed, parted per pale embattled Gules and Argent
Motto Dominus providebit (The Lord will provide)

BRODIE
Crest A right hand holding a bunch of arrows all Proper
Motto Unite

BRUCE
Crest A lion statant Azure armed and langued Gules
Motto Fuimus (We have been)
Plant Badge Rosemary

BUCHAN
Crest (upon a chapeau Gules furred Ermine) A sun shining upon a sunflower full blown Proper
Motto Non inferiora secutus (Not having followed mean pursuits)
Plant Badge Sunflower

BURNETT
Crest (on a chapeau Gules furred Ermine) A cubit arm, the hand naked, vested Vert doubled Argent pruning a vinetree with a pruning knife Proper
Motto Virescit vulnere virtus (Her virtue flourishes by her wounds); on Compartment: Alterius non sit qui suus esse potest (Let not him be another's who can be his own)
Plant Badge A sprig of holly leaves.

CAMERON
Crest A sheaf of five arrows points upwards Proper tied with a band Gules
Motto Aonaibh ri chéile (Unite); on Compartment: Pro rege et patria (For my King and country)

CAMPBELL
Crest A boar's head fessways erased Or, armed Argent, langued Gules
Motto Ne obliviscaris (Do not forget)
Plant Badge Bog myrtle

CARMICHAEL
Crest A dexter hand and arm in pale armed and holding a broken spear Proper
Motto Tout jour prest (Always ready)

CARNEGIE
Crest A thunderbolt Proper, winged Or
Motto Dred God

CATHCART
Crest A dexter hand couped above the wrist and erect Proper, grasping a crescent Argent
Motto I hope to speed

CHARTERIS
Crest A dexter hand holding up a dagger paleways Proper
Motto This is our Charter

CHATTAN
Crest A cat salient Proper

Motto Touch not the catt but a glove
Plant Badge Red whortleberry

CHISHOLM
Crest A dexter hand holding a dagger erect Proper, the point thereof transfixing a boar's head erased Or
Motto Feros ferio (I am fierce with the fierce); on Compartment: Vi aut virtute (By force or virtue)

COCHRANE
Crest A horse passant Argent
Motto Virtute et labore (By valour and exertion)

COLQUHOUN
Crest A hart's head couped Gules, attired Argent
Motto Si je puis (If I can); on Compartment: Cnoc Ealachain
Plant Badge Hazel saplings

COLVILLE
Crest A hind's head couped at the neck Argent
Motto Oublier ne puis (I cannot forget)

CRANSTOUN
Crest A crane Proper dormant holding a stone in her claw
Motto Thou shalt want ere I want
Plant Badge A bunch of strawberries Proper

CRICHTON
Crest A dragon spouting out fire Proper.
Motto God send grace

CUMMING
Crest A lion rampant Or holding in his dexter paw a dagger Proper
Motto Courage

DARROCH
Crest On a chapeau Gules furred miniver a demi-Negro, in his dexter hand a dagger Proper
Motto Be watchfull

DAVIDSON
Crest A stag's head erased Proper.
Motto Sapienter si sincere (Wisely if sincerely)

DEWAR
Crest Issuant from a Crest-cornet Or of four (three visible) strawberry leaves, a dexter arm vambraced, brandishing a sword Proper, hilted and pommelled Or
Motto Quid non pro patria (What will a man not do for his country); on Compartment: Virtute et solertia (By virtue and by skill)

DRUMMOND
Crest On a crest coronet Or, a goshawk, wings displayed Proper, armed and belled

Or, jessed Gules
Motto Virtutem coronat honos (Honour crowns virtue); on Compartment: Gang warily
Plant Badge Holly

DUNBAR
Crest A horse's head Argent, bridled and reined Gules
Motto In promptu (In readiness); on Compartment: Candoris praemium honos (Honour is the reward of sincerity)

DUNDAS
Crest A lion's head affrontée looking through a bush of oak Proper
Motto Essayez (Try)

DURIE
Crest A crescent Or
Motto Confido (I trust)

ELIOTT
Crest A hand couped at the wrist in armour holding a cutlass in bend Proper
Motto Fortiter et recte (Boldly and rightly); on Compartment: Soyez sage (Be wise)
Plant Badge White hawthorn

ELPHINSTONE
Crest A lady, from the waist upwards, richly habited in red, her arms extended, the right hand supporting a tower and the left holding a branch of laurel, all Proper
Motto Cause causit (Cause caused it)

ERSKINE
Crests Dexter, on a chapeau Gules furred Ermine, a hand holding up a skene in pale Argent, hilted and pommelled Or (Erskine); sinister, on a chapeau Gules furred Ermine, a demi-lion rampant guardant Gules, langued Azure, armed Argent (Kellie)
Mottoes Dexter, Je pense plus (I think more); sinister, Decori decus addit avito (He adds honour to that of his ancestors); on Compartment: Unione fortior (Stronger through unity)

FARQUHARSON
Crest On a chapeau Gules furred Ermine, a demi-lion Gules holding in his dexter paw a sword Proper
Motto Fide et fortitudine (By fidelity and fortitude); on Compartment: I force nae freen, I fear nae foe
Plant Badge Seedling Scots firs Proper

FERGUSSON
Crest Upon a chapeau Gules furred Ermine, a bee on a thistle Proper
Motto Dulcius ex asperis (Sweeter after difficulties); on Compartment: Ut prosim aliis (That I may be of use to others)
Plant Badge Poplar seedlings

FORBES
Crest A stag's head attired with ten tines Proper
Motto Grace me guide

FORSYTH
Crest A griffin segreant Azure, armed and membered Sable, crowned Or
Motto Instaurator ruinae (A repairer of ruin)
Plant Badge Forsythia flower

FRASER
Crests Dexter, on a mount a flourish of strawberries leaved and fructed Proper; sinister, an ostrich holding in its beak a horseshoe Proper
Mottoes Dexter, All my hope is in God; sinister, In God is all

FRASER OF LOVAT
Crest A buck's head erased Proper
Motto Je suis prest (I am ready)

GORDON
Crest Issuant from a crest coronet Or a stag's head (affrontée) Proper attired with 10 tines Or
Motto Bydand (Remaining); on Compartment: Animo non astutia (By courage not by stratagem)
Plant Badge Rock ivy

GRAHAM
Crest A falcon Proper, beaked and armed Or, killing a stork Argent, armed Gules
Motto Ne oublie (Do not forget)
Plant Badge Spurge laurel

GRANT
Crest A burning hill Proper
Motto Craig Elachie (The rock of alarm): on Compartment: Stand Fast
Plant Badge Seedling Scots pines fructed Proper

GRIERSON
Crest A fetterlock Argent
Motto Hoc securior (More secure by this)
Plant Badge A stem of bluebells Proper

GUTHRIE
Crest A dexter arm holding a drawn sword Proper
Motto Sto pro veritate (I stand for the truth)

HAIG
Crest A rock Proper
Motto Tyde what may

HALDANE
Crest An eagle's head erased Or
Motto Suffer

HAMILTON
Crests Dexter, in a ducal coronet an oak tree fructed and penetrated transversely in the main stem by a frame saw Proper, the frame Or (Hamilton); sinister, on a chapeau

Gules turned up Ermine a salamander in flames Proper (Douglas)
Mottoes Dexter, Through; sinister, Jamais arrière (Never behind)

HANNAY
Crest A cross crosslet fitchée issuing out of a crescent Sable
Motto Per ardua ad alta (Through difficulties to higher things)
Plant Badge Periwinkle

HAY
Crest Issuing out of a Crest Coronet a falcon volant Proper, armed, jessed and belled Or
Motto Serva jugum (Keep the yoke)
Plant Badge Mistletoe

HENDERSON
Crest A cubit arm Proper the hand holding an estoile Or surmounted by a crescent Azure
Motto Sola virtus nobilitat (Virtue alone ennobles)
Plant Badge Stem of cotton grass (Eriophorum augustifolium)

HOME
Crests Dexter, on a cap of maintenance Proper, a lion's head erased Argent (Home); sinister, on a cap of maintenance Proper, a salamander Vert, encircled with flames of fire Proper
Mottoes Dexter, A Home • A Home • A Home; sinister, Jamais arrière (Never behind)

HOPE
Crest A broken terrestrial globe surmounted by a rainbow issuing out of a cloud at each end all Proper
Motto At spes infracta (But hope is unbroken)

HUNTER
Crest A greyhound sejant Proper, gorged with an antique crown Or
Motto Cursum perficio (I accomplish the hunt)
Plant Badge Stem of thrift (armeria maritima) Proper

IRVINE
Crest A sheaf of holly consisting of nine leaves Vert slipped and banded Gules
Motto Sub sole sub umbra virens (Flourishing both in sunshine and in shade)

JARDINE
Crest A spur rowel of six points Proper
Motto Cave adsum (Beware I am present)
Plant Badge Sprig of apple-blossom

JOHNSTONE
Crest A winged spur Or
Motto Nunquam non paratus (Never unprepared)

KEITH
Crests Dexter, on a Wreath Or and Gules, a noble lady from the middle richly

attired holding in her right hand a garland of laurel Proper (Earldom of Kintore); sinister, out of a Crest Coronet Or, a roebuck's head Proper, attired Or (Keith)
Mottoes Dexter, Quae amissa salva (What has been lost is safe); sinister, Veritas vincit (Truth conquers); on Compartment: Thay say: quhat say they: thay haif sayd: lat thame say
Plant Badge White rose

KENNEDY
Crest A dolphin naiant Proper
Motto Avise la fin (Consider the end)

KERR
Crests Dexter, the sun in his splendour Or (Lothian); sinister, a stag's head erased Proper (Kerr)
Mottoes Dexter, Sero sed serio (Late but in earnest); sinister, Forward in the name of God

KINCAID
Crest A triple towered castle Argent, masoned Sable, and issuing from the centre tower a dexter arm from the shoulder embowed, vested in the proper tartan of Kincaid and grasping a drawn sword all Proper
Motto This I'll defend

LAMONT
Crest A dexter hand couped at the wrist Proper
Motto Ne parcas nec spernas (Neither spare nor dispose)

LEASK
Crest A crescent Argent
Motto Virtute cresco (I grow by virtue); on Compartment: Leskgaronne

LENNOX
Crest Two broadswords in saltire behind a swan's head and neck all Proper
Motto I'll defend
Plant Badge A rose slipped Gules

LESLIE
Crest A demi griffin Proper, beaked, armed and winged Or
Motto Grip fast
Plant Badge Rue, in flower

LINDSAY
Crest Issuing from an antique ducal coronet Or, the head, neck and wings of a swan Proper
Motto Endure fort (Endure boldly)
Plant Badge Lime tree

LOCKHART
Crest On a chapeau Gules furred Ermine a boar's head erased Argent, langued Gules

Motto Corda serrata pando (I open locked hearts); on Compartment: Semper pugnare paratus pro patria (Always ready to fight for my country)

LUMSDEN
Crests Dexter, issuant from a crest coronet Or a naked arm grasping a sword Proper (Lumsden of that Ilk); sinister, an earne devouring a salmon Proper (Lumsden of Blanerne)
Mottoes Dexter, Amor patitur moras (Love endures delays); sinister, Beware in tyme
Plant Badge Sprig of hazel fructed Proper

LYON
Crest Within a garland of bay leaves, a lady from the middle richly attired, holding in her dexter hand a thistle all Proper (in allusion to the alliance of Sir John Lyon with Princess Jean, daughter of King Robert II
Motto In te domine speravi (In Thee O Lord have I put my trust)

MACALISTER
Crest A dexter arm in armour erect, the hand holding a dagger in pale all Proper
Motto Fortiter (Boldly); on Compartment: Per mare per terras (By sea and by land)

MACBAIN
Crest A grey demi-cat-a-mountain salient, on his sinister foreleg a Highland targe Gules
Motto Touch not a catt bot a targe; on Compartment: Kinchyle
Plant Badge Boxwood plants

MACDONALD OF MACDONALD
Crest On a crest coronet Or, a hand in armour fessways couped at the elbow Proper holding a cross crosslet fitchée Gules
Motto Per mare per terras (By sea and by land); on Compartment: Fraoch Eilean
Plant Badge Heather

MACDONALD OF CLANRANALD
Crest A triple-towered castle Argent masoned Sable, and issuing from the centre tower a dexter arm in armour embowed grasping a sword all Proper
Motto My hope is constant in thee; on Compartment: Dh' aindeòin cò theireadh e (Gainsay who dare)
Plant Badge Common heather

MACDONALD OF SLEAT
Crests Dexter, a hand in armour fesswise holding a cross crosslet fitchée Gules; sinister, a bull passant Argent, armed Or, issuing from a hurst of oak, charged on the shoulder with a rose proper
Mottoes Dexter, Per mare per terras (By sea and by land) (Macdonald); sinister, Virtus propter se (Virtue for its own sake) (Bosville)

MACDONNELL OF GLENGARRY
Crest A raven Proper perching on a rock Azure
Motto Cragan an Fhithich (The rock of the raven); on Compartment: Per mare per terras (By sea and by land)

MACDOUGALL
Crest (on a chapeau Gules furred Ermine) A dexter arm in armour embowed fess-ways couped Proper, holding a cross crosslet fitchée erect Gules
Motto Buaidh no bas (To conquer or die)
Plant Badge Bell heather

MACDOWALL
Crest (issuant from a crest coronet Or) A lion's paw erased and erected Proper holding a dagger point upwards Proper, hilted and pommelled Or
Motto Vincere vel mori (To conquer or die)
Plant Badge A sprig of oak Proper

MACGREGOR
Crest A lion's head erased Proper, crowned with an antique crown Or
Motto 'S rioghal mo dhream (My race is royal); on Compartment: E'en do and spair nocht
Plant Badge Scots pine

MACINTYRE
Crest A dexter hand holding a dagger in pale Proper
Motto Per ardua (Through difficulties)
Plant Badge White heather

MACKAY
Crest A dexter arm erect couped at the elbow the hand grasping a dagger also erect all Proper
Motto Manu forti (With a strong hand)
Plant Badge Great bullrush

MACKENZIE
Crest A mount in flames Proper
Motto Luceo non uro (I shine, not burn)
Plant Badge Stagshorn clubmoss

MACKINNON
Crest A boar's head erased and holding in its mouth the shank of a deer all Proper
Motto Audentes fortuna juvat (Fortune assists the daring); on Compartment: Cumhnich bas Alpin (Remember the death of Alpin)

MACKINTOSH
Crest A cat-a-mountain salient guardant Proper
Motto Loch Moigh; on Compartment: Touch not the cat bot a glove
Plant Badge Red whortleberry fructed Proper

MACLACHLAN
Crest (issuant from a crest coronet of four (three visible) strawberry leaves Or) A castle set upon a rock all Proper
Motto Fortis et fidus (Brave and faithful)
Plant Badge Rowan seedlings fructed Proper

MACLAINE OF LOCHBUIE
Crest A branch of laurel and a branch of cypress in saltire surmounted of a battle axe in pale all Proper
Motto Vincere vel mori (To conquer or die)

MACLAREN
Crest A lion's head erased Sable crowned with an antique crown of six (four visible) points Or, between two branches of laurel issuing from the Wreath at either side of the head both Proper
Motto Creag an Tuirc (The boar's rock); on Compartment Ab origine fidus (Faithful from the first)

MACLEAN
Crest A tower embattled Argent
Motto Virtue mine honour

MACLENNAN
Crest A demi-piper all Proper, garbed in the proper tartan of the Clan MacLennan
Motto Dum spiro spero (While I breathe I hope)
Plant Badge Furze

MACLEOD
Crest A bull's head cabossed Sable, horned Or, between two flags Gules, staved of the First
Motto Hold fast; on Compartment: Murus aheneus esto (Be a wall of brass)
Plant Badge Juniper

MACMILLAN
Crest A dexter and a sinister hand issuing from the Wreath grasping and brandishing aloft a two-handed sword Proper
Motto Miseris succurere disco (I learn to succour the unfortunate); on Compartment: Fhad's a bhuaileas tonn ri crag (As long as the wave beats against the rock)
Plant Badge Holly seedlings fructed Proper

MACNAB
Crest The head of a savage affrontée Proper
Motto Timor omnis abesto (Let fear be far from all)
Plant Badge Stone-bramble

MACNAGHTEN
Crest A tower embattled Gules
Motto I hoip in God
Plant Badge Trailing azalea Proper

MACNEACAIL
Crest A hawk's head erased Gules
Mottoes (above) Sgorr-a-bhreac; (below) Generositate non ferocitate (By generosity not ferocity)

MACNEIL
Crest On a chapeau Gules furred Ermine, a rock Proper

Motto Buaidh no bas (To conquer or die)
Plant Badge Plants of dryas

MACPHERSON
Crest A cat sejant Proper
Motto Touch not the cat but a glove
Plant Badge White heather

MACTHOMAS
Crest A demi-cat-a-mountain rampant guardant Proper, grasping in his dexter paw a serpent Vert, langued Gules, its tail environing the sinister paw
Motto Deo juvante invidiam superabo (I will overcome envy with God's help); on Compartment: Clach na coileach (The stone of the cock)

MAITLAND
Crest A lion sejant affrontée Gules, ducally crowned Proper, in his dexter paw a sword Proper hilted and pommelled Or, in his sinister a fleur de lis Azure
Motto Consilio et animis (By wisdom and courage)
Plant Badge Honeysuckle

MAKGILL
Crest A phoenix in flames Proper
Motto Sine fine (Without end)

MALCOLM (MACCALLUM)
Crest A tower Argent, window and port Azure
Motto In ardua tendit (He has attempted difficult things); on Compartment: Dens refugium nostrum (God is our refuge)

MAR
Crest On a chapeau Gules furred Ermine, two wings, each of ten pen feathers, erected and addorsed, both blazoned as in the Arms
Motto Pans plus (Think more)

MARJORIBANKS
Crest A demi-griffin Proper, issuant from a crest coronet Or
Motto Et custos et pugnax (Both a preserver and a champion)

MATHESON
Crest Issuant from an antique crown Or, a hand brandishing a scimitar fessways all Proper
Motto Fac et spera (Do and hope); on Compartment: O'Chian

MENZIES
Crest A savage head erased Proper
Motto Vil God I zal
Plant Badge Menzies heath

MOFFAT
Crest A crest coronet and issuing therefrom a cross crosslet fitchée Sable surmounted of a saltire Argent
Motto Spero meliora (I hope for better things)

MONCREIFFE
Crest Issuing from a crest coronet Or, a demi-lion rampant Gules, armed and langued Azure
Motto Sur esperance (Upon hope)
Plant Badge Oak

MONTGOMERY
Crests Dexter, a lady dressed in ancient apparel Azure holding in her dexter hand an anchor and in her sinister the head of a savage couped suspended by the hair all Proper; sinister, issuing from a ducal coronet Or, a wyvern vomiting fire his wings elevated Proper
Mottoes Dexter, Garde bien (Watch well); sinister, Hazard yet forward

MORRISON
Crest Issuant from waves of the sea Azure crested Argent, a mount Vert, thereon an embattled wall Azure masoned Argent, and issuing therefrom a cubit arm naked Proper, the hand grasping a dagger hilted Or
Motto Teaghlach Phabbay (Pabbay family); on Compartment: Dun Eistein
Plant Badge Driftweed

MUNRO
Crest An eagle perching Proper
Motto Dread God; on Compartment: Caisteal Fotais 'n a theine (Foulis Castle in flames)
Plant Badge Common Club Moss

MURRAY
Crests Dexter, on a Wreath Argent and Azure a mermaid holding in her dexter hand a mirror and in her sinister a comb all Proper (Murray); centre, on a Wreath Or and Sable a demi-savage Proper wreathed about the temples and waist with laurel, his arms extended and holding in the right hand a dagger, in the left a key all Proper (Atholl); sinister, on a Wreath Argent and Azure, a peacock's head and neck Proper, accompanied (one on either side) by two arms from the elbows Proper, vested in maunches Azure doubled Argent
Mottoes Dexter, Tout prest (Quite ready); centre, Furth fortune and fill the fetters; sinister, Praite (Ready)
Plant Badges Juniper, for Atholl and butcher's broom, for Murray

NAPIER
Crest A dexter arm erect couped below the elbow Proper, grasping a crescent Argent
Motto Sans tache (Without stain); on Compartment: Ready aye ready

NESBITT
Crest A boar passant Sable, armed Argent and langued Gules
Motto I byd it

NICOLSON
Crest A lion issuant Or armed and langued Gules
Motto Generositate (By generosity); on Compartment: Nil sistere contra (Nothing to oppose us)
Plant Badge Sprig of juniper

OGILVY
Crest A lady affrontée from the middle upward Proper in Azure vestments richly attired holding a portcullis Gules
Motto A fin (To the end)

PRIMROSE
Crest A demi-lion rampant Gules holding in his dexter paw a primrose Or
Motto Fide et fidacia (By faith and trust)

RAMSAY
Crest A unicorn's head couped Argent armed Or
Motto Ora et labora (Pray and work)

RATTRAY
Crest Issuant from a crest coronet Or, a star Or and thereon a flaming heart Proper
Motto Super sidera votum (My wishes are above the stars)

RIDDELL
Crest A demi greyhound Proper
Motto I hope to share

ROBERTSON
Crest A dexter hand holding up an imperial crown Proper
Motto Virtutis gloria merces (Glory is the reward of valour); on Compartment: Garg 'n uair dhuisgear (Fierce when roused)
Plant Badge Bracken

ROLLO
Crest A stag's head couped Proper
Motto La fortune passe partout (Fortune passes over everywhere)

ROSE
Crest On a chapeau Gules furred Ermine, a harp Azure
Motto Constant and true
Plant Badge Wild rosemary

ROSS
Crest A hand holding a garland of juniper Proper
Motto Spem successus alit (Success nourishes hope)
Plant Badge Juniper plant fructed Proper

RUTHVEN
Crest A ram's head couped Sable armed Or
Motto Deid schaw

SANDILANDS
Crest An eagle displayed Proper
Motto Spero meliora (I hope for better things)

SCOTT
Crest A stag trippant Proper, attired and unguled Or
Motto Amo (I love)

SCRYMGEOUR
Crest A lion's paw erased in bend Or holding a crooked sword or scymitar Argent
Motto Dissipate (Disperse)
Plant Badge Rowan

SEMPILL
Crest A stag's head Argent attired with ten tynes Azure and collared with a prince's crown Or
Motto Keep tryst

SHAW OF TORDARROCH
Crest A dexter cubit arm couped and holding a dagger erect all Proper
Motto Fide et fortitudine (By faith and fortitude)

SINCLAIR
Crest A cock Proper, armed and beaked Or
Motto Commit thy work to God
Plant Badge Whin

SKENE
Crest A dexter arm issuing from the shoulder out of a cloud, holding forth in the hand a triumphal crown, Proper
Motto Virtutis regia merces (A palace the reward of bravery)

SPENS
Crest A hart's head erased Proper
Motto Si deus quis contra (If God is for us, who is against us)

STIRLING
Crest Issuing out of an antique coronet Or a hart's head couped Azure
Motto Gang forward; on Compartment: Castrum et nemus strivelense (The castle and wood of Stirling)

STRANGE
Crest Dexter, on a Wreath Argent and Sable a cluster of grapes Proper; sinister, on a Wreath Argent and Sable a castle Proper, masoned Sable.
Motto Dexter, Dulce quod utile (That which is useful is sweet); sinister, Stet fortuna domus (The good fortune of the house stands)

STUART OF BUTE
Crests Dexter, a dragon Vert spouting out fire Or, crowned with an open crown of four strawberry leaves of the Last (Crichton); centre, a demi-lion rampant Gules, armed and langued Azure (Stuart); sinister, a wyvern Proper holding in the mouth a sinister hand couped Gules (Lordship of Cardiff)
Mottoes Dexter, God send grace; centre, Nobilis est ira leonis (The lion's anger is noble); sinister, Ung je serviram (I will serve one); on Compartment: Avito viret honore (He flourishes by ancestral honours)

SUTHERLAND
Crest A cat-a-mountain sejant rampant Proper

Motto Sans peur (Without fear)
Plant Badge Cotton-sedge plant

SWINTON
Crest A boar chained to a tree Proper
Motto J'espere (I hope): on Compartment: Je pense (I think)

TROTTER
Crest A knight in armour Proper, holding his courser Argent caparisoned Gules.
Motto God send grace

URQUHART
Crest Issuant from a crest coronet Or, a naked woman from the waist upwards
Proper, brandishing in her dexter hand a sword Azure, hilted and pommelled Gules,
and holding in her sinister hand a palm sapling Vert
Motto Meane weil speak weil and doe weil

WALLACE
Crest Issuant from a crest coronet of four (three visible) strawberry leaves Or, a dexter arm vambraced, the hand brandishing a sword all Proper
Motto Pro libertate (For liberty)
Plant Badge A sprig of oak fructed Proper

WEDDERBURN
Crest An eagle's head erased Proper
Motto Non degener (Not degenerate)
Plant Badge Beech

WEMYSS
Crest A swan Proper
Motto Je pense (I think)

• HERALDIC TERMS •

Many of the terms used in the descriptions of the clan arms and crests are heraldic. The language is very stylised, but the short glossary below outlines some of the terms that recur frequently in the lists on the previous pages.

affrontée facing towards the onlooker
argent silver or white
azure blue; one of the main heraldic colours, with **gules**, **sable** and **vert**.
banner a flag, rectangular or square, showing the part of the coat of arms that appears on the shield. Banners are carried in procession or flown from a flagpole.
bend A band running from **dexter chief** to **sinister** base. One of the main heraldic charges, or ordinaries; a bend sinister runs in the opposite direction.
bezant a golden roundel
charge a figure or device set on a shield

charged anything with a charge on it

chevron an upside-down V; one of the main heraldic charges, or ordinaries.

chief a broad band running horizontally across the top of a shield; one of the main heraldic charges, or ordinaries.

coronet a lesser crown. A different style of coronet is assigned to each of the five ranks of the peerage.

couped cut off with a straight line along the lower edge. But close couped has the outline of a head only, with no neck seen.

cross the commonest of heraldic charges, or ordinaries; there are several types

demi half; usually the upper half of a human or animal charge.

dexter right-hand side of the shield as seen by the bearer; left side to the onlooker.

displayed describing outstretched wings

dormant describing a sleeping pose

erased with a jagged edge, as if it had been torn

fess a band running across the shield centre; one of the main heraldic charges, or ordinaries; *fessways* describes any feature running across the shield centre

field the shield background or surface that the charges appear on

fitchée describing a cross with a pointed lower spar

garb a wheat sheaf

guardant describing a creature with its head turned out towards the onlooker

gules red; one of the main heraldic colours, with *azure*, *sable* and *vert*.

gyronny see *partition, line of*

issuant issuing from or coming out of

lymphad a single-masted galley with oars

or gold

ordinary any one of the main heraldic charges, usually a geometric shape. The main ones are *bend*, *bend sinister*, *chevron*, *chief*, *cross*, *fess*, *pale*, *pall*, *pile* and *saltire*

overall describing a feature superimposed on all the others

pale a broad band running vertically down the centre of a shield; one of the main heraldic charges, or ordinaries.

pall a Y shape; one of the main heraldic charges, or ordinaries.

pile a triangular shape pointing towards the base of a shield; one of the main heraldic charges, or ordinaries.

partition, line of dividing line of a shield or edge of a charge; these can take various patterns, often along the lines of a particular shield's *ordinary*. So, for example, if a shield is described as parted per pale, it is divided vertically down the middle. Other terms used to describe partitions include *tierced* – divided into three – and *gyronny*, with triangular shapes radiating from the centre.

proper in natural colours

rampant describing a creature rearing or standing on its back leg

respectant describing two creatures looking at one another

sable black; one of the main heraldic colours, with *azure*, *gules* and *vert*.

saltire an X-shaped cross; one of the main heraldic charges, or ordinaries.

sinister left-hand side of the shield as seen by the bearer; right side to the onlooker

surmounted describing a charge or feature with another one over it

tierced see **partition, line of**

vert green; one of the main heraldic colours, with **azure**, **gules** and **sable**

volant flying

wyvern a two-legged dragon-like monster (dragons are depicted with four legs in heraldry)

• THE SEPTS •

Septs – usually regarded as branches of a 'parent' clan or family – are generally associated with particular clans. Although there is some dispute over the nature of the relationships between particular septs and clans, the list that follows shows commonly accepted groupings.

Name	Associated Clan	Name	Associated Clan
Abbot	Macnab	Begg	Macdonald
Abbotson	Macnab	Berry	Forbes
Addison	Gordon	Beton	Macleod
Adie	Gordon	Binnie	Macbain
Airlie	Ogilvy	Black	Lamont, Macgregor, Maclean
Airth	Graham	Blake	Lamont
Aitcheson	Gordon	Bonar	Graham
Aitken	Gordon	Bontein	Graham
Alexander	Macalister, Macdonald	Bontine	Graham
Alistair	Macalister	Bowers	Macgregor
Allan	Macdonald, Macfarlane	Bowie	Macdonald
Allanson	Macdonald, Macfarlane	Bowmaker	Macgregor
Allison	Macalister	Bowman	Farquharson
Arrol	Hay	Boyes	Forbes
Arthur	Macarthur	Brebner	Farquharson
Askey	Macleod	Brewer	Drummond, Macgregor
Austin	Keith	Brieve	Morrison
Ayson	Mackintosh	Brown	Lamont, Macmillan
Bain	Macbain, Mackay	Bryce	Macfarlane
Balloch	Macdonald	Bryde	Brodie
Barrie	Farquharson, Gordon	Buntain	Graham
Barron	Rose	Bunten	Graham
Bartholomew	Macfarlane, Leslie	Buntine	Graham
Bean	Macbain	Burdon	Lamont
Beath	Macdonald, Maclean	Burk	Macdonald
Beattie	Macbain	Burnes	Campbell

Name	Associated Clan	Name	Associated Clan
Burns	Campbell	Crombie	Macdonald
Caddell	Campbell	Crookshanks	Stewart
Caird	Sinclair, Macgregor	Cruickshanks	Stewart
Cariston	Skene	Crum	Macdonald
Carlyle	Bruce	Cullen	Gordon
Carr	Kerr	Cumin	Cumming
Carrick	Kennedy	Dallas	Mackintosh
Carson	Macpherson	Daniels	Macdonald
Cassels	Kennedy	Davie	Davidson
Cattanach	Macpherson	Davis	Davidson
Caw	Macfarlane	Davison	Davidson
Cessford	Kerr	Dawson	Davidson
Charles	Mackenzie	Day	Davidson
Christie	Farquharson	Dean	Davidson
Clanachan	Maclean	Denoon	Campbell
Clark	Cameron, Macpherson	Denune	Campbell
Clarke	Cameron, Macpherson	Deuchar	Lindsay
Clarkson	Cameron, Macpherson	Dickson	Keith
Clement	Lamont	Dingwall	Munro, Ross
Clerk	Cameron, Macpherson	Dinnes	Innes
Cluny	Macpherson	Dis	Skene
Clyne	Sinclair	Dixon	Keith
Cobb	Lindsay	Dobbie	Robertson
Collier	Robertson	Dobson	Robertson
Colman	Buchanan	Dochart	Macgregor
Colson	Macdonald	Docharty	Macgregor
Colyear	Robertson	Doig	Drummond
Combie	Macthomas	Doles	Mackintosh
Comine	Cumming (Comyn)	Donachie	Robertson
Comrie	Macgregor	Donaldson	Macdonald
Conacher	Macdougall	Donillson	Macdonald
Connall	Macdonald	Donleavy	Buchanan
Connell	Macdonald	Donlevy	Buchanan
Conochie	Campbell	Donnellson	Macdonnell
Constable	Hay	Dove	Buchanan
Cook	Stewart	Dow	Buchanan, Davidson
Corbet	Ross	Dowe	Buchanan
Cormack	Buchanan	Downie	Lindsay
Coull	Macdonald	Drysdale	Douglas
Coulson	Macdonald	Duff	Macduff
Cousland	Buchanan	Duffie	Macfie
Coutts	Farquharson	Duffus	Sutherland
Cowan	Colquhoun, Macdougall	Duffy	Macfie
Cowie	Fraser	Duilach	Stewart
Crerar	Mackintosh	Duncanson	Robertson

Name	Associated Clan	Name	Associated Clan
Dunnachie	Robertson	Gilfillan	Macnab
Duthie	Ross	Gill	Macdonald
Dyce	Skene	Gillanders	Ross
Eadie	Gordon	Gillespie	Macpherson
Eaton	Home	Gillies	Macpherson
Edie	Gordon	Gillon	Maclean
Elder	Mackintosh	Gilroy	Grant, Macgillivray
Ennis	Innes	Glennie	Mackintosh
Enrick	Gunn	Gorrie	Macdonald
Esson	Mackintosh	Goudie	Macpherson
Ewing	Maclachlan	Gow	Macpherson
Fair	Ross	Gowan	Macdonald
Fairbairn	Armstrong	Gowrie	Macdonald
Federith	Sutherland	Greenlaw	Home
Fee	Macfie	Gregorson	Macgregor
Fergus	Ferguson	Gregory	Macgregor
Ferries	Ferguson	Greig	Macgregor
Ferson	Macpherson	Greusach	Farquharson
Fife	Macduff	Grewar	Macgregor, Drummond
Findlater	Ogilvie	Grier	Macgregor
Findlay	Farquharson	Griesck	Macfarlane
Findlayson	Farquharson	Grigor	Macgregor
Finlay	Farquharson	Gruamach	Macfarlane
Finlayson	Farquharson	Gruer	Macgregor, Drummond
Fisher	Campbell	Haddon	Graham
Foulis	Munro	Haggart	Ross
France	Stewart	Hallyard	Skene
Francis	Stewart	Hardie	Farquharson, Mackintosh
Frew	Fraser	Hardy	Farquharson, Mackintosh
Frissell	Fraser	Harold	Macleod
Frizell	Fraser	Harper	Buchanan
Fyfe	Macduff	Harperson	Buchanan
Gallie	Gunn	Harvey	Keith
Galt	Macdonald	Hastings	Campbell
Garrow	Stewart	Hawes	Campbell
Garvie	Maclean	Haws	Campbell
Gaunson	Gunn	Hawson	Campbell
Geddes	Gordon	Hawthorn	Macdonald
Georgeson	Gunn	Hendrie	Macnaughton
Gibb	Buchanan	Hendry	Macnaughton
Gifford	Hay	Hewitson	Macdonald
Gilbert	Buchanan	Hewitt	Macdonald
Gilbertson	Buchanan	Higginson	Mackintosh
Gilbride	Macdonald	Hobson	Robertson
Gilchrist	Maclachlan, Ogilvy	Hossack	Mackintosh

Name	Associated Clan	Name	Associated Clan
Howe	Graham	Leckie	Macgregor
Howie	Graham	Lecky	Macgregor
Howison	Macdonald	Lees	Macpherson
Hudson	Macdonald	Leitch	Macdonald
Hughson	Macdonald	Lemond	Lamont
Huntly	Gordon	Lennie	Buchanan
Hutchenson	Macdonald	Lenny	Buchanan
Hutcheson	Macdonald	Lewis	Macleod
Hutchinson	Macdonald	Limond	Lamont
Hutchison	Macdonald	Limont	Lamont
Inches	Robertson	Linklater	Sinclair
Ingram	Colquhoun	Lobban	Maclennan
Innie	Innes	Lockerbie	Douglas
Isles	Macdonald	Lombard	Stewart
Jameson	Gunn, Stewart	Lonie	Cameron
Jamieson	Gunn, Stewart	Lorne	Stewart, Campbell
Jeffrey	Macdonald	Loudoun	Campbell
Kay	Davidson	Low	Maclaren
Kean	Gunn, Macdonald	Lowson	Maclaren
Keene	Gunn, Macdonald	Lucas	Lamont
Kellie	Macdonald	Luke	Lamont
Kendrick	Macnaughton	Lyall	Sinclair
Kenneth	Mackenzie	MacA'challies	Macdonald
Kennethson	Mackenzie	Macachounich	Colquhoun
Kerracher	Farquharson	Macadam	Macgregor
Kilgour	Macduff	Macadie	Ferguson
King	Colquhoun	Macaindra	Macfarlane
Kinnell	Macdonald	Macaldonich	Buchanan
Kinnieson	Macfarlane	Macalduie	Lamont
Knox	Macfarlane	Macallan	Macdonald, Macfarlane
Lachie	Maclachlan	Macalonie	Cameron
Laidlaw	Scott	Macandeoir	Buchanan, Macnab
Lair	Maclaren	Macandrew	Mackintosh
Lamb	Lamont	Macangus	Macinnes
Lambie	Lamont	Macara	Macgregor, Macrae
Lammond	Lamont	Macaree	Macgregor
Lamondson	Lamont	Macaskill	Macleod
Landers	Lamont	Macaslan	Buchanan
Lang	Leslie	Macauselan	Buchanan
Lansdale	Home	Macauslan	Buchanan
Lauchlan	Maclachlan	Macausland	Buchanan
Lawrence	Maclaren	Macauslane	Buchanan
Lawrie	Maclaren	Macay	Shaw
Lawson	Maclaren	Macbaxter	Macmillan
Lean	Maclean	Macbean	Macbain

Name	Associated Clan	Name	Associated Clan
Macbeath	Macbain, Macdonald, Maclean	Maccombe	Macthomas
		Maccombich	Stewart (of Appin)
Macbeolain	Mackenzie	Maccombie	Macthomas
Macbeth	Macbain, Macdonald, Maclean	Maccomie	Macthomas
		Macconacher	Macdougall
Macbheath	Macbain, Macdonald, Maclean	Macconachie	Macgregor, Robertson
		Macconchy	Mackintosh
Macbride	Macdonald	Maccondy	Macfarlane
Macbrieve	Morrison	Macconnach	Mackenzie
Macburie	Macdonald	Macconnechy	Campbell, Robertson
Maccaa	Macfarlane	Macconnell	Macdonald
Maccabe	Macleod	Macconochie	Campbell, Robertson
Maccaig	Farquharson, Macleod	Maccooish	Macdonald
Maccaishe	Macdonald	Maccook	Macdonald
Maccall	Macdonald	Maccorkill	Gunn
Maccalman	Buchanan	Maccorkindale	Macleod
Maccalmont	Buchanan	Maccorkle	Gunn
Maccamie	Stewart	Maccormack	Buchanan
Maccammon	Buchanan	Maccormick	Maclean of Lochbuie
Maccammond	Buchanan	Maccorrie	Macquarrie
Maccanish	Macinnes	Maccorry	Macquarrie
Maccansh	Macinnes	Maccosram	Macdonald
Maccartney	Farquharson, Mackintosh	Maccoull	Macdougall
Maccartair	Campbell	Maccowan	Colquhoun, Macdougall
Maccarter	Campbell	Maccrae	Macrae
Maccash	Macdonald	Maccrain	Macdonald
Maccaskill	Macleod	Maccraken	Maclean
Maccasland	Buchanan	Maccraw	Macrae
Maccaul	Macdonald	Maccreath	Macrae
Maccause	Macfarlane	Maccrie	Mackay
Maccaw	Macfarlane	Maccrimmor	Macleod
Maccay	Mackay	Maccrindle	Macdonald
Macceallaich	Macdonald	Maccririe	Macdonald
Macchlerich	Cameron	Maccrouther	Macgregor, Drummond
Macchlery	Cameron	Maccruithein	Macdonald
Macchoiter	Macgregor	Maccuag	Macdonald
Macchruiter	Buchanan	Maccuaig	Farquharson, Macleod
Maccloy	Stewart	Maccubbin	Buchanan
Macclure	Macleod	Maccuish	Macdonald
Maccluskie	Macdonald	Maccune	Macewan
Macclymont	Lamont	Maccunn	Macpherson
Maccodrum	Macdonald	Maccurrach	Macpherson
Maccoll	Macdonald	Maccutchen	Macdonald
Maccolman	Buchanan	Maccutcheon	Macdonald
Maccomas	Macthomas, Gunn	Macdade	Davidson

Name	Associated Clan	Name	Associated Clan
Macdaid	Davidson	Macgilvray	Macgillivray
Macdaniell	Macdonald	Macglashan	Mackintosh, Stewart
Macdavid	Davidson	Macglasrich	Maciver, Campbell
Macdermid	Campbell	Macgorrie	Macdonald
Macdiarmid	Campbell	Macgorry	Macdonald
Macdonachie	Robertson	Macgoun	Macdonald, Macpherson
Macdonleavy	Buchanan	Macgowan	Macdonald, Macpherson
Macdrain	Macdonald	Macgown	Macdonald, Macpherson
Macduffie	Macfie	Macgrath	Macrae
Macdulothe	Macdougall	Macgreusich	Buchanan, Macfarlane
Maceachan	Macdonald of Clanranald	Macgrewar	Macgregor, Drummond
Maceachern	Macdonald	Macgrime	Graham
Maceachin	Macdonald of Clanranald	Macgrory	Maclaren
Maceachran	Macdonald	Macgrowther	Macgregor, Drummond
Macearachar	Farquharson	Macgruder	Macgregor, Drummond
Macelfrish	Macdonald	Macgruer	Fraser
Macelheran	Macdonald	Macgruther	Macgregor, Drummond
Maceoin	Macfarlane	Macguaran	Macquarrie
Maceol	Macnaughton	Macguffie	McFie
Macerracher	Macfarlane	Macgugan	Macneil
Macfadzean	Maclaine of Lochbuie	Macguire	Macquarrie
Macfall	Macpherson	Machaffie	Macfie
Macfarquhar	Farquharson	Machardie	Farquharson, Mackintosh
Macfater	Maclaren	Machardy	Farquharson, Mackintosh
Macfeat	Maclaren	Macharold	Macleod
Macfergus	Ferguson	Machendrie	Macnaughton
Macgaw	Macfarlane	Machendry	Macnaughton, Macdonald
Macgeachie	Macdonald of Clanranald	Machowell	Macdougall
Macgeachin	Macdonald of Clanranald	Machugh	Macdonald
Macgeoch	Macfarlane	Machutchen	Macdonald
Macghee	Mackay	Machutcheon	Macdonald
Macghie	Mackay	Macian	Gunn, Macdonald
Macgilbert	Buchanan	Macildowie	Cameron
Macgilchrist	Maclachlan, Ogilvie	Macilduy	Macgregor, Maclean
Macgill	Macdonald	Macilreach	Macdonald
Macgilledon	Lamont	Macilleriach	Macdonald
Macgillegowie	Lamont	Macilriach	Macdonald
Macgillivantic	Macdonald	Macilrevie	Macdonald
Macgillivour	Macgillivray	Macilvain	Macbean
Macgillonie	Cameron	Macilvora	Maclaine of Lochbuie
Macgilp	Macdonald	Macilvrae	Macgillivray
Macgilroy	Grant, Macgillivray	Macilvride	Macdonald
Macgilvernock	Graham	Macilwhom	Lamont
Macgilvra	Macgillivray, Maclaine of Lochbuie	Macilwraith	Macdonald
		Macilzegowie	Lamont

Name	Associated Clan
Macimmey	Fraser
Macinally	Buchanan
Macindeor	Menzies
Macindoe	Buchanan
Macinroy	Robertson
Macinstalker	Macfarlane
Maciock	Macfarlane
Macissac	Campbell, Macdonald
Maciver	Maciver, Campbell
Macivor	Maciver, Campbell
Macjames	Macfarlane
Mackail	Cameron
Mackames	Gunn
Mackaskill	Macleod
Mackeachan	Macdonald
Mackeamish	Gunn
Mackean	Gunn, Macdonald
Mackechnie	Macdonald of Clanranald
Mackee	Mackay
Mackeggie	Mackintosh
Mackeith	Macpherson
Mackellachie	Macdonald
Mackellaig	Macdonald
Mackellaigh	Macdonald
Mackellar	Campbell
Mackelloch	Macdonald
Mackelvie	Campbell
Mackendrick	Macnaughton
Mackenrick	Macnaughton
Mackeochan	Macdonald of Clanranald
Mackerchar	Farquharson
Mackerlich	Mackenzie
Mackerracher	Farquharson
Mackerras	Ferguson
Mackersey	Ferguson
Mackessock	Campbell, Macdonald of Clanranald
Mackichan	Macdonald of Clanranald, Macdougall
Mackieson	Mackintosh
Mackiggan	Macdonald
Mackilligan	Mackintosh
Mackillop	Macdonald
Mackim	Fraser

Name	Associated Clan
Mackimmie	Fraser
Mackindlay	Farquharson
Mackinlay	Buchanan, Farquharson, Macfarlane, Stewart of Appin
Mackinley	Buchanan
Mackinnell	Macdonald
Mackinney	Mackinnon
Mackinning	Mackinnon
Mackinven	Mackinnon
Mackirdy	Stewart
Mackissock	Campbell, Macdonald of Clanranald
Macknight	Macnaughton
Maclae	Stewart of Appin
Maclagan	Robertson
Maclaghlan	Maclachlan
Maclairish	Macdonald
Maclamond	Lamont
Maclardie	Macdonald
Maclardy	Macdonald
Maclarty	Macdonald
Maclaverty	Macdonald
Maclaws	Campbell
Maclea	Stewart of Appin
Macleay	Stewart of Appin
Maclehose	Campbell
Macleish	Macpherson
Macleister	Macgregor
Maclergain	Maclean
Maclerie	Cameron, Mackintosh, Macpherson
Macleverty	Macdonald
Maclewis	Macleod
Maclintock	Macdougall
Maclise	Macpherson
Macliver	Macgregor
Maclucas	Lamont, Macdougall
Maclugash	Macdougall
Maclulich	Macdougall, Munro, Ross
Maclure	Macleod
Maclymont	Lamont
Macmanus	Colquhoun, Gunn
Macmartin	Cameron
Macmaster	Buchanan, Macinnes

Name	Associated Clan	Name	Associated Clan
Macmath	Matheson	Macpetrie	Macgregor
Macmaurice	Buchanan	Macphadden	Maclaine of Lochbuie
Macmenzies	Menzies	Macphater	Maclaren
Macmichael	Stewart of Appin, Stewart	Macphedran	Campbell
Macminn	Menzies	Macphedron	Macaulay
Macmonies	Menzies	Macpheidiran	Macaulay
Macmorran	Mackinnon	Macphillip	Macdonald
Macmunn	Stewart	Macphorich	Lamont
Macmurchie	Buchanan, Mackenzie	Macphun	Matheson, Campbell
Macmurchy	Buchanan, Mackenzie	Macquaire	Macquarrie
Macmurdo	Macpherson	Macquartie	Macquarrie
Macmurdoch	Macpherson	Macquey	Mackay
Macmurray	Murray	Macquhirr	Macquarrie
Macmurrich	Macdonald of Clanranald,	Macquire	Macquarrie
	Macpherson	Macquistan	Macdonald
Macmutrie	Stewart	Macquisten	Macdonald
Macnair	Macfarlane, Macnaughton	Macquoid	Mackay
Macnamell	Macdougall	Macra	Macrae
Macnayer	Macnaughton	Macrach	Macrae
Macnee	Macgregor	Macraild	Macleod
Macneilage	Macneil	Macraith	Macrae, Macdonald
Macneiledge	Macneil	Macrankin	Maclean
Macneilly	Macneil	Macrath	Macrae
Macneish	Macgregor	Macritchie	Mackintosh
Macneur	Macfarlane	Macrob	Gunn, Macfarlane
Macney	Macgregor	Macrobb	Macfarlane
Macnider	Macfarlane	Macrobbie	Robertson, Drummond
Macnie	Macgregor	Macrobert	Robertson, Drummond
Macnish	Macgregor	Macrobie	Robertson, Drummond
Macniter	Macfarlane	Macrorie	Macdonald
Macniven	Cumming, Mackintosh,	Macrory	Macdonald
	Macnaughton	Macruer	Macdonald
Macnuir	Macnaughton	Macrurie	Macdonald
Macnuyer	Buchanan, Macnaughton	Macrury	Macdonald
Macomie	Macthomas	Macshannachan	Macdonald
Macomish	Macthomas	Macshimes	Fraser of Lovat
Maconie	Cameron	Macsimon	Fraser of Lovat
Macoran	Campbell	Macsorley	Cameron, Macdonald
MacO'Shannaig	Macdonald	Macsporran	Macdonald
Macoull	Macdougall	Macswan	Macdonald
Macourlic	Cameron	Macsween	Macdonald
Macowen	Campbell	Macswen	Macdonald
Macowl	Macdougall	Macsymon	Fraser
Macpatrick	Lamont, Maclaren	Mactaggart	Ross

Name	Associated Clan	Name	Associated Clan
Mactary	Innes	Meyners	Menzies
Mactause	Campbell	Michie	Forbes
Mactavish	Campbell	Miller	Macfarlane
Mactear	Ross, Macintyre	Milne	Gordon, Ogilvy
Mactier	Ross	Milroy	Macgillivray
Mactire	Ross	Minn	Menzies
Maculric	Cameron	Minnus	Menzies
Macure	Campbell	Mitchell	Innes
Macvail	Cameron, Mackay	Monach	Macfarlane
Macvanish	Mackenzie	Monzie	Menzies
Macvarish	Macdonald of Clanranald	Moodie	Stewart
Macveagh	Maclean	Moray	Murray
Macvean	Macbean	Morgan	Mackay
Macvey	Maclean	Morren	Mackinnon
Macvicar	Macnaughton	Morris	Buchanan
Macvinish	Mackenzie	Morton	Douglas
Macvurich	Macdonald of Clanranald,	Munn	Stewart, Lamont
	Macpherson	Murchie	Buchanan, Menzies
Macvurie	Macdonald of Clanranald	Murchison	Buchanan, Menzies
Macwalrick	Cameron	Murdoch	Macdonald, Macpherson
Macwalter	Macfarlane	Murdoson	Macdonald, Macpherson
Macwattie	Buchanan	Murphy	Macdonald
Macwhannell	Macdonald	Neal	Macneil
Macwhirr	Macquarrie	Neil	Macneil
Macwhirter	Buchanan	Neill	Macneil
Macwilliam	Gunn, Macfarlane	Neilson	Macneil
Malcolmson	Malcolm (Maccallum)	Nelson	Gunn, Macneil
Malloch	Macgregor	Neish	Macgregor
Mann	Gunn	Nish	Macgregor
Manson	Gunn	Niven	Cumming, Mackintosh
Mark	Macdonald	Nixon	Armstrong
Marnoch	Innes	Noble	Mackintosh
Marshall	Keith	Norie	Macdonald
Martin	Cameron, Macdonald	Norman	Sutherland
Mason	Sinclair	O'Drain	Macdonald
Massey	Matheson	Oliver	Fraser
Masterson	Buchanan	O'May	Sutherland
Mathie	Matheson	O'Shaig	Macdonald
Mavor	Gordon	O'Shannachan	Macdonald
May	Macdonald	O'Shannaig	Macdonald
Means	Menzies	Park	Macdonald
Meikleham	Lamont	Parlane	Macfarlane
Mein	Menzies	Paton	Macdonald, Maclean
Meine	Menzies	Patrick	Lamont
Mennie	Menzies		

Name	Associated Clan	Name	Associated Clan
Paul	Cameron, Mackintosh	Simpson	Fraser of Lovat
Pearson	Macpherson	Simson	Fraser of Lovat
Peterkin	Macgregor	Skinner	Macgregor
Petrie	Macgregor	Small	Murray
Philipson	Macdonald	Smart	Mackenzie
Pinkerton	Campbell	Smith	Macpherson, Mackintosh
Piper	Murray	Sorely	Cameron, Macdonald
Pitullich	Macdonald	Spence	Macduff
Pollard	Mackay	Spittal	Buchanan
Polson	Mackay	Spittel	Buchanan
Porter	Macnaughton	Sporran	Macdonald
Pratt	Grant	Stalker	Macfarlane
Purcell	Macdonald	Stark	Robertson
Raith	Macrae	Stenhouse	Bruce
Randolf	Bruce	Stewart	Stewart
Reidfurd	Innes	Storie	Ogilvie
Reoch	Farquharson, Macdonald	Stringer	Macgregor
Revie	Macdonald	Summers	Lindsay
Riach	Farquharson, Macdonald	Suttie	Grant
Richardson	Ogilvie, Buchanan	Swan	Gunn
Risk	Buchanan	Swanson	Gunn
Ritchie	Mackintosh	Syme	Fraser
Robb	Macfarlane	Symon	Fraser
Roberts	Robertson	Taggart	Ross
Robinson	Gunn, Robertson	Tarrill	Mackintosh
Robison	Gunn, Robertson	Tawesson	Campbell
Robson	Gunn, Robertson	Tawse	Farquharson
Rome	Johnstone	Thain	Innes, Macintosh
Ronald	Macdonald, Gunn	Todd	Gordon
Ronaldson	Macdonald, Gunn	Tolmie	Macleod
Rorison	Macdonald	Tonnochy	Robertson
Roy	Robertson	Torry	Campbell
Rusk	Buchanan	Tosh	Mackintosh
Ruskin	Buchanan	Toward	Lamont
Russell	Russell, Cumming	Towart	Lamont
Sanderson	Macdonald	Train	Ross
Sandison	Gunn	Turner	Lamont
Saunders	Macalister	Tyre	Macintyre
Scobie	Mackay	Ure	Campbell
Shannon	Macdonald	Vass	Munro, Ross
Sharp	Stewart	Wallis	Wallace
Sherry	Mackinnon	Walters	Forbes
Sim	Fraser of Lovat	Wass	Munro, Ross
Sime	Fraser of Lovat	Watt	Buchanan
Simon	Fraser of Lovat	Weaver	Macfarlane

Name	Associated Clan	Name	Associated Clan
Webster	Macfarlane	Will	Gunn
Whannell	Macdonald	Williamson	Gunn, Mackay
Wharrie	Macquarrie	Wilson	Gunn, Innes
Wheelan	Macdonald	Wright	Macintyre
White	Macgregor, Lamont	Wylie	Gunn, Macfarlane
Whyte	Macgregor, Lamont	Yuill	Buchanan
Wilkie	Macdonald	Yuille	Buchanan
Wilkinson	Macdonald	Yule	Buchanan

• CLAN CHIEFS •

These are the current chiefs of the clans recognised by the Lyon Court. Not all are members of the Standing Council of Scottish Chiefs.

AGNEW
Sir Crispin Agnew of Lochnaw, Bt, 6 Palmerston Road, Edinburgh EH9 ITN

ANSTRUTHER
Sir Ralph Anstruther of that Ilk, Bt, Balcaskie, Pittenweem, Fife

ARBUTHNOTT
The Viscount of Arbuthnott, KT, Arbuthnott House, By Laurencekirk, Kincardineshire AB3 1PA

BANNERMAN
Sir David Bannerman of Elsick, Bt, 3 St George's Road, St Margarets, Twickenham, Middlesex TW1 1QS

BARCLAY
Peter C. Barclay of Towie Barclay and of that Ilk, 28A Gordon Place, London W8 4JE

BORTHWICK
The Lord Borthwick, Crookston, Heriot, Midlothian EH38 5YS

BOYD
The Lord Kilmarnock, 194 Regent's Park Road, London NW1 8XP

BOYLE
The Earl of Glasgow, Kelburn, Fairlie, Ayrshire

BRODIE
Ninian Brodie of Brodie, Brodie Castle, Forres, Morayshire IV36 0TE

BROUN
Sir Lionel Broun of Colstoun, Bt, 23 Clan Alpine Street, Mosman, NSW 2088, Australia

BRUCE
The Earl of Elgin and Kincardine, KT, Broomhall, Dunfermline, Fife KY11 3DV

BUCHAN
Capt. David Buchan of Auchmacoy, Auchmacoy House, Ellon, Aberdeenshire AB41 3RB

BURNETT
James Burnett of the Leys, Crathes Castle, Banchory, Kincardineshire

BUTTER
Major Sir David Butter of Pitlochry, Cluniemore, Pitlochry, Perthshire

CAMERON
Sir Donald Cameron of Lochiel, KT, Achnacarry, Spean Bridge, Inverness-shire

CAMPBELL
The Duke of Argyll, Inverary Castle, Inveraray, Argyll PA32 8XF

CARMICHAEL
Richard Carmichael of Carmichael, Carmichael, Thankerton, Biggar, Lanarkshire ML12 6PG

CARNEGIE
The Duke of Fife, Elsick House, Stonehaven, Kincardineshire AB3 2NT

CATHCART
The Earl Cathcart, Gately Hall, Dereham, Norfolk

CHARTERIS
The Earl of Wemyss and March, KT, Gosford House, Longniddry, East Lothian

CHISHOLM
Hamish Chisholm of Chisholm, The Chisholm, Elmpine, Beck Row, Bury St Edmunds, Suffolk IP28 8BT

COCHRANE
The Earl of Dundonald, Lochnell Castle, Ledaig, Argyll

COLQUHOUN
Sir Ivor Colquhoun of Luss, Bt, Camstradden, Luss, Dunbartonshire G83 8NX

COLVILLE
The Viscount Colville of Culross, House of Lords, London SW1A 0PW

CRANSTOUN
David Cranstoun of that Ilk, Corehouse, Lanark

CRICHTON
David Crichton of that Ilk, Monzie Castle, Crieff

CUMMING
Sir William Cumming of Altyre, Bt, Altyre, Forres, Moray

DARROCH
Capt. Duncan Darroch of Gourock, The Red House, Branksome Park Road, Camberley, Surrey

DAVIDSON
Alister Davidson of Davidston, 21 Winscombe Street, Takapuna, Auckland, New Zealand

DEWAR
Kenneth Dewar of that Ilk and Vogrie, The Dower House, Grayshott, Near Hindhead, Surrey

DRUMMOND
The Earl of Perth, Stobball, By Perth, Perthshire

DUNBAR
Sir James Dunbar of Mochrum, Bt, 211 Gardenville Drive, Yorktown, Virginia, USA

DUNDAS
David Dundas of Dundas, 8 Derna Road, Kenwyn 7700, South Africa

DURIE
Andrew Durie of Durie, Finnich Malise, Croftamie, Stirlingshire

ELIOTT
Madam Margaret Eliott of Redheugh, Newcastleton, Roxburghshire

ELPHINSTONE
The Lord Elphinstone, Whitberry House, Tyninghame, Dunbar EH42 1XL

ERSKINE
The Earl of Mar and Kellie, Claremont House, Alloa, Clackmannanshire FK10 2JF

FARQUHARSON
Capt. Alwyn Farquharson of Invercauld Braemar, Invercauld, Braemar, Aberdeenshire AB35

FERGUSSON
Sir Charles Fergusson of Kilkerran, Bt, Kilkerran, Maybole, Ayrshire

FORBES
The Lord Forbes, Balforbes, Alford, Aberdeenshire AB33 8DR

FORSYTH
Alistair Forsyth of that Ilk, Ethie Castle, By Arbroath, Angus DD11 5SP

FRASER
Lady Saltoun, Inverey House, Aberdeenshire AB35 5YB

FRASER OF LOVAT
The Lord Lovat, Beaufort Lodge, Beauly, Inverness-shire IV4 7AZ

GAYRE
R. Gayre of Gayre and Nigg, 3 Gloucester Lane, Edinburgh EH3 6ED

GORDON
The Marquess of Huntly, Aboyne Castle, Aberdeenshire

GRAHAM
The Duke of Montrose, Buchanan Auld House, Drymen, Stirlingshire

GRANT
The Lord Strathspey, The House of Lords, London SW1A 0PW

GRIERSON
Sir Michael Grierson of Lag, Bt, 40c Palace Road, London SW2 2NJ

HAIG
The Earl Haig, Bemersyde, Melrose, Roxburghshire TP6 9DP

HALDANE
Martin Haldane of Gleneagles, Gleneagles, Auchterarder, Perthshire

HAMILTON
The Duke of Hamilton, Lennoxlove, Haddington, East Lothian

HANNAY
Maj. Ramsey Hannay of Kirkdale and of that Ilk, Cardoness House, Gatehouse-of-Fleet, Kirkcudbrightshire

HAY
The Earl of Erroll, Woodbury Hall, Sandy, Bedfordshire SG19 2HR

HENDERSON
John Henderson of Fordell, 'Rossyth', 7 Owen Street, Toowoomba, Queensland 4359, Australia

HOPE
Sir John Hope of Craighall, Bt, 9 Westleigh Avenue, London SW15 6RF

HUNTER
Madam Pauline Hunter of Hunterston, Plovers Ridge, Lon Cecrist, Treaddur Bay, Anglesey LL65 2AZ

IRVINE OF DRUM
David Irvine of Drum, 20 Enville Road, Bowden, Altrincham, Cheshire WA14 2PQ

JARDINE
Sir Alexander Jardine of Applegirth, Bt, Ash House, Thwaites, Millom, Cumbria LA18 5HY

JOHNSTONE
The Earl of Annandale and Hartfell, St Anns, Raehills, By Lockerbie, Dumfriesshire DG11 1HQ

KEITH
The Earl of Kintore, The Stables, Keith Hall, Inverurie, Aberdeenshire AB5 0LD

KENNEDY
The Marquess of Ailsa, Cassillis, Maybole, Ayrshire KA19 7JN

KERR
The Marquess of Lothian, Ferniehurst Castle, Jedburgh, Roxburghshire TD8 6NX

LAMONT
Fr Peter Lamont of that Ilk, 309 Bungarribee Road, Blacktown, NSW 2148, Australia

LEASK
Madam Leask of Leask, 1 Vincent Road, Sheringham, Norfolk

LENNOX
Edward Lennox of that Ilk, Pools Farm, Downton on the Rock, Near Ludlow, Shropshire SY8 2LL

LESLIE
The Earl of Rothes, Tanglewood, West Tytherley, Salisbury, Wiltshire

LINDSAY
The Earl of Crawford, Balcarres, Colinsburgh, Fife KY9 1HL

LOCKHART
Angus Lockhart of the Lee, Newholme, Dunsyre, Lanark

LUMSDEN
Gillem Lumsden of that Ilk and Blanerne, Stapely Howe, Hoe Benham, Newbury, Berkshire

LYON
The Earl of Strathmore and Kinghorne, Glamis Castle, Angus

MACALESTER
William MacAlester of Loup and Lennox, 'Dun Skeig', 27 Burnham Road, Burton, Christchurch, Dorset BH23 7ND

MCBAIN
James McBain of McBain, 7025 North Finger Rock Place, Tucson, Arizona 85718, USA

MACDONALD OF MACDONALD
The Lord Macdonald, The Macdonald of Macdonald, Kinloch Lodge, Sleat, Isle of Skye

MACDONALD OF CLANRANALD
The Captain of Clanranald, Morenish House, Killin, Perthshire FK21 8TX

MACDONALD OF SLEAT
Sir Ian Macdonald of Sleat, Bt, Thorpe Hall, Rudston, Driffield, East Yorkshire

MACDONELL OF GLENGARRY
Ranald MacDonell of Glengarry, 74 Haverhill Road, London SW12 0HB

MACDOUGALL
Madam Morag MacDougall of MacDougall, Dunollie Castle, Oban, Argyll PA34 5TU

MACDOWALL
Fergus Macdowall of Garthland, 9170 Ardmore Drive, North Saanich, BC, Canada

MACGREGOR
Brig. Sir Gregor MacGregor of MacGregor, Bt, Bannatyne, Newtyle, Angus PH12 8TR

MACINTYRE
James MacIntyre of Glencoe, 15301 Pine Orchard Drive, Apartment 3H, Silver Spring, Maryland, USA

MACKAY
The Lord Reay, 11 Wilton Crescent, London SW1

MACKENZIE
The Earl of Cromartie, Castle Leod, Strathpeffer, Ross-shire

MACKINNON
Madam Ann Mackinnon of Mackinnon, 16 Purleigh Road, Bridgewater, Somerset TA6 7HR

MACKINTOSH
The Mackintosh of Mackintosh, Moy Hall, Tomatin, Inverness-shire IV13

MACLACHLAN
MacLachlan of MacLachlan, Castle Lachlan, Strathlachlan, Argyll

MACLAINE OF LOCHBUIE
Lorne Maclaine of Lochbuie, 4 Stormont Close, Kloof 3630, Natal, South Africa

MACLAREN
Donald MacLaren of MacLaren, Achleskine, Kirkton, Balquhidder, Near Lochearnhead, Argyllshire

MACLEAN
The Hon. Sir Lachlan Maclean of Duart and Morvern, Bt, Arngask House, Glenfarg, Perthshire PH2 9QA

MACLENNAN
Ruairidh MacLennan of LacLennan, The Old Mill, Dores, Inverness

MACLEOD
John MacLeod of MacLeod, Dunvegan Castle, Dunvegan, Isle of Skye

MACLEOD OF THE LEWES
Torquil Roderick MacLeod of the Lewes, 6 Lambert Avenue, Sandy Bay, Tasmania 7006, Australia

MACMILLAN
George MacMillan of MacMillan, Finlaystone, Langbank, Renfrewshire

MACNAB
James Macnab of Macnab, Leuchars Castle Farmhouse, Leuchars, St Andrews, Fife KY16 0EY

MACNAGHTEN
Sir Patrick Macnaghten of Macnaghten, Bt, Dundarave, Bushmills, Co. Antrim, N. Ireland BT57 8ST

MACNEACAIL
Iain Macneacail of Macneacail and Scorrybreac, 12 Fox Street, Ballina, NSW, Australia

MACNEIL OF BARRA
Prof. Ian Macneil of Barra, 95/6 Grange Loan, Edinburgh

MACPHERSON
Sir William Macpherson of Cluny-MacPherson, Newton Castle, Blairgowrie, Perthshire

MACTAVISH
Dugald MacTavish of Dunardry, 3049 Bolin Lane, Sebring, FL 33870, USA

MACTHOMAS
Andrew MacThomas of Finegand, Roslin Cottage, Pitmedden, Aberdeenshire AB41 7NY

MAITLAND
The Earl of Lauderdale, 12 Vincent Street, Edinburgh

MAKGILL
The Viscount of Oxfuird, Hill House, St Mary Bourne, Andover, Hampshire

MALCOLM (MACCALLUM)
Robin Malcolm of Poltalloch, Duntrune Castle, Kilmartin, Argyll PA31 8QQ

MAR
The Countess of Mar, St Michael's Farm, Stourport Road, Great Witley, Worcestershire WR6 6JB

MARJORIBANKS
Andrew Marjoribanks of that Ilk, 10 Newark Street, Greenock, Renfrewshire

MATHESON
Major Sir Fergus Matheson of Matheson, Bt, Hendenham Old Rectory, Bungay, Norfolk NR35 2LD

MELVILLE
The Earl of Leven and Melville, Glenferness, Nairn

MENZIES
David Menzies of Menzies, Wester Auchnagallin Farmhouse, Braes of Castle Grant, Grantown-on-Spey, Moray PH26 3PL

MOFFAT
Madam Jean Moffat of that Ilk, St Jasual, Wheeler End Common, High Wycombe, Buckinghamshire HP14 3NH

MONCREIFFE
Peregrine Moncreiffe of Moncreiffe, Easter Moncreiffe, Perthshire PH2 8QA

MONTGOMERIE
The Earl of Eglinton and Winton, Balhomie, Cargill, Perth PH2 6DS

MORRISON
Ian Morrison of Ruchdi, Magnolia Cottage, The Street, Walberton, Arundel, Sussex BN18 0PJ

MUNRO
Hector Munro of Foulis, Foulis Castle, Evanton, Ross-shire

MURRAY
The Duke of Atholl, Blair Castle, Blair Atholl, Perthshire

NAPIER
The Lord Napier and Ettrick, Down House, Wylye, Wiltshire BA12 0QN

NESBITT
Robert Nesbitt of that Ilk, Upper Roundhurst Farm, Roundhurst, Haslemere, Surrey

NICOLSON
The Lord Carnock, 90 Whitehall Court, London SW1A 2EL

OGILVY
The Earl of Airlie, Cortachy Castle, Kirriemuir, Angus

PRIMROSE
The Earl of Rosebery, Dalmeny House, South Queensferry, West Lothian

RAMSAY
The Earl of Dalhousie, Brechin Castle, Brechin, Angus

RATTRAY
Capt. James Rattray of Rattray, Stragirth Cottage, Craighall-Rattray, Perthshire

RIDDELL
Sir John Riddell of that Ilk, Hepple, Morpeth, Northumberland

ROBERTSON
Gilbert Robertson of Struan, Breach Farm, Goudhurst Road, Cranbrook, Kent

ROLLO
The Lord Rollo, Pitcairns, Dunning, Perthshire

ROSE
Miss Elizabeth Rose of Kilravock, Kilravock Castle, Croy, Inverness

ROSS
David Ross of Ross, 'Shandwick', Perth Road, Stanley, Perthshire PH1 4NF

SCOTT
The Duke of Buccleuch, Bowhill, Selkirk

SCRYMGEOUR
The Earl of Dundee, Birkhill, Cupar, Fife

SEMPILL
The Lord Sempill, 3 Vanburgh Place, Edinburgh EH6

SHAW OF TORDARROCH
John Shaw of Tordarroch, East Craig an Ron, 22 Academy Street, Fortrose IV10 8TW

SINCLAIR
The Earl of Caithness, 137 Claxton Grove, London W6 8HB

SKENE
Danus Skene of Skene, Pitlour House, Strathmiglo, Fife

STIRLING
Fraser Stirling of Cader, 44A Oakley Street, London SW3 5HA

STRANGE
Major Timothy Strange of Balcaskie, Little Holme, Porton Road, Amesbury, Wiltshire

STUART OF BUTE
The Marquess of Bute, Mount Stuart, Rothesay, Isle of Bute PA20 9LR

SUTHERLAND
The Countess of Sutherland, House of Tongue, By Lairg, Sutherland

SWINTON
William Swinton of that Ilk, 123 Superior Avenue SW, Calgary, Alberta TC3 2HA, Canada

TROTTER
Alexander Trotter of Mortonhall, Charterhall, Duns, Berwickshire

URQUHART
Kenneth Urquhart of Urquhart, 507 Jefferson Park Avenue, Jefferson, Louisiana 70121, USA

WALLACE
Ian Wallace of that Ilk, 5 Lennox Street, Edinburgh EH4 lQB

WEDDERBURN OF THAT ILK
The Lord Scrymgeour, Birkhill, Cupar, Fife

WEMYSS
Capt. David Wemyss of that Ilk, Invermay, Forteviot, Perthshire

ARISTOCRACY

• THE ROYAL HOUSEHOLD IN SCOTLAND •

Hereditary Lord High Constable of Scotland (The Earl of Erroll)
Hereditary Master of the Household in Scotland (The Duke of Argyll)
Lord Lyon King of Arms (Sir Malcolm Rognvald Innes of Edingight, KCVO, WS)
Hereditary Standard Bearer for Scotland (The Earl of Dundee)
Hereditary Bearer of the National Flag of Scotland (The Earl of Lauderdale)
Hereditary Keepers
  Palace of Holyroodhouse (The Duke of Hamilton)
  Falkland Palace
  Rothesay (The Marquess of Bute)
  Stirling Castle (The Earl of Mar and Kellie)
  Dunstaffnage Castle (The Duke of Argyll)
  Dunconnell Castle
Hereditary Carver
Governor of Edinburgh Castle
Keeper of Dumbarton Castle
Historiographer
Botanist
Painter and Limner
Sculptor in Ordinary
Astronomer
Heralds and Pursuivants

ECCLESIASTICAL HOUSEHOLD
Dean of the Order of the Thistle
Dean of the Chapel Royal
Domestic Chaplain, Balmoral
Chaplains in Ordinary

MEDICAL HOUSEHOLD
Physicians in Scotland
Surgeons in Scotland
Apothecary to the Household at Balmoral,
Apothecary to the Household at the Palace of Holyroodhouse

ROYAL COMPANY OF ARCHERS (THE QUEEN'S BODYGUARD FOR SCOTLAND)
Captain-General and Gold Stick for Scotland
President of the Council and Silver Stick for Scotland
Members on the active list: c. 400

• HER MAJESTY'S OFFICERS OF ARMS IN SCOTLAND •

THE COURT OF THE LORD LYON

Dating from the 14th century, if not earlier, the Court of the Lord Lyon King of Arms is the Scottish court of heraldry and genealogy. The Court has full legal jurisdiction over questions of heraldry and the right to bear arms, and decides on issues of pedigree. The Lord Lyon is also responsible for preparing all state ceremonial in Scotland such as royal proclamations and the investiture of Knights of the Thistle.

Lord Lyon King of Arms
(Sir Malcolm Innes of Edingight, KCVO, WS)

Heralds (Senior Officers of the Court)
Albany (J.A. Spens, MVO, RD,WS)
Rothesay (Sir Crispin Agnew of Lochnaw, Bt., QC)
Ross (C.J. Burnett, FSA SCOT)
Marchmont
Islay
Snowdon

Pursuivants (Junior Officers of the Court)
Kintyre (J.C.G. George, FSA SCOT)
Unicorn (Alastair Campbell of Airds, FSA SCOT)
Carrick (Mrs C.G.W Roads, MVO, FSA SCOT)
Dingwall
Bute
Ormond

Other Officials of the Court
Lyon Clerk and Keeper of the Records
   (Mrs C.G.W Roads, MVO, FSA Scot)
Procurator-Fiscal

Herald Painter
Macer

PURSUIVANTS OF EARLS

Some of Scotland's senior aristocratic families maintain private officers of arms, who are recognised by the Lord Lyon but who do not come under his control and do not form part of the royal household.

Slains Pursuivant to the Earl of Erroll
Garioch Pursuivant to the Countess of Mar

Endure Pursuivant to the Earl of Crawford

• ORDER OF PRECEDENCE IN SCOTLAND •

The Sovereign
The Prince Philip, Duke of Edinburgh
The Lord High Commissioner to the General Assembly of the Church of Scotland (while the Assembly is sitting)
The Duke of Rothesay (eldest son of the Sovereign)
The Sovereign's younger sons
The Sovereign's grandsons
The Sovereign's cousins
Lord-Lieutenants (during their term of office and within their own counties)
Lord Provosts of Cities (being *ex officio* Lord-Lieutenants of Counties of Cities, applying during term of office and within their own cities)
Sheriffs Principal (during term of office and within their own sheriffdoms)
Lord Chancellor of Great Britain
Moderator of the General Assembly of the Church of Scotland (during office)
The Prime Minister
Keeper of the Great Seal (The First Minister) if a Peer
Secretary of State for Scotland if a Peer
Keeper of the Privy Seal of Scotland if a Peer
Hereditary High Constable of Scotland
Hereditary Master of the Household in Scotland
Dukes, according to their patent of creation:
    (1) of England
    (2) of Scotland
    (3) of Great Britain
    (4) of the United Kingdom
    (5) those of Ireland created since the Union between Great Britain and Ireland
Eldest sons of Dukes of the Blood Royal
Marquesses, according to their patent of creation:
    (1) of England
    (2) of Scotland
    (3) of Great Britain
    (4) of the United Kingdom
    (5) those of Ireland created since the Union between Great Britain and Ireland

Dukes' eldest sons
Earls, according to their patent of creation:
    (1) of England
    (2) of Scotland
    (3) of Great Britain
    (4) of the United Kingdom
    (5) those of Ireland created since the Union between Great Britain and Ireland
Younger sons of Dukes of Blood Royal
Marquesses' eldest sons
Dukes' younger sons
Keeper of the Great Seal (The First Minister) if not a Peer
Secretary of State for Scotland if not a Peer
Keeper of the Privy Seal of Scotland if not a Peer
Lord Justice-General
Lord Clerk Register
Lord Advocate
Lord Justice-Clerk
Viscounts, according to their patent of creation
    (1) of England
    (2) of Scotland
    (3) of Great Britain
    (4) of the United Kingdom
    (5) those of Ireland created since the Union between Great Britain and Ireland
Earls' eldest sons
Marquesses' younger sons
Barons or Lords of Parliament (Scotland), according to their patent of creation:
    (1) of England
    (2) of Scotland
    (3) of Great Britain
    (4) of the United Kingdom
    (5) those of Ireland created since the Union between Great Britain and Ireland
Viscounts' eldest sons
Earls' younger sons
Barons' or Lords of Parliament's eldest sons
Knights of the Garter
Knights of the Thistle
Privy Counsellors
Senators of College of Justice (Lords of Session)
Viscounts' younger sons
Barons' or Lords of Parliament's younger sons
Baronets
Knights Grand Cross of the Order of the Bath
Knights Grand Commanders of the Order of the Star of India
Knights Grand Cross of the Order of St Michael and St George
Knights Grand Commanders of the Order of the Indian Empire
Knights Grand Cross of the Royal Victorian Order

Knights Commanders of the Order of the Bath
Knights Commanders of the Order of the Star of India
Knights Commanders of the Order of St Michael and St George
Knights Commanders of the Order of the Indian Empire
Knights Commanders of the Royal Victorian Order
Solicitor-General for Scotland
Lyon King of Arms
Sheriffs Principal (when outwith their own county)
Knights Bachelor
Sheriffs
Commanders of the Royal Victorian Order
Companions of the Order of the Bath
Companions of the Order of the Star of India
Companions of the Order of St Michael and St George
Companions of the Order of the IndianEmpire
Lieutenants of the Royal Victorian Order
Companions of the Distingnished Service Order
Eldest sons of younger sons of Peers
Baronets' eldest sons
Knights' eldest sons, in the same order as their fathers
Members of the Royal Victorian Order
Baronets' younger sons
Knights' younger sons, in the same order as their fathers
Queen's Counsel
Esquires
Gentlemen

• SCOTTISH PEERS •

Dukes
1701   Argyll (12th), Ian Campbell
1703   Atholl (11th), John Murray
1663   Buccleuch (9th) and Queensberry (11th), Walter Francis John Montagu
       Douglas Scott, KT, VRD
1900   Fife (3rd), James George Alexander Bannerman Carnegie
1643   Hamilton (15th) and Brandon (12th), Angus Alan Douglas Douglas-Hamilton
       (**Premier Peer of Scotland**)
1707   Montrose (8th), James Graham
1707   Roxburghe (10th), Guy David Innes-Ker (**Premier Baronet of Scotland**)

Marquesses
1831   Ailsa (8th), Archibald Angus Charles Kennedy
1796   Bute (7th), John Colum Crichton-Stuart
1599   Huntly (13th), Granville Charles Gomer Gordon (**Premier Marquess of
       Scotland**)
1784   Lansdowne (8th), George John Charles Mercer Nairne Petty-Fitzmaurice PC

1902 Linlithgow (4th), Adrian John Charles Hope
1701 Lothian (12th), Peter Francis Walter Kerr KCVO
1682 Queensberry (12th), David Harrington Angus Douglas
1694 Tweeddale (13th), Edward Douglas John Hay

Earls
1639 Airlie (13th), David George Coke Patrick Ogilvy KT, GCVO, PC
1662 Annandale and Hartfell (11th), Patrick Andrew Wentworth Hope Johnstone
1922 Balfour (4th), Gerald Arthur James Balfour
1677 Breadalbane and Holland (10th), John Romer Boreland Campbell
1469 Buchan (17th), Malcolm Harry Erskine
1455 Caithness (20th), Malcolm Ian Sinclair
1827 Cawdor (7th), Colin Robert Vaughan Campbel
1398 Crawford (29th) and Balcarres (12th), Robert Alexander Lindsay KT, PC
1861 Cromartie (5th), John Ruaridh Blunt Grant Mackenzie
1633 Dalhousie (16th), Simon Ramsay KT, GCVO, CBE, MC
1660 Dundee (12th), Alexander Henry Scrymgeour
1669 Dundonald (15th), Iain Alexander Douglas Blair Cochrane
1686 Dunmore (12th), Malcohn Kenneth Murray
1507 Eglinton (18th) and Winton (9th), Archibald George Montgomerie
1633 Elgin (11th) and Kincardine (15th), Andrew Douglas Alexander Thomas Bruce KT
1452 Erroll (24th), Merlin Sereld Victor Gilbert Hay (**Hereditary Lord High
      Constable and Knight Marischal of Scotland**)
1623 Galloway (13th), Randolph Keith Reginald Stewart
1703 Glasgow (10th), Patrick Robin Archibald Boyle
1619 Haddington (13th), John George Baillie-Hamilton
1919 Haig (2nd), George Alexander Eugene Douglas Haig OBE
1605 Home (15th), David Alexander Cospatrick Douglas-Home CVO
1633 Kinnoull (15th), Arthur William George Patrick Hay
1677 Kintore (13th), Michael Canning William John Keith
1624 Lauderdale (17th), Patrick Francis Maitland
1641 Leven (14th) and Melville (13th), Alexander Robert Leslie Melville
1633 Lindsay (16th), James Randolph Lindesay-Bethufle
1838 Lovelace (5th), Peter Axel William Locke King
1776 Mansfield and Mansfield (8th), William David Mungo James Murray
1565 Mar (14th) and Keilie (16th), James Thorne Erskine
1813 Minto (6th), Gilbert Edward George Lariston Elliot-Murray-Kynynmound OBE
1562 Moray (20th), Douglas John Moray Stuart
1458 Morton (22nd), John Charles Sholto Douglas
1660 Newburgh (12th), Don Filippo Giambattista Camillo Francesco Aldo Maria
      Rospigliosi
1647 Northesk (14th), David John MacRae Carnegie
1696 Orkney (9th), (Oliver) Peter St John
1605 Perth (17th), John David Drummond PC
1703 Rosebery (7th), Neil Archibald Primrose
1457 Rothes (21st), Ian Lionel Malcolm Leslie

1701   Seafield (13th), Ian Derek Francis Ogilvie-Grant
1646   Selkirk. Disclaimed for life by the Rt Hon Lord James Douglas-Hamilton, 1994
1703   Stair (14th), John David James Dalrymple
1606   Strathmore and Kinghorne (18th), Michael Fergus Bowes Lyon
1633   Wemyss (12th) and March (8th), Francis David Charteris KT

Countesses in their own right

1643   Dysart (11th in line), Rosamund Agnes Greaves
1633   Loudoun (13th in line), Barbara Huddleston Abney-Hastings
1115   Mar (31st in line), Margaret of Mar
1235   Sutherland (24th in line), Elizabeth Millicent Sutherland

Viscounts

1642   of Arbuthnott (16th), John Campbell Arbuthnott KT, CBE, DSC
1902   Colville of Culross (4th), John Mark Alexander Colville QC
1620   Falkland (15th), Lucius Edward William Plantagenet Cary (**Premier Scottish Viscount on the Roll**)
1651   of Oxfuird (13th), George Hubbard Makgill CBE
1959   Stuart of Findhorn (2nd), David Randolph Moray Stuart
1952   Thurso (3rd), John Archibald Sinclair
1938   Weir (3rd), William Kenneth James Weir
1923   Younger of Leckie (4th), George Kenneth Hotson Younger KT, KCVO,TD, PC

Barons/Lords

1607   Balfour of Burleigh (8th), Robert Bruce
1647   Belhaven and Stenton (13th), Robert Anthony Carmichael Hamilton
1903   Biddulph (5th), (Anthony) Nicholas Cohn Maitland Biddulph
1452   Borthwick (24th), John Hugh Borthwick
1942   Bruntisfield (2nd), John Robert Warrender OBE, MC, TD
1948   Clydesmuir (3rd), David Ronald Colville
1919   Cochrane of Cults (4th), (Ralph Henry) Vere Cochrane
1509   Elphinstone (19th), Alexander Mountstuart Elphinstone
1627   Fairfax of Cameron (14th), Nicholas John Albert Fairfax
1445   Forbes (22nd), Nigel Ivan Forbes KBE (**Premier Lord of Scotland**)
1917   Forteviot (4th), John James Evelyn Dewar
1918   Glenarthur (4th), Simon Mark Arthur
1445   Gray (22nd), Angus Diarmid Ian Campbell-Gray
1902   Kinross (5th), Christopher Patrick Balfour
1458   Lovat (16th), Simon Fraser
1914   Lyell (3rd), Charles Lyell
1776   Macdonald (8th), Godfrey James Macdonald of Macdonald
1951   Macpherson of Drumochter (2nd), (James) Gordon Macpherson
1873   Moncreiff (5th), Harry Robert Wellwood Moncreiff
1627   Napier (14th) and Ettrick (5th), Francis Nigel Napier KCVO
1690   Polwarth (10th), Henry Alexander Hepbume-Scott TD
1932   Rankeillour (4th), Peter St Thomas More Henry Hope
1628   Reay (14th), Hugh William Mackay

1651   Rollo (14th), David Eric Howard Rollo
1911   Rowallan (4th), John Polson Cameron Corbett
1489   Sempill (21st), James William Stuart Whitemore Sempill
1449   Sinclair (17th), Charles Murray Kennedy St Clair CVO
1955   Strathclyde (2nd), Thomas Galloway Dunlop du Roy de Blicquy Galbraith PC
1564   Torphichen (15th), James Andrew Douglas Sandilands

Baronesses/Ladies in their own right
1490   Herries of Terregles (14th in line), Anne Elizabeth Fitzalan-Howard
1602   Kinloss (12th in line), Beatrice Mary Grenville Freeman-Grenville
1445   Saltoun (20th in line), Flora Marjory Frase
1628   Strange (16th in line), (Jean) Cherry Drummond of Megginch; title called out of abeyance, 1986

Life Peers
1974   Balniel, Earl of Crawford and Balcarres. See **Earls**.
1977   Cameron of Lochbroom, Kenneth John Cameron PC
1981   Campbell of Alloway, Alan Robertson Campbell QC
1974   Campbell of Croy, Gordon Thomas Calthrop Campbell MC, PC
1983   Carmichael of Kelvingrove, Neil George Carmichael
1996   Clyde, James John Clyde
1980   Emslie, George Carlyle Emslie MBE, PC
1992   Ewing of Kirkford, Harry Ewing
1999   Forsyth of Drumlean, Michael Forsyth PC
1989   Fraser of Carmyllie, Peter Lovat Fraser PC, QC
1997   Gordon of Strathblane, James Stuart Gordon CBE
1983   Gray of Contin, James (Hamish) Hector Northey Gray PC
1997   Hardie, Andrew Rutherford Hardie QC, PC
1997   Hogg of Cumbernauld, Norman Hogg
1995   Hope of Craighead (James Arthur) David Hope PC
1978   Howie of Troon, William Howie
1997   Hughes of Woodside, Robert Hughes
1961   Hughes, William Hughes CBE, PC
1987   Irvine of Lairg, Alexander Andrew Mackay Irvine PC, QC
1988   Jauncey of Tullichettle, Charles Eliot Jauncey, PC
1987   Jenkins of Hillhead, Roy Jenkins, PC
1975   Kirkhill, John Farquharson Smith
1977   Keith of Kinkel, Henry Shanks Keith, GBE, PC; b. 1922
1991   Laing of Dunphail, Hector Laing; b 1923
1997   Lang of Monkton, Ian Bruce Lang PC
1984   Macaulay of Bragar, Donald Macaulay QC
1976   McCluskey, John Herbert McCluskey
1998   Macdonald of Tradeston, Gus Macdonald
1991   Macfarlane of Bearsden, Norman Somerville Macfarlane KT
1991   Mackay of Ardbrecknish, John Jackson Mackay, PC
1979   Mackay of Clashfern, James Peter Hymers Mackay, PC
1995   Mackay of Drumadoon, Donald Sage Mackay

1999	Mackenzie of Culkein, Hector Uisdean Mackenzie
1988	Mackenzie-Stuart, Alexander John Mackenzie Stuart
1974	Mackie of Benshie, George Yull Mackie CBE, DSO, DFC
1982	MacLehose of Beoch, (Crawford) Murray MacLehose KT, GBE, KCMG, KCVO
1997	Monro of Langholm, Hector Monro
1994	Nickson, David Wigley Nickson KBE
1990	Pearson of Rannoch, Malcolm Everard MacLaren Pearson
1999	Robertson of Port Ellen. George Robertson PC
1992	Rodger of Earlsferry, Alan Ferguson Rodger PC, QC
1997	Russell-Johnston, (David) Russell-Johnston
1985	Sanderson of Bowden, Charles Russell Sanderson
1997	Selkirk of Douglas, James Alexander Douglas-Hamilton
1997	Steel of Aikwood, David Martin Scott Steel KBE, PC
1981	Stodart of Leaston, James Anthony Stodart, PC
1968	Taylor of Gryfe, Thomas Johnston Taylor
1977	Thomson of Monifieth, George Morgan Thomson KT, PC
1974	Wallace of Campsie, George Wallace
1997	Watson of Invergowrie, Michael Goodall Watson
1992	Wilson of Tillyorn, David Clive Wilson, GCMG
1992	Younger of Prestwick. See *Viscounts*.

Baronesses

1982	Carnegy of Lour, Elizabeth Patricia Carnegy of Lour
1971	Macleod of Borve, Evelyn Hester MacLeod
1995	Smith of Gilmorehill, Elizabeth Margaret Smith
1997	Linklater of Butterstone, Veronica Linklater

• THE MOST ANCIENT AND MOST NOBLE ORDER OF THE THISTLE •

The Order of the Thistle is an exclusively Scottish order of knighthood. Chivalric orders in Scotland date from at least the Middle Ages but the present Order was established by James VII and II in 1687, comprising the sovereign and eight knights. In 1703 this was increased to 12 knights and since 1827 the maximum number of knights has been 16. Conferment of the Order also confers a knighthood on the recipient. Knights of the Thistle carry the postnomial initials of 'KT' while Ladies are styled 'LT'. The Order's motto is the same as that carried by many Scottish regiments, *Nemo Me Impune Laccessit* (No-one Provokes Me With Impunity).

Sovereign of the Order
HM The Queen

Royal Knights and Lady
HM Queen Elizabeth the Queen Mother, 1937
HRH The Prince Philip, Duke of Edinburgh, 1952
HRH The Prince Charles, Duke of Rothesay, 1977

Knights Brethren and Ladies

The Earl of Wemyss and March (1966)

Sir Donald Cameron of Lochiel (1973)

The Duke of Buccleuch and Queens-berry (1978)

The Earl of Elgin and Kincardine (1981)

The Lord Thomson of Monifieth (1981)

The Lord MacLehose of Beoch (1983)

The Earl of Airlie (1985)

Capt. Sir Iain Tennant (1986)

The Viscount Younger of Leckie (1995)

The Viscount of Arburhnott (1996)

The Earl of Crawford and Balcarres (1996)

Lady Marion Fraser (1996)

The Lord Macfarlane of Bearsden (1996)

The Lord Mackay of Clashfern (1997)

Chancellor: The Duke of Buccleuch and Queensberry KT, VRD

Secretary and Lord Lyon King of Arms: Sir Malcolm Innes of Edingight KCVO, WS

Usher of the Green Rod, Rear-Adm. C.H. Layman CB, DSO, LVO

Dean: The Very Revd G.I. Macmillan

• LORDS LIEUTENANT •

The Lord Lieutenant of a county is the local representative of the Crown in that county and is appointed by the sovereign on the recommendation of the Prime Minister. The Lord Lieutenant's responsibilities include attending on royalty during official visits and making presentations and awards on behalf of the Crown.

Aberdeenshire

Captain A. Farquharson

Angus

Earl of Airlie KT, GCVO, PC

Argyll and Bute

The Duke of Argyll

Ayrshire and Arran

Major R.Y. Henderson TD

Banffshire

J.A.S. McPherson CBE

Berwickshire

Maj-Gen. Sir John Swinton KCVO, OBE

Caithness

Major G.T. Dunnett TD

Clackmannan

Lt-Col R.C. Stewart CBE, TD

Dumfries

Captain R.C. Cunningham-Jardine

Dunbartonshire

Brigadier D.D.G. Hardie TD

East Lothian

Sir Hew Hamilton-Dalrymple BT, KCVO

Fife

Mrs C.M. Dean

Inverness

Lord Gray of Contin PC

Kincardineshire

Viscount of Arbuthnott KT, CBE, DSC, FRSE

Lanarkshire

H.B. Sneddon CBE

Midlothian

Captain G.W. Bumet LVO

Moray

Air Vice-Marshal G.A. Chesworth CB, OBE, DFC

Nairn

E.J. Brodie

Orkney

G.R. Marwick

Perth and Kinross

Sir David Montgomery Bt

Renfrewshire

C.H. Parker OBE

Ross and Cromarty
Captain R.W.K. Stirling of Fairburn, TD
Roxburgh, Ettrick and Lauderdale
Dr June Paterson-Brown
Shetland
J.H. Scott
Stirling and Falkirk
Lt-Col I Stirling of Garden CBE, TD
Sutherland
Maj-Gen. D. Houston CBE

The Stewartry of Kirkcudbright
Lt-Gen Sir Norman Arthur KCB
Tweeddale
Captain J.D.B. Younger
West Lothian
The Earl of Morton
Wigtown
Major E.S. Orr-Ewing

• LORD HIGH COMMISSIONERS •

The Lord High Commissioneer is the sovereign's representative at the General Assembly of the Church of Scotland.

1995 Lady Marion Fraser
1996 HRH Princess Royal
1997 Rt Hon Lord Macfarlane of
      Bearsden

1998 Lord Hogg of Cumbernauld
1999 Lord Hogg of Cumbernauld

• ROYAL SALUTES IN SCOTLAND •

The firing of royal salutes are authorised at both Edinburgh and Stirling Castles. In practice, however, Edinburgh Castle is the only operating saluting station in Scotland.

A 21-gun salute is fired on:
• the anniversaries of the birth, accession and coronation of The Queen
• the anniversary of the birth of HM Queen Elizabeth the Queen Mother
• the anniversary of the birth of HRH Prince Philip, Duke of Edinburgh

A 21-gun salute is also fired in Edinburgh to mark the opening of the General Assembly of the Church of Scotland and to mark the arrival of HM The Queen, HM Queen Elizabeth the Queen Mother or another Royal Highness on an official visit.

• TERRITORIAL TITLES •

Territorial title	Family Name	Territorial title	Family Name
Duke of Albany	Stewart	Earl of Atholl	Stewart
Earl of Angus	Douglas	Earl of Balcarres	Lindsay
Duke of Argyll	Campbell	Lord Balermino	Elphinstone
Earl of Arran	Hamilton	Lord Belhaven	Hamilton
Duke of Atholl	Murray	Earl of Bothwell	Hepburn

Territorial title	Family Name	Territorial title	Family Name
Earl of Breadalbane	Campbell	Lord Lovat	Fraser
Duke of Buccleuch	Scott	Earl of Mar	Erskine
Earl of Bute	Stuart	Earl of Marchmont	Hume
Earl of Caithness	Sinclair	Earl Marischal	Keith
Earl of Cassillis	Kennedy	Earl of Melfort	Drummond
Duke of Chatelherault	Hamilton	Earl of Melville	Leslie
Earl of Crawford	Lindsay	Earl of Menteith	Graham
Earl of Cromarty	Mackenzie	Lord Methven	Stewart
Viscount Dundee	Graham	Duke of Montrose	Graham
Earl of Eglinton	Montgomery	Earl of Moray	Stewart
Earl of Errol	Hay	Earl of Morton	Douglas
Lord Glamis	Lyon	Lord Ochiltree	Stewart
Earl of Glencairn	Cunningham	Earl of Perth	Drummond
Earl of Gowrie	Ruthven	Earl of Queensferry	Douglas
Earl of Huntly	Gordon	Earl of Rothes	Leslie
Lord Innermeath	Stewart	Duke of Roxburgh	Kerr
Earl of Islay	Campbell	Earl of Seafield	Ogilvie
Duke of Lauderdale	Maitland	Earl of Seaforth	Mackenzie
Earl of Lennox	Stewart	Earl of Stair	Dalrymple
Earl of Leven	Leslie	Earl of Sutherland	Gordon
Lord Lorne	Campbell	Viscount Tarbat	Mackenzie
Earl of Lothian	Kerr	Earl of Tweedale	Hay
Earl of Loudon	Campbell	Lord Yester	Hay

Famous Scots

• By Profession •

Actors
Sean Connery
Billy Connolly
James Robertson-Justice

Adventurers
Captain Kidd
Rob Roy Macgregor
Peter Williamson

Anthropologists
James Frazer
Lord Monboddo

Architects
Robert Adam
William Bruce
Robert Lorimer
Charles Rennie Mackintosh
Alexander 'Greek' Thomson

Artists
David Octavius Hill
Charles Rennie Mackintosh
Henry Raeburn
Allan Ramsay
David Wilkie

Athletes
Eric Liddell

Astronomers
Thomas Henderson

Biographers
James Boswell
Samuel Smiles

Broadcasters
John Reith

Castaways
Alexander Selkirk

Chemists
Joseph Black
Charles Macintosh
Charles Tennant
James Young

Clerics
Thomas Chalmers
St Columba
Duns Scotus
John Knox
George MacLeod
Andrew Melville
St Mungo
St Ninian
St John Ogilvie

Collectors
William Burrell

Conservationists
John Muir

Criminals
Sawney Bean
Deacon Brodie

Designers
Charles Rennie Mackintosh

Detectives
Allan Pinkerton

Economists
Adam Smith

Emigrés
Alexander Graham Bell

Andrew Carnegie
John Paul Jones
John Macdonald
John Muir
Allan Pinkerton

Engineers
John Logie Baird
John Loudon McAdam
The Stevenson Family
Thomas Telford
Robert Watson-Watt
James Watt

Entertainers
Billy Connolly
Harry Lauder

Entrepreneurs
Andrew Carnegie
Kate Cranston
David Dale
Charles Tennant
James Young

Explorers
James Bruce
Hugh Clapperton
David Livingstone
Mungo Park

Factors
Patrick Sellar

Film-makers
Bill Forsyth
John Grierson

Financiers
William Paterson

Football managers & players
Matt Busby
Jock Stein

Geologists
James Hutton
Hugh Miller

Inventors
John Logie Baird

Alexander Graham Bell
James Dewar
John Dunlop
David Gregory
Charles Macintosh
Robert Watson-Watt
James Watt

Jacobites
Viscount Dundee
Flora Macdonald
Lord George Murray
Lady Nairne

Lawyers
Lord Cockburn
Lord Monboddo
Lord Stair

Martyrs
Patrick Hamilton
St John Ogilvie

Mathematicians
John Napier

Meteorologists
Alexander Buchan

Missionaries
St Columba
Eric Liddell
David Livingstone
St Mungo
St Ninian
Mary Slessor

Motor racing champions
Jim Clark

Nobles
Earl of Bothwell
Lord Darnley
Sir James Douglas
Viscount Dundee
Marquess of Montrose
Lord George Murray
Lady Nairne
Duke of Queensberry

Nutritionists
John Boyd Orr

Outlaws
Rob Roy Macgregor

Patriots
William Wallace
Robert I, the Bruce

Philanthropists
Andrew Carnegie
David Dale

Philosophers
Duns Scotus
David Hume
Adam Smith

Physicists
James Clerk Maxwell
William Thompson

Photographers
David Octavus Hill

Physicians
Dugald Baird
Alexander Fleming
John & William Hunter
Elsie Inglis
Robert Knox
Robert Liston
William MacEwen
J. J. R. Macleod
James Young Simpson
Nora Wattie

Pirates
Captain Kidd

Poets
Robert Burns
William Dunbar
David Lyndsay
Hugh MacDiarmid
William McGonagall
James Macpherson
Marquess of Montrose
Robert Tannahill

Thomas the Rhymer

Politicians
John Buchan
Henry Campbell-Bannerman
James Connolly
R. B. Cunninghame Graham
Keir Hardie
John Macdonald
Ramsay MacDonald
John Maclean
James Maxton
John Wheatley

Prodigies
James Crichton

Publishers
William Blackwood
William Collins

Rakes
Duke of Queensberry

Royals
Alexander III
Prince Charles Edward Stuart
James I
James II
James III
James IV
James V
James VI
Macbeth
St Margaret
Mary
Robert I, the Bruce

Sailors
Thomas Cochrane
John Paul Jones
Captain Kidd
Alexander Selkirk

Saints
St Columba
St Margaret
St Mungo
St Ninian
St John Ogilvie

Scholars
George Buchanan
Alexander Cruden

Seers
Thomas the Rhymer

Servants
John Brown

Social reformers
Samuel Smiles

Society figures
Margot Asquith
Madeleine Smith

Soldiers
Ralph Abercromby
Sir James Douglas
Viscount Dundee
Douglas Haig
Duke of Hamilton
Marquess of Montrose
Lord George Murray
William Wallace

Songwriters
Lady Nairne

Suffragettes
Elsie Inglis

Theologians
Duns Scotus

Weavers
Robert Tannahill

Whisky distillers
John Dewar
George Smith of Glenlivet

Wits
Margot Asquith

Wizards
Michael Scott

Writers
J. M. Barrie
James Boswell
John Buchan

Thomas Carlyle
A. J. Cronin
R. B. Cunninghame Graham
Arthur Conan Doyle
Lewis Grassic Gibbon
James Hogg
David Lyndsay
Compton Mackenzie
Alistair Maclean
Margaret Oliphant
Walter Scott
Tobias Smollet
Robert Louis Stevenson

• BY PERSONALITY •

A BIOGRAPHICAL A–Z

Ralph Abercromby (1734–1801) Army general and reformer
Born at Menstrie near Tullibody. Highly regarded general who reformed the army after its defeat in the American Revolutionary Wars, allowing talent rather than political influence to determine promotions.

Robert Adam (1728–92) Architect
Born in Kirkcaldy to a family of architects: his father and three brothers all went into the profession. Adam's neoclassical work. with its unified exteriors and interiors, were fashionable in their day and have recently again been recognised as the work of genius. Some of his buildings include Culzean Castle in Ayrshire and Charlotte Square in Edinburgh.

Alexander III (1241–1286) King of Scots
A direct descendant of the first Scots king, Kenneth MacAlpin, and last of the Celtic kings. Alexander saw off threats from the Vikings and the English; the Scots economy was strong; and his self-assured reign was seen as a golden age for Scotland. But the successive deaths of his heirs plunged Scotland into a struggle for its existence, resolved only with the victory at Bannockburn in 1314.

Margot Asquith (1864–1945) Society figure and wit
Great-great granddaughter of the chemist Charles Tennant. She was one of the starring figures in London society of her day, and a great talker and wit. When the actress Jean Harlow mispronounced her first name, Margot corrected her: 'The "t" is silent, as in "Harlow".' She said of Kitchener, whom she disliked, that if he was not a great man, he was, at least, a great poster. Margot married Herbert Asquith, later Liberal Prime Minister.

Dugald Baird (1899–1986) Pioneer of maternity and neonatal care
Greenock-born obstetrician who did pioneering research into maternal and infant mortality, and neonatal care. He advocated universal access to contraception and was a leading advocate of reform of the abortion laws in the 1960s. His findings and methods still influence maternity care today.

John Logie Baird (1888–1946) Inventor of television
Born in Helensburgh, Baird was a serial inventor, devising a diverse range of products, from as an all-weather sock to a working television in 1924. He also worked with colour, 3D and the forerunner of what would become CDs. He provided the BBC with its first sight and sound broadcast and its first outside broadcast, of the Derby in 1931.

J. M. Barrie (1860–1937) Novelist and playwright
The child of a Kirriemuir weaver, James Barrie never grew taller than 5ft 1in in height. He was one of the most successful writers of his day, but it is for Peter Pan, the story of the boy who never grew up, that he is mostly remembered today.

Sawney Bean (lived late 13th–early 14th century) Cannibal

Notorious leader of a savage family 45 members strong who lived in a cave at Bennane Head near Ballantrae in Ayrshire. The Bean family robbed and passing travellers, eating their remains. One victim escaped the cave to tell the tale, and James I personally led the party who rounded up the family. All the adults were executed.

Alexander Graham Bell (1847–1922) Inventor of the telephone

Although the telephone was Bell's most famous invention, his life's work was dedicated to improving systems of communication for the deaf and for deaf mutes. He worked with machines to transmit sounds telegraphically, allowing deaf people to hear them. This led directly to the development of the telephone which he patented in February 1876, only days ahead of several rivals. The first telephone message was sent on 10 March 1876, to his assistant – 'Mr Watson, come here; I want you,'; and it was publicly demonstrated at a fair in Philadelphia that year, when he recited Hamlet's 'To be or not to be' soliloquy over the telephone to the Emperor of Brazil. His other inventions included flying machines, a universal language, a phonograph, hydrofoils, an iron lung, and a new method of sheep breeding.

Joseph Black (1728–1799) Chemist

Chemist Black identified carbon dioxide for the first time. A friend of James Watt, he passed on to him his most famous advance, the theory of latent heat, used by Watt in his own work.

William Blackwood (1776–1834) Publisher

Blackwood's Edinburgh Magazine was one of the most influential periodicals of its day, bringing on the undiscovered talents of contributors like James Hogg and, later, George Eliot and Joseph Conrad. He first hit upon the idea of publishing stories in serial form, and made contemporary writing available at a low cost.

James Boswell (1740–1795) Writer, and biographer of Dr Johnson

Friend and biographer of Dr Samuel Johnson. Boswell's 1791 Life of Johnson, proved him to be, according to one critic words, 'the Shakespeare of biographers'. Johnson's is famous today largely because of Boswell's work.

John Boyd Orr (1880–1971) Nutritionist

John Boyd Orr's work at the Rowett Research Institute in Aberdeen in the 1940s brought the first applications of modern scientific methods to farming. The visible health benefits to children of his 1927 free school milk experiment led the government to apply it nationally. Orr's work helped improve the nation's diet and health during the food rationing of the Second World War. He worked with the UN to improve Third World food production, and he won the Nobel Peace Prize in 1949.

Deacon Brodie (1741–1788) Thief

By day a respected Edinburgh artisan and town councillor, by night a gambler and burglar, William Brodie led the archetypal double life. He was only caught when one of his gang turned king's evidence and was hanged in Edinburgh. Robert Louis Stevenson was said to have based Dr Jekyll and Mr Hyde on his life.

John Brown (1826–1883) Royal retainer

A gillie in 1849 who eventually became Queen Victoria's personal servant and groom. He was uncompromising, unceremonial and devoted to the queen but their relationship aroused jealously in the royal household and scandal in the country. Victoria was buried with a photo of him.

James Bruce (1730–1794) Explorer

One of the explorers seeking the source of the Nile, adventure-seeking James Bruce discovered the source of its tributary, the Blue Nile, instead. His accounts of African life caused outrage and scandal in genteel Georgian society.

William Bruce (1630–1710) Architect

Fife-born founding figure of British Palladianism. Bruce's Stuart sympathies led to his fall from royal favour after James VII's deposition in 1689. Hopetoun House, ultimately completed by William Adam, was one of his works.

Alexander Buchan (1829–1907) Meteorologist

Pioneer of meteorology and proposer of the Buchan Spells – the statistically based observation that the British climate undergoes a series of cold and warm periods which fall approximately between certain dates each year. He made valuable contributions to every aspect of climatology and meteorology.

John Buchan (1875–1940) Writer and statesman

Perth-born Buchan worked in a series of political-related jobs, including civil servant, war correspondent and MP, ultimately becoming Canadian Governor-General in 1936. It is for his writing that he remains famous today, notably The Thirty-Nine Steps.

George Buchanan (1506–1582) Scholar

Brilliant but deeply flawed scholar of European standing. He was tutor to the toddler James VI, whom he taught by fear and terror. And his severe personality problems led him to write a scurrilous and libellous pamphlet about Queen Mary, and to try to poison her young son's mind against her

Robert Burns (1759–1796) Poet

Born in Alloway on 25 January 1759, Burns is one of Scotland's most celebrated children. His first book, Poems, Chiefly in the Scottish Dialect, saved him from financial disaster; he also produced in two collections of songs – one of his own, and one of old Scots airs. But heavy drinking broke his fragile health and left him dead at 37. Burns had many children, legitimate and illegitimate, all of whom he loved and took responsibility for. His politics, despite a romantic Jacobitism, were republican: he passionately supported the French Revolution of 1789. Burns' appeal is enduring and international, and his birthday is celebrated each year by fans of his life and works.

William Burrell (1861–1958) Shipping magnate and art collector

Glasgow-born William Burrell was a lifelong art collector, ultimately retiring at 56 from the family shipping business to spend his time to amassing a collection of over 8,500 art objects and spending up to £80,000 a year on his hobby. The collection was bequeathed to Glasgow, opening in 1983 in a magnificent new gallery. The Burrell Collection has been one of the top Scottish tourist attractions ever since.

Matt Busby *(1909–1994)* **Football Manager**

A football player, then manager of Manchester United, Busby overcame disaster at Munich Airport in 1958 when most of his brilliant young side died in a plane crash and he himself almost lost his life, to lead his new side to the European Championship 10 years later. He remained influential at the club until his death.

Henry Campbell-Bannerman *(1836–1908)* **Prime Minister steered his** party to its 1906 landslide in the General Election. He was a radical: he keenly supported Irish devolution and wanted to extend trade union rights and reform education. When the Lords blocked his policies he laid the plans to curb their power. An opponent of the Boer War, he supported women's suffrage and introduced the Old Age Pension.

Thomas Carlyle *(1795–1881)* **Essayist and historian**

One of the foremost writers and intellectuals of his era, Carlisle wrote influential works on The French Revolution, Cromwell and Frederick the Great, emphasising the cult of a great man as national moral leader.

Andrew Carnegie *(1835–1919)* **American industrialist and philanthropist**

Scots-American who worked his way from railway clerk to the head of his company in 10 years. He consolidated his wealth in the oil and steel industries until in 1900, he began spending it on charitable and philanthropic projects. Libraries, trusts and educational establishments benefitted, as did his home town of Dunfermline.

Thomas Chalmers *(1780–1847)* **Founder of the Free Church of Scotland**

The most famous and dynamic minister of his day, a vociferous advocate of social and religious reform through self-reliance, and the leader of the party whose walk-out of General Assembly in 1843, sensationally split the Church of Scotland.

Prince Charles Edward Stuart, 'Bonnie Prince Charlie' *(1720–1788)* **de jure King Charles III**

Centre of hopes of a Stuart restoration from his childhood, Charles landed in the Hebrides in 1745; in weeks he had won a crushing victory at Prestonpans and held the whole of Scotland. Charles' army marched south as far as Derby before, cut off from their own support, they turned north again. The Duke of Cumberland's army caught up with them at Culloden in April of 1746, where Charles, against the advice of his brilliant General Lord George Murray, chose to fight. The Jacobites were decimated, hopes of a Stuart restoration crushed. After five months on the run, Charles finally escaped on a French ship. The Highlands were punished terribly by the British Government, who dismantled the social and cultural fabric of Scottish Gaeldom and Charles lived out his days in fading hope, guilt and drunken dissolution.

Hugh Clapperton *(1788–1827)* **Explorer**

A 19th-century hero who lived a life of travel and excitement, from his time as a 13-year-old cabin boy on a cross-Atlantic ship to a spell as a navy captain; his adoption by the Hurons in Canada; through his stint as an explorer searching for the source of the Niger in the 1820s. He died of dysentery in Africa without reaching his goal.

Jim Clark *(1936–1968)* **World champion racing driver**

Berwickshire farmer turned Formula 1 driver, Clark won the world championship in

1963 and again in 1965, when he also won the Indianapolis 500. He died in an unexplained crash in practice at Hockenheim in 1968.

Thomas Cochrane (1775–1860) Naval commander

A famed naval commander in the Napoleonic Wars. But his lack of political cunning made him enemies, and he was found guilty of a fraud charge he always denied. Released from prison, he led the navies of Chile, Brazil and Greece before becoming Earl of Dundonald, succeeding his father and winning public rehabilitiation.

Lord Cockburn (1779–1854) Judge

Noted defence counsel who became Solicitor General. His published journals present an invaluable picture of Scotland in the time of the French Revolution and reform upheavals.

William Collins (1789–1853) Publisher

Glasgow bookseller, anti-slavery campaigner, supporter of Thomas Chalmers and committed temperance campaigner. Bibles and schoolbooks formed the core of his bookselling business.

St Columba (521–597) Missionary to Scotland

Born into a Donegal chiefly family, Columba had an early reputation as a miracleworker, despite his martial background. His exile from Ireland was said to have been a penance for belligerence. In 561 he and 12 followers were washed ashore at Iona where he built his monastery and the basis for his conversion of the Picts. Iona is still a venerated island today.

Sean Connery (Born 1930) Actor

Edinburgh-born Thomas Connery worked in a variety of jobs, including coffin polisher and milkman before breaking into showbusiness. His big break was as James Bond in Dr No (1962), a part he made his own. He broke from Bond to do a range of work, and has won a BAFTA for his part in The Name of the Rose, and an Oscar for The Untouchables. He is the world's most famous living Scot.

Billy Connolly (Born 1942) Entertainer

The most successful and popular all-round entertainer to emerge from Scotland in recent years. Originally a professional musician, he is known for his comedy act, observing life's banalities with a keen line in lavatorial humour. He has long been a target for criticism by the Scottish press.

James Connolly (1868–1916) Socialist and Irish rebel leader

One the most original and influential socialist thinkers of his days. He settled in Ireland and In 1916 led his Irish Citizen Army in the Easter Rising against British rule. The government crushed the rising and executed its leaders, turning them into martyrs: the wounded Connolly being tied to a chair to be shot by firing squad.

Kate Cranston (1850–1934) Tearoom owner and patron of the arts

Proprietor of the most famous of the temperance-influenced tearooms in turn-of-the-century Glasgow, Miss Cranston commissioned designs from Charles Rennie Mackintosh, Margaret Macdonald and George Walton. She sold off her tearooms after the early death of her husband in 1917.

James Crichton (1560–1585) Prodigy

The original boy wonder whose name has become a byword for complete accomplishment – handsome, a brilliant student, a superb horseman and fencer, and accomplished in all social graces. He died in a street brawl in Italy in 1582.

A. J. Cronin (1896–1981) Writer

Originally a doctor who took to writing while recuperating from illness, Cronin wrote The Citadel and Keys of the Kingdom, but found real fame with tales of his own medical experiences, in Dr Finlay's Casebook.

R. B. Cunninghame Graham (1852–1936) Traveller, writer, socialist and nationalist

Larger-than-life figure of a wide range of talents and interests: descended from Robert II on one side and Spanish nobility on the other, he spoke Spanish as his first language and rode with the gauchos in South America where he was highly regarded. He was also a Lanarkshire Liberal MP and set up the Scottish Labour Party with Keir Hardie. He was possibly the only person to be president of both the Scottish Labour Party (1888) and the Scottish National Party (1934), where his interests later drifted. A witty and charming man, he travelled widely, wrote and was a friend of figures like Morris, Whistler, Shaw, Wells and Buffalo Bill.

David Dale (1739–1806) Industrialist and philanthropist

Successful industrialist who went into partnership with Richard Arkwright, inventor of the mechanised spinning machine, to establish the spinning mills and model village of New Lanark. He also established mills in the Highlands to help victims of the Clearances, and much of his personal wealth went on poor relief.

Lord Darnley (1545–1567) Second husband of Mary, Queen of Scots

Henry Stewart, Lord Darnley, was the cousin of Queen Mary, whom he married in July 1565. But Mary needed a strong and wise advisor in her husband, and the weak and vain Darnley was neither. He took part in the murder of David Rizzio, the queen's secretary, and the couple were estranged by the time of the christening of their son, the future James VI. An apparent reconciliation in 1567 was abruptly ended when Darnley's house was blown up and he was killed. Both the queen and the Earl of Bothwell, whom she later married, were suspected of the murder.

James Dewar (1842–1923) Inventor of the vacuum flask

An experimental scientist Dewar's speciality was liquefying and freezing gasses, and he devised a vacuum jacket to maintain their temperature. Known as the Dewar flask, it was later marketed commercially as the Thermos flask. He also developed cordite, the explosive propellant.

John Dewar (1856–1929) Spirit merchant and distiller

Son of a licensed grocer who followed into and transformed his family business. He and his brother, Tommy, were the first to bottle whiskies for sale (they had always been sold from the keg, in licensed premised). They popularised blends, making whisky more palatable and accepted outside Scotland. Their firm joined the Distillers Company conglomerate in 1925 and Dewar's White Label is still one of the world's best-selling Scotches.

James Douglas (c. 1286–1330) Commander in the Wars of Independence
Robert I's lieutenant and right-hand man, Douglas was with the king constantly throughout his darkest period in 1306–7. He raided the north of England regularly, and his martial feats in the War of Independence make thrilling reading. At Robert's request, Douglas took the dead king's heart on pilgrimage to the Holy Land but was killed en route fighting the Moors in Andalucía.

Arthur Conan Doyle (1859–1930) Writer
A doctor most famous for his literary work, particularly his character of Sherlock Holmes. He was a firm supporter of the Boer War and his diverse range of interests included boxing, seafaring, spiritualism and fairies, in which he believed totally.

William Dunbar (c.1460–1520) Poet
A cleric who became poet laureate under James IV, his sympathetic, humorous, satirical and human poetry was part of a flowering of culture in early-16th-century Scotland. No record remains of his whereabouts after the Battle of Flodden.

Viscount Dundee (1648–1689) Royalist commander
Professional soldier and kinsman of the Marquis of Montrose, John Graham helped suppress the Covenanters, the extremist rump of the presbyterian party, and championed the cause of James VII in Scotland. His forces won a stunning victory at Killiecrankie, but Dundee was killed at the point of victory; James VII's cause in Scotland died with him.

John Dunlop (1840–1921) Inventor and pioneer of the pneumatic tyre
A vet who developed the pneumatic tyre to cushion his son's bike rides on bumpy cobbled streets. He patented his invention in 1888.He went into partnership with Harvey du Cros, and their Dublin-based company later became the Dunlop Rubber Company Ltd. Dunlop did not make much money out of his invention.

Duns Scotus (c. 1265–c.1308) Philosopher and theologian
Franciscan John Duns Scotus was among the greatest medieval thinkers, his ideas emphasising the primacy of the individual and of individual will. He fell from favour in the 16th century, by when his followers had acquired the name 'Dunses', meant to denote their dullness and obstinacy, and from which evolved the modern word 'dunce'. Duns Scotus has since been canonised.

Alexander Fleming (1881–1955) Discoverer of penicillin
Fleming is famous for his discovery of penicillin, possibly the single biggest drug advance in the history of medicine, but which came about by what he called a 'triumph of accident and shrewd observation'. He saw that a culture of staphylococcus bacteria had accidentally become infected with mould – and the mould, Penicillum notatum, which commonly grows on stale food – was killing the bacteria. Tests showed it to have unprecedented antibacterial properties while being harmlessness to human cells. It took another 15 years to find a manufacturing process. Fleming won the Nobel Prize in 1945, and never patented his discovery so it could remain cheap and widely available to benefit as many people as possible.

Bill Forsyth (Born 1946) Film-maker

Glasgow-born film director who first came to public notice in the late '70s and early '80s with That Sinking Feeling and Gregory's Girl, a teenage comedy romance. Local Hero, starring Burt Lancaster, established his name internationally. A stay in the US failed to live up to his expectations, and he ultimately returned to the UK.

James Frazer (1854–1941) Anthropologist

Author of The Golden Bough: A Study in Comparative Religion, a 12-volume work stuffed with customs and practices from around the world, and source of great inspiration for many writers, including Conrad, Eliot, Lawrence and Yeats, as well as an enormous popular success. Despite the breadth of his scope, his ideas soon fell out of date.

Lewis Grassic Gibbon (1901–1935) Writer

James Leslie Mitchell is best remembered for the trilogy A Scots Quair, written under the pen-name of Lewis Grassic Gibbon. These deeply symbolic works – Sunset Song, Cloud Howe and Grey Granite – took an innovative and evocative look at the land and the upheaval of the country way of life.

John Grierson (1898–1972) Film-maker

A pioneering figure in non-fiction film-making and one of the greatest directors and producers of his day, he became known as 'the father of documentary'. Some of his most famous work was done at the GPO, such as the superb Night Mail, with commentary by W. H. Auden. He worked internationally during and after the war.

Douglas Haig (1861–1928) First World War commander

This Sandhurst-educated son of a Borders landed family rose to become commander of the British armies on the Western Front in the 1914–18 war; as such, he was responsible for the policy of attrition which was followed to the exclusion of any other strategy by the British forces on the Western Front for the next three years. It cost the lives of almost a million British troops alone, and its use has been the subject of great controversy ever since. Haig was honoured after the war. His family had interests in the whisky industry, and he became a director of the Distillers Company Ltd until his death.

Patrick Hamilton (1503–1528) Lutheran martyr

Scotland's first Protestant martyr. A Catholic cleric who turned Lutheran view during his stays on the continent, he wrote his own interpretation of Luther's works, known as Patrick's Places. Hamilton was asked by Cardinal Beaton to come to preach in St Andrews in 1528 but was soon seized, tried and convicted of heresy. On 29 February he was burned at the stake, his body taking six hours to burn. Ultimately, his death did more to publicise Lutheranism than his life would have done.

Keir Hardie (1836–1915) Socialist and labour leader

Christianity, trade unionism and temperance were three of the most important early influences on Hardie. His early politics were Liberal but he saw the need of a party to represent working people's interests. He and Cunninghame Graham founded the Scottish Labour Party in 1888; by 1900 the British Labour Party grew out of this. Hardie himself became an MP, turning up for work in casual tweeds and cloth cap which, with his politics and his plain Scots accent, made him a figure of hatred. He is seen as the father of the Labour Party.

Thomas Henderson (1789–1844) Astronomer

An enthusiastic amateur astronomer who turned his passion into his life's work, Henderson became professor of astronomy at Edinburgh University and first Astronomer Royal for Scotland.

David Octavius Hill (1802–1870) Painter and photographer

Painter who moved into the new field of photography. Hill, with his partner Robert Adamson, was a pioneer of the new medium, using it for portrait work as well as recording landscapes, buildings and scenes around Edinburgh.

James Hogg (1770–1835) Writer

Uneducated shepherd poet and writer who published intermittently, becoming a friend of Walter Scott and a regular contributor to the Edinburgh literary scene. He is most famed today for The Private Memoirs and Confessions of a Justified Sinner, a book of great power which his contemporaries found too disturbing.

David Hume (1711–1776) Philosopher

One of the world's great philosophers and the most notorious agnostic of his day, Hume was a leading figure in the Edinburgh Enlightenment. Scotland was intolerant of agnosticism, however, and Hume's views on religion meant he was debarred from ever taking up an academic appointment.

John and William Hunter (John 1728–1793; William 1718–1783) Anatomists

Noted surgeons with a competitive and often quarrelsome relationship, the Hunter brothers made their names in London. John was the more naturally gifted of the two, and the more brilliant surgeon with a particular interest in dissection. He helped make surgery a science, raising its status from that of a barber's profession. William was an obstetrician who ultimately became physician to Queen Charlotte and professor of anatomy to the Royal Academy.

James Hutton (1726–1797) Founder of modern geological science

A self-taught geologist whose work established geology as a science. Hutton deduced from his own observations the igneous origins and nature of the earth, and that it was governed by still-continuing laws. His views were in line with those of Galileo, Newton and other great scientists and were published in his most important work, The Theory of the Earth.

Elsie Inglis (1864–1917) Medical reformer and suffragette

One of the first women doctors, Elsie Inglis's experience of bigotry in the medical profession and of the poverty of maternity provision led her in 1901 to establish a maternity hospital staffed entirely by women (later the Elsie Inglis Memorial Maternity Hospital). She founded the Scottish Women's Suffrage Federation in 1906, and was the driving force behind the organisation of all-women mobile surgical units sent to the front in the First World War.

James I (1394–1437) King of Scots

Held prisoner in England from the age of 12, James I returned to his country as king in 1424, heralding the return of effective government for the first time in over 30 years. He was the first in a series of effective and intelligent Stewart kings who energetically took royal authority to all corners of the country, and he introduced a mass of reforming legislation. But his avaricious appropriation of land made him unpopular, and he was assassinated in Perth by disgruntled nobles.

James II (1430–1460) King of Scots

King in name at age six, James came into his authority in 1450 and marked the event by crushing the nobles who wielded power during his minority. He re-enacted many of his father's laws and brought peace and prosperity to the country for a short time before his untimely death, killed in a freak explosion by one of his expensive imported cannons.

James III (1451–1488) King of Scots

Another active, able and voracious Stewart ruler, James's seemingly incessant demands for money alienated the nobles, and his policy of pursuing peace with England, though visionary, was deeply unpopular. He was accidentally killed in a revolt by his nobles, led by his son, the future James IV.

James IV (1473–1513) King of Scots

The charismatic, charming and intelligent James IV was Scotland's renaissance prince. A patron of the arts, he kept one of the foremost courts of his day; introduced legal reforms and expanded education; and travelled the country extensively to exercise his personal power. The humanist scholar Erasmus said of him, 'He had a wonderful intellectual power, an astonishing knowledge of everything, and unconquerable magnanimity, and the most abundant generosity.' James's marriage to Margaret Tudor, daughter of Henry VII of England, ultimately brought the Stewarts to the throne of England. But it was the Auld Alliance with France that caused James to invade England in September 1513; James and many of his nobles died in pointless and muddy defeat at Flodden, leaving Scotland rudderless before the stormy winds of change blowing in from Europe.

James V (1512–1542) King of Scots

James V shared the Stewart traits of efficiency and energy, and was another effective ruler. Like his father, he was a patron of the arts, but unlike him he was also avaricious and vindictive. In 1538 he married Mary of Guise; tragically, the couple's first children, two sons, died within a month of one another in 1541. Relations with England deteriorated into war in 1542, but the Scots were defeated at Solway Moss. James's already strained health was broken by the defeat, and he died six days after the birth of his new daughter.

James VI (1566–1625) King of Scots

Learned, moderate, vigorous and possessed of a first-class mind, James VI has stood the tests of history to emerge as one of the most successful of all Scottish monarchs. His parentless early years were bleak, and when he came into his power James was forced to take on not just powerful nobles but the ambitious new Church of Scotland, too. He was more than a match for all, proving himself in the process the shrewdest of political operators. He ruled the country as effectively from Edinburgh as his hard-working and far-travelled predecessors had done by personal authority. In 1603 James succeeded to the English throne, but the more intimate and personal Scots style of rule did not suit the sense of dignity and reserve demanded of the English monarch, and James was often ridiculed and misunderstood. His policies in Ireland were also disastrous, with repercussions that continue to the present day.

John Paul Jones (1747–1792) Hero of the War of American Independence

Originally a gardener's son, John Paul, as he started out, began his seafaring life early, working from 12 years on a slave ship. An inheritance in Virginia let him settle in America, and he volunteered for the US navy at the outbreak of war with Britain. He led several daring raids into British and European waters. He later fought with the French and Russian navies, and was made a rear-admiral by Catherine the Great.

Captain Kidd (c. 1645–1701) Pirate, adventurer and merchant

Greenock-born minister's son and privateer-turned pirate. He was betrayed and hanged after a shamelessly rigged show trial. Kidd never revealed the location of his stores of buried treasure.

John Knox (c. 1513–1572) Protestant reformer

A man with an immense sense of his own place in history, who equated his own will with the will of God and who let everyone else know about it, Knox was as extreme a fundamentalist zealot as it is possible to find anywhere today. He managed to antagonise powerful interests, including Queen Elizabeth of England, and showed a calculated disrespect to Queen Mary in Scotland; even many of his natural allies, including his Geneva mentor, John Calvin, distanced themselves from him. He had a strong influence on the course of the Reformation in Scotland, especially as the driving force behind setting up a 'godly discipline' which let the Church and its representatives interfere in every corner of the private lives of ordinary people. Knox's own private life raised a few eyebrows: he had a penchant for young women, and his second trophy wife was a 16-year-old girl, a relative of the queen, chosen when he himself was in his 50s.

Robert Knox (1791–1862) Anatomist

One of Edinburgh's most successful anatomists, Robert Knox was one of those dependent on the city's 'resurrection men' for his subjects. In 1827–28 he became a customer of Burke and Hare, who got their corpses by murder, not from the grave. Knox was cleared of knowledge of their crimes but the doubts that remained about his complete innocence damaged his career. Bridie's play The Anatomist and Stevenson's horror story The Body Snatcher, are both based on Knox's life.

Harry Lauder (1870–1950) Entertainer

Lauder's bekilted, singing, Scotch caricature was popular inside Scotland as well as outside, bringing him phenomenal success worldwide. His success was based on talent and hard work, and he wrote some of the most famous Scots songs, including Stop Yer Ticklin', Jock, Roamin' in the Gloamin' and I Love a Lassie (for his wife). His caricature image is so strong that he is still the most famous of Scottish entertainers.

Eric Liddell (1902–1945) Athlete and missionary

Son of a missionary, who became a missionary himself, Eric Liddell shot to fame as the athlete who refused to run an Olympic 100 metres on a Sunday – something his Sabbatarianism could not countenance. He took bronze in the 200 metres at the games, and entered the 400, in which he was inexperienced. Sensationally, he took the gold medal with a new world record. Liddell's story, and that of Harold Abrahams, the victor in the 100 metres, was told in the 1981 film, Chariots of Fire. Liddell died in a Japanese internment camp.

Robert Liston (1794–1847) Surgeon and pioneer of anaesthetics

One of the most skilled surgeons of his day, at a time when surgery was dreaded and universally avoided. Liston became the first to use general anaesthetic, in a public operation in London in 1846. He also gave his name to the Liston Splint, the treatment he devised for dislocation of the thigh.

David Livingstone (1813–1873) Missionary and explorer

Doctor, missionary and one of the first to explore the Dark Continent, Livingstone was a 19th-century hero. He explored and mapped much of central Africa, discovering the Victoria Falls in 1855. He ultimately abandoned his missionary work in favour of exploration. He also became a vehement anti-slavery campaigner, having witnessed the horrors of the slave-trade first-hand. He was presumed lost on his final trip, to find the source of the Nile, and only found by investigative reporter H. M. Stanley of the New York Herald; Stanley's first words, 'Dr Livingstone, I presume?', have passed into history. Livingstone would not be persuaded to leave Africa and he died the following year. He is buried in Westminster Abbey.

Robert Lorimer (1864–1929) Architect

One of Scotland's most noted architects. Along with Mackintosh's, his was the first distinctively Scottish style to emerge for over a century. He took on a variety of commissions, from Rowallan Castle in Ayrshire, to rows of colonies cottages for craftsmen in Edinburgh. Two of Lorimer's most famous public works are also in Edinburgh: in the Thistle Chapel in St Giles' Cathedral, and the National War Memorial at the Castle.

David Lyndsay (c. 1486–1555) Poet and playwright

Appointed by James IV as usher and general companion to his baby son, the future James V, Lyndsay came to the fore in the reign of his young charge as head of the College of Heralds, and court poet. He satirised the vices of court life and he was comfortable enough to rebuked the king for his licentiousness and susceptibility to flattery, but he remained one of James' favourites. His 1540 masterpiece, Ane Pleasant Satyre of the Thrie Estatis, was a morality play which is still performed today. Despite his sympathy for the reformers, Lyndsay died a Catholic.

John Loudon McAdam (1756–1836) Road builder

McAdam experimented with ideas for improved road construction, with large stones at the bottom and small ones at the surface, laid on drained soil and with a camber to allow drainage. His revolutionary roads were inexpensive, flexible, almost waterproof and silent. Years of research and work saw him spend thousands of pounds of his own money before his ideas were finally accepted and put into general use. The terms 'macadamised' and 'macadamisation' were used to describe the new roads and their building.

Macbeth (c. 1005–1057) King of Scots

Not the great villain portrayed by Shakespeare, Macbeth was no worse and probably better than many medieval kings and the country was relatively stable under his government. He went to Rome on pilgrimage in 1050 and is said to have 'scattered alms like seed corn'. He is buried on the island of Iona.

Hugh MacDiarmid (1892–1978) Poet

His first poetry was written in English, but after studying a Scots dictionary, he used words from different dialects to build up a literary Scots language. His best-known work, A Drunk Man Looks at the Thistle, was published in 1926, a self-parodic poem of meditation and introspection. But the work he did in the 1930s was acknowledged as his best. He swayed between political parties, at times joining Labour, the Communists, and helping found the SNP.

Flora Macdonald (1725–1789) Jacobite heroine

Flora Macdonald gained lasting fame by helping the fugitive Bonnie Prince Charlie evade capture. She took him from Benbecula to Skye, although she was unhappy that he was disguised as a woman. As a gift Charles gave Flora a gold locket with his portrait. Flora was later arrested and imprisoned in the Tower of London until the Jacobite amnesty of 1747. She later entertained and favourably impressed Dr Johnson on his Hebridean tour. She returned home after a few years in America. Her shroud was the sheet Prince Charles and Dr Johnson had slept in.

John Macdonald (1815–91) Canadian statesman

Glasgow-born Canadian politician who became a successful lawyer. Macdonald was a leading light in the Conservative Party and in his 34 years as premier, his influence helped bring the Maritime provinces, Manitoba and BC into the Dominion. He also secured the construction of the Canadian Pacific railroad, an enterprise vital in a country so vast.

Ramsay MacDonald (1866–1937) First Labour Prime Minister

Ramsay MacDonald went from desperately poor beginnings to become first Labour PM. He joined Keir Hardie's ILP, becoming an MP in 1906 and party leader in 1911. He was a moderate and visionary in international affairs, including the First World War and its aftermath. In 1924 he became leader of the first, minority, Labour Government. PM again in 1929, he was dissuaded from resigning with the rest of his colleagues over the economic crisis, to head up a 'National' coalition Government; the break with his party was permanent. He eventually resigned as PM in 1935.

William MacEwen (1848–1924) Pioneer of neurosurgery

Under the influence of Lister, William MacEwen became a surgeon, becoming the first dedicated neurosurgeon. But his success and advances were not just in neurosurgery, and he devised procedures from a cure knock-knees and hernias, to bone grafts.

William McGonagall (c. 1825–1902) Poet

McGonagall was a amateur showman, and his love of the dramatic was evident in his poetry, which he printed on sheets, to be sold across the country, and enthusiastically recited on stage. Typical is The Death of Lord and Lady Dalhousie: 'Alas! Lord and

Lady Dalhousie are dead, and buried at last, / Which causes many people to feel a little downcast.' McGonagall's poetry has been called some of the worst ever written.

Rob Roy Macgregor (1671–1734) Outlaw and adventurer
Known as 'Roy' because of his thick, dark red curly hair, Macgregor was a grazier who raided cattle and took protection money from neighbours to safeguard their herds. His lawlessness meant he had to live rough in caves and woods, and tales of his exploits, hair's-breadth escapes and Robin Hood-style wealth redistribution are well worth reading. In 1727, on the point of being transported, he was pardoned for his past deeds. his luck seemed to have run out when he was sentenced to transportation; instead, he received a pardon.

Charles Macintosh (1766–1843) Inventor of waterproof materials
Most of Macintosh's work was done in the bleaching and dyeing industry but his main claim to fame was his invention and patenting in 1823 of a fabric-waterproofing process which has ensured the survival of his name as a household word.

Compton Mackenzie (1883–1972) Writer
A Scot by inclination, English-born Compton Mackenzie was regarded as one of the most promising writing talents of his generation. His output was prolific, and his most famous comedy, Whisky Galore, used the backdrop of his Barra home. It was based on the real-life story of the wartime wrecking of the SS Politician. Mackenzie was a founder member of the SNP.

Charles Rennie Mackintosh (1868–1928) Architect, designer and artist
Glasgow's most famous child and an acknowledged architectural and design genius, Mackintosh's work was a fusion of Scottish vernacular, Art Nouveau and the modern. But his style was too avant garde for home consumption, and he and his wife Margaret Macdonald settled in France, where he concentrated on watercolours and emerged as one of the finest British exponents of the medium. He is now seen as a prophet of the Modern Movement and a founder of modern architecture.

John Maclean (1879–1923) Marxist politician
A revolutionary socialist and teacher, Maclean's lectures and open classes regularly attracted over a thousand people; he went on to found the Scottish Labour College. He was vehemently anti-war and anti-conscription, and was made Soviet Consul in Scotland by the new Moscow government. His views left him isolated from democratic socialists, and his health was broken by long periods in jail.

George MacLeod (1895–1991) Founder of the Iona Community
Socialist George MacLeod was one of the Church of Scotland's foremost clerics. His fame came from two sources, each achieved in the teeth of opposition from the Church establishment: he led a group to restore Columba's monastery on Iona; and founded the Iona Community, reviving in a 20th-century context the missionary spirit of Iona's first settlers in deprived city areas.

J. J. R. Macleod (1876–1935) Co-discoverer of insulin
Macleod and his University of Toronto colleague, Dr Frederick Banting, led the team that identified the pancreatic malfunction and isolated the hormone which controlled blood sugar levels; Macleod called the hormone 'insulin'. In 1923 the pair won the

Nobel Prize for Medicine, which they shared with their fellow researchers.

St Margaret (c. 1046–1093) Saint and Queen of Scots

Margaret, canonised in 1251, is the only Scottish royal saint. The English-born wife of Malcolm III, she had a great influence over her devoted husband, bringing anglicisation to court and church and ousting Gaelic. She was personally pious and cared especially for orphans. She died four days after her husband and eldest son were killed in battle.

Mary I (1542–1587) Queen of Scots

Queen when she was just six days old, Mary went to France for safety as a child, marrying the Dauphin Francis in 1558, and the couple became king and queen on the death of his father in 1559. But with Francis's death in 1560, Mary returned to her northern realm. The zealous heat of reformation raged in Scotland and Mary depended on the political skills of her half-brother, James Stewart, for the first few years. It was an attempt to break free of him and to strengthen her claim to the English throne led her to marry her cousin, Henry Stewart, Lord Darnley; but the man was a political and personal disaster. His active part in the murder of Mary's secretary, David Rizzio, in the pregnant queen's presence just months after their marriage, was an unforgivable betrayal. Mary was suspected of playing a part in her husband's subsequent assassination, and made her situation worse by marrying Bothwell, the chief murder suspect, in May 1567, so uniting all her opponents at a stroke. She was captured and forced to abdicate in favour of her infant son. Defeat at Langside followed her escape, and she fled to England, never to return. Mary remained a centre of Catholic intrigue until she was trapped into the Babbington Plot to assasinate Elizabeth. Her trial at Fotheringay Castle was rigged, and Elizabeth finally signed her cousin's death warrant on 1 February 1587. Mary was executed seven days later and has remained one of the most romantic figures in Scottish history.

James Maxton (1885–1946) Labour politician

A socialist politician of great oratorial skills and personal charm. Maxton was a student of John Maclean and one of the foremost of the fiery 'Red Clydesiders'. He never used dry, formulaic political dogma, preferring to entertain and persuade his audiences with wit and humour. He emerged after early battles as one of the best-loved politicians.

James Clerk Maxwell (1831–1879) Physicist

A brilliant theoretical physicist whose immense intellect and work rank him on a par with Newton and Einstein. His Treatise on Electricity and Magnetism examined the nature of electromagnetism and laid the way for the work of Einstein and Planck. Other diverse research examined the nature of Saturn's rings, whose composition he proved mathematically, to the perception of colour and a demonstration of colour photography, using as his subject a piece of tartan ribbon.

Andrew Melville (1545–1622) Religious and academic reformer

Like Knox, an Ayatollah of the Scottish Reformation. Melville was an ardent believer in a presbyterian government for the Church of Scotland, and directly opposed James VI's plans for episcopacy. In his most famous outburst, Melville told James that he was merely 'God's silly vassal', and 'not a king, nor a lord, nor a head, but a member' of the kingdom of Christ in Scotland. For James, revenge was sweet: he summoned Melville to London in 1606 and threw him in the Tower for five years. On his release Melville went abroad to teach.

Hugh Miller (1802–1856) Geologist

Originally a stonemason, Hugh Miller was a self-taught palaeantologist who indulged a lifelong interest in fossils and single-handedly popularised the new science of geology. But Miller also had a literal approach to the Bible, which sat uneasily with the scientific and logical consequences of his discoveries. Miller was prone to fits of depression and, unable to reconcile the old certainties with his researches, he killed himself. Darwin's The Origin of Species appeared three years after Miller's death.

Marquess of Montrose (1612–1650) Royalist soldier and poet

One of the most dashing and glamorous figures of Scottish history, Montrose was Charles I's champion, winning a series of battles for the king. A final defeat in 1646 sent him into exile for four years, only to return after Charles I's execution, at the request of the new king. But his luck had run out and after several reverses he was finally betrayed for £25,000 by Macleod of Assynt, from whom he had sought shelter. His trial was a foregone conclusion; for his execution on 21 May, he dressed and conducted hiimself with panache, appearing, as one observer said, more like a bridegroom than a criminal.

As well as a soldier, Montrose was also a talented poet and Scotland's only composer of Cavalier courtly poetry.

John Muir (1838–1914) American ecologist and conservationist

Scots-American who emigrated in childhood. A period in Canada escaping the Civil War draft led to a passion for wilderness, and he roamed the American backwoods on foot, taking notes and sketching. He began a public crusade to save the remaining forests and wilderness, championing the conservation of Yosemite Valley in California. He is now recognised as the founder of the national parks movement.

St Mungo (c. 520–612) Patron saint of Glasgow

Kentigern, nicknamed Mungo (meaning 'dear friend'), was the son of St Thenew and was brought up under the influence of St Serf. He became a missionary, building on the Christian legacy left in southern Scotland by the Romans and preaching in Strathclyde, Cumbria and Wales, meeting St David and St Columba on his travels. He was buried in his cathedral in Glasgow and as the city's patron saint, appears on its arms along with pictorial mementoes of his miracles.

Lord George Murray (c. 1700–1760) Jacobite commander

A brilliant general who was the key to the Jacobites' stunning successes in the 1745 rising: he supervised the winning of battles, the avoidance of engagements and the superb tactical retreat to Scotland. But Murray disagreed with Charles' decision to march to Inverness, and to fight at Culloden; however, he still took part, resigning his post only the day after. Forced into exile, he was rewarded by the prince's father in Rome, but his unhealed breach with Charles remained.

Lady Nairne (1766–1845) Songwriter

Daughter of a staunchly Jacobite family, Carolina Oliphant, whose married name was

Lady Nairne, first became interested in old Scots songs through the work of Burns. She collected old airs, setting her own words to them; her work includes the Jacobite classics, Charlie is my Darlin', and the haunting lament for the lost cause, Will ye no' come back again?, as well as others such as The Rowan Tree and The Auld Hoose. Her work was published posthumously.

John Napier (1550–1617) Discoverer of logarithms

Napier was a man of great intellect, persistence and will, leading a solitary lifestyle; his interests in subjects like divination acquired him a reputation as a necromancer. But his true genius lay in mathematics: he developed theories of logarithms, computing them and constructing tables He was the first to devise the use of the decimal point. He also invented the world's first mechanical computing device in the form of a series of rods which were nicknamed 'Napier's Bones'. Napier was also an enthusiastic religious controversialist who wasted much time and talent inventing war machines to fend off his particular Spanish Catholic bogeyman.

St Ninian (Lived c. 400) Missionary and saint

The first missionary sent out to Scotland from Rome to convert the people to Christianity. He chose Roman Carlisle as his first base, eventually setting up his church in Whithorn. He built on some of the networks the Romans had left, converting in the south west, as far north as Perth and west into Ireland. Ninian is said to have been buried at Whithorn, which later became one of the foremost centres of pilgrimage in Scotland.

St John Ogilvie (1579–1615) Catholic martyr

Catholic convert from Calvinism, Banffshire-born John Ogilvie joined the Society of Jesus, the shock-troops of the Catholic Church's Counter-Reformation movement. Saying Mass in Scotland was a penal offence, but Ogilvie chose to return. He was in the country a year before he was betrayed in 1614. Ogilvie was tortured and sleep-deprived to make him convert or reveal his co-religionists. He was hanged in 1615 at Glasgow Cross, canonised in 1976 and is Scotland's only post-Reformation saint.

Margaret Oliphant (1828–97) Writer

Prodigious writer who by her efforts supported her invalid husband, the families of her two dissolute brothers, and her own children, all of whom predeceased her. The supernatural was her particular interest, and she wrote 93 novels, over 30 short stories, biographies, histories, reviews, essays and articles.

Mungo Park (1771–1806) Explorer

Trained botanist and physician who first explored the African interior, sailing up the Gambia River, in 1795. His trip was a catalogue of disasters, but his account of it was a huge success. Despite his attempts to settle in the Borders, he set off once more in 1805 for Africa on a fateful trip whose participants were decimated by malaria and native attacks; neither Park nor his journals were ever found again.

William Paterson (1658–1719) Founder of the Bank of England

In 1691 Paterson, a London trader, devised a scheme to let the government borrow at good rates of interest; lenders were part of the Company of the Bank of England. His plans became a reality four years later. Paterson was also involved in the Darien debacle in Panama, where Scots tried to establish a colony; he sailed out in 1698 and was among the few bedraggled and broken survivors who came back the next year. He was a vocal supporter of the union in 1707, and established a fund to convert the National Debt in later years.

Allan Pinkerton (1819–1884) Founder of the Pinkerton Detective Agency

A trained cooper, Pinkerton sailed for the US at 23 to avoid arrest for his Chartist political activities. Success in uncovering a local counterfeiting ring led him to set up his own group of young and morally upright detectives in Chigaco in 1852. They pulled off some spectacular feats, including breaking up the Molly Maguires, a Pennsylvania-Irish secret society, and saving President-elect Abraham Lincoln from assassination. Pinkerton headed the US secret service during the Civil War (1861–65) and was a fervent abolitionist; his own home was a station on the Underground Railroad.

Duke of Queensberry (1724–1810) Rake

William Douglas, fourth Duke of Queensberry's main claims to fame were his passions for gambling, horse racing and womanising. He had his own Newmarket stables and won huge sums of money betting on almost anything. He was also a member of the notorious Hellfire Club, whose motto was, 'Do what you please; dare to despise convention.' Like the other club members, his sexual habits were promiscuous and scandalous. He was also very careful of his health, and his doctor, was paid on a daily basis for keeping his master alive and healthy. Almost universally reviled, Queensberry managed to die with a personal fortune of over a million pounds.

Henry Raeburn (1756–1823) Artist

Trained as a goldsmith, Raeburn's talents led him into painting, particularly portraits; he became the foremost Scottish portrait painter of his day. His subjects included some of the richest and most powerful figures in the land, including Cockburn, Hume, Boswell, Smith, Braxfield and Scott.

Allan Ramsay (1713–1784) Artist

Son of Allan Ramsay the poet, Allan junior showed a precocious talent for drawing. After three years' study in Rome he established himself as one of the most successful and talented portrait painters, and by the time he moved to London in 1762 he was a rich man whose reputation was secure. He was appointed George III's portrait painter five years later. He moved to Italy in his later years and died at Dover on his way home during a bout of homesickness.

John Reith (1889–1971) Broadcasting pioneer

A minister's son whose early upbringing influenced his own outlook and those of the broadcasting organisation which was essentially his creation, the BBC. His engineering background brought him the new job of general manager of the British Broadcasting Company in 1922, in charge of a staff of four people. He saw the BBC's potential for influence and was determined to ensure it impartiality of government, refusing to broadcast anti-General Strike propaganda in 1926 and successfully fighting to have the BBC publicly funded. For 16 years he dominated the infant company, influencing on its every action, and his stamp on the corporation and its reputation has proved lasting. The succession of jobs he took on in later life never suited his talents quite so well.

Robert I, the Bruce (1274–1329) King of Scots

Of Scots-Norman lineage, the Bruce family had been strong contenders for the throne in 1292 when they lost out to John Balliol. Robert Bruce was pragmatic rather than patriotic, serving with Wallace then Edward, wherever he saw his own interests best served. His moment of no return came in 1306 when in the Greyfriars Church in Dumfries he murdered John Comyn, leader of the Balliol faction. He was hurriedly crowned King of Scots at Scone, bringing down Edward's full fury on his family. The old king died before he reached Scotland, but Robert's forces were scattered and he and his supporters fugitives. It was at this low point that, sheltering in a cave, he was said to have learned the effectiveness of endurance from a spider struggling repeatedly to climb a wall to build her web.

In 1307 Robert began the long haul of driving the English out of the country, waging a seven-year campaign of guerrilla warfare. By 1314 only Berwick and Stirling were still held by the English. Robert's greatest victory was at Bannockburn in June 1314: against a larger, better equipped force, his superior tactics won the day. The English army was decimated, losing three-quarters of its 20,000-strong force, and Edward II ignominiously fled the field in disgrace, chased by James Douglas.

Robert was confirmed king by Parliament, who agreed a detailed act of succession. War with England continued intermittently until Scottish independence was recognised in 1328 in the Treaty of Northampton. Bannockburn was a turning point, and Scotland was never again subject to the overlordship of England.

The most important recognition of Scottish independence came from the papacy after the 1320 Declaration of Arbroath – a letter from the Scots nobles to the pope, which has stood as a poignant declaration of Scottish patriotism and independence: 'While there exist a hundred of us we will never submit to England. For we fight not for glory, wealth, or honour, but for that liberty which no virtuous man lays down but with his life.'

For such a superb general, Robert was a surprisingly successful peacetime king, reconciling alienated factions, introducing legal reforms, reasserting royal authority and caring for the rights of ordinary people. He died at Cardross in 1329, ravaged, it is said, by leprosy, contracted during the hardships of his life on the run. He was the man to whom Scotland owed its continuing independence, and he is probably the single most important figure in Scottish history.

James Robertson-Justice (1905–1975) Actor

The multi-talented James Robertson-Justice turned his hand to many jobs before settling on acting fairly late in life. A committed socialist, he fought in the International Brigades in Spain during the Civil War, and was an officer in the Royal Navy during the Second World War. His acting break came in 1944, but his most distinctive role was as Sir Lancelot Sprat, in Doctor in the House and its follow-up series. He was also an active conservationist and trained and flew falcons.

Michael Scott (c. 1175–c. 1234) Wizard

A Borders-born European scholar, Scott joined Emperor Frederick the Great's glittering court at Palermo. Through his Arabic translations, many works which had been lost to or were unknown in Christendom were reintroduced and discovered. Scott's own interests lay more in astrology and the occult, including alchemy, sorcery, physiognomy and prophesy. He was said to have magical powers, and was respected and feared. Scott appeared among the enchanters in the eighth circle of Hell in Dante's Inferno; he was mentioned by Boccaccio; and Walter Scott wrote about him.

Walter Scott (1771–1832) Writer

Scotland's most prolific writer and a founder of the historical novel. A lawyer who wrote fiction, his first novel, Waverley, enjoyed instant success, as did the series that followed. Scott had a high social profile and was the prime organiser of George IV's visit to Scotland in 1822. His spending on property and various collections, as well as a series of poor investment, left him £100,000 in debt, and his ultimately successful battle to write to pay off his debts ultimately broke his health.

Alexander Selkirk (1676–1721) Castaway and model for Robinson Crusoe

A high-spirited young man, Selkirk first ran away to sea in 1695, ultimately joining a privateer in 1703. But an unwise quarrel with the captain left him marooned on the uninhabited South Pacific island of Juan Fernandez. He had to survive on his own until, in 1709, he was rescued by a passing ship. Daniel Defoe based Robinson Crusoe on Selkirk's adventures.

Patrick Sellar (1780–1851) Sutherland factor during the Clearances

Patrick Sellar was the factor of the Duke of Sutherland, one of the most notorious landlords for clearing off the land tenants whose families had farmed there for generations. Sellar was in the front line of the duke's dirty work, and showed great enthusiasm and brutality in his ruthless evictions. He was eventually tried for oppression in 1816, and although acquitted, his name became synonymous with the Clearances.

James Young Simpson (1811–1870) Pioneer of anaesthesia

Bathgate-born Simpson was a high-flying young doctor whose major medical preoccupation was the alleviation of physical pain in his patients, particularly those undergoing surgery and childbirth. In 1847 he and two assistants tested chloroform on themselves; in a minute, he delightedly reported, all three were under the table. The anaesthetic was introduced two weeks later to Edinburgh Infirmary, but the forces of superstition fought a strong rearguard action, believing it to be God's will that humans should suffer. Anaesthesia gained full respectability when Queen Victoria used it in childbirth in 1853.

Mary Slessor (1848–1915) Missionary

Mary Slessor was the most important Scots African missionary, but she had an unpromising start when her behaviour scandalised genteel missionary society: she mixed with the natives and she wore light, cool clothing appropriate to the hot climate. She was in constant conflict with the missionary authorities. But the benefits she brought were immeasurable, outlawing ritualised rape, infanticide and human sacrifice. She saved many women and children from enslavement and terrible death, and adopted many children in the process. She died in 1915, having done invaluable work to alleviate suffering and raise the local people from the mire of savagery.

Samuel Smiles (1812–1904) Social reformer
Author of one of the inspirational Bibles of Victorian society, Self-Help, a collection of biographies of contemporary men of achievement. A quarter of a million copies were sold.

Adam Smith (1723–1790) Economist and philosopher
Kirkcaldy-born academic at Glasgow University and one of David Hume's circle of Edinburgh intellectuals, Adam Smith gained lasting and world fame for his treatise on laissez-faire, The Wealth of Nations. It was instantly influential and successful, and has never been out of print. Smith's ideas continue to influence economists today.

George Smith of Glenlivet (1792–1871) Whisky distiller
First of the licensed distillers of Speyside in an era when the trade was largely illicit. Smith's persistence and financial success eventually carried the day for the pro-licensers and, with the help of Edinburgh merchant Andrew Usher, the Glenlivet whisky became the most popular whisky in the country. Ironically, success brought its own complications and Smith had to fight to retain exclusive use of the name Glenlivet. The settlement still stands: other companies could use the name Glenlivet as a hyphenated suffix but only Smith's family company could use the direct article, as The Glenlivet.

Madeleine Smith (1835–1928) Alleged poisoner
Daughter of a well-to-do Glasgow architect and the defendant in one of the most sensational murder trials ever held in a Scottish court. She had an illicit affair with a clerk but when she dropped him for a more wealthy suitor, her ex-lover threatened to expose the affair to her father by showing him her love letters. Madeleine was known to have bought arsenic three times in early 1857; her lover died weeks later; and a post-mortem showed he died of arsenic poisoning. Madeleine was arrested and tried for murder. Public interest in the trial was unprecedented, especially when the explicit love letters were read out. But she was brilliantly defended and the jury returned a 'Not Proven' verdict. Madeleine became a figure in fashionable London society and later emigrated to New York, aged 80.

Tobias Smollett (1721–1771) Writer
A ship's doctor-turned-writer, the witty and outspoken Tobias Smollet is best known today and the author of The Expedition of Humphrey Clinker, a delightful and enduring comic novel that remains his most entertaining.

Jock Stein (1922–1985) Football manager
Burnbank-born Stein was the greatest football manager Scotland has ever produced and a man who acquired messianic status. A mediocre player himself, he moved through coaching and managerial appointments before joining Celtic as manager in 1965. His success at Celtic will never be equalled: 10 league titles (nine won consecutively), eight Scottish Cups and six League Cups. He led the side to two European Cup finals, winning the competition in 1967, the year his team won every competition they entered. In later years, as manager, he steered the national team to qualification for the 1982 World Cup but tragically and dramatically died at the trackside during a crucial match.

The Stevenson Family (18th–20th centuries) Engineers

The most famous family of all Scots engineers. Patriarch Robert Stevenson (1772–1850) followed in the footsteps of his step-father Thomas Smith, an Edinburgh lampmaker and first engineer of the Northern Lighthouse Board, set up to build new lighthouses and make Scottish coastal waters safer for shipping. He built over 20 lighthouses, most famously the ingeniously designed lighthouse on the treacherous Bell Rock off the east coast. Three of his sons – Alan (1807–65), David (1815–86) and Thomas (1818–87), father of author Robert Louis – also became engineers, working both in the Northern Lighthouse Board and in their own firm where they diversified into other areas of civil engineering. The brothers also designed lighthouses for waters from Newfoundland to Japan. Their sons and grandson entered the profession; the final Stevenson engineer, D. Alan, was responsible for deepening the Clyde to accommodate the newly built Queen Mary after her launch in 1934.

Robert Louis Stevenson (1850–1894) Writer

A sickly and imaginative only child, Lewis (later Louis) turned off the family career path of engineering to study law, but writing was always his first love. Travels abroad to escape the Edinburgh cold gave him material for his writing, and it was on a trip to France that he met his future wife, an American divorcée with two young children. Almost all of Stevenson's most famous work was written after his marriage: Treasure Island was written in 1882 for Lloyd, his stepson. Kidnapped and Catriona followed, and The Strange Case of Dr Jekyll and Mr Hyde, which explored the duality of good and evil present in all his works; it shot him to fame in 1886. With his family and mother he eventually left Scotland for good, ultimately settling on Samoa in the South Seas. He was writing Weir of Hermiston at the time of his death; unfinished, it remains his masterpiece.

Robert Tannahill (1774–1810) Poet and weaver

Immensely popular weaver-poet from Paisley who wrote, initially for Glasgow periodicals and was later published. Some of his poems and songs are not unlike those of Burns, whom he admired. But he suffered ill-health and ultimately drowned himself in a Paisley canal over difficulties with his publishers.

Thomas Telford (1757–1834) Engineer

An uneducated Dumfriesshire stonemason who went on to become a giant of the Industrial Revolution. His first break was landing an important surveying job in Shropshire, where his designs for canal aqueducts were innovative. Government road- and bridge-building schemes in the Highlands followed, while work in England and Europe also helped make his reputation as the foremost civil engineer of his day, earning him the nickname, 'the Colossus of Roads'. One of his most famous structures is the Menai Bridge at Anglesey, one of the few in Britain to use the suspension principle. Despite his success he was never personally wealthy, choosing projects which were in the public, rather than his own, interest.

Charles Tennant (1768–1838) Chemist

Textiles was one of the key industries of the Industrial Revolution and a chemist like Tennant, who learned his trade in the bleaching industry, was well placed to exploit it. His patented bleaching powder – which was probably devised by his partner,

Charles Macintosh – had the benefit of being portable, so could could easily supply the burgeoning textile industry. In 1800 Tennant and his partners moved to the St Rollox chemical works, the largest in the world.

Thomas the Rhymer (Lived in the mid–late 13th century) Poet and seer

A Borders poet who also appears in the eponymous ballad Thomas the Rhymer. He was said to have been captivated by the Queen of the Fairies in the Eildon Hills, but the three days he spent with her was actually three years. On parting, she gave him the gift of prophesy, apparently allowing him to foretell Flodden and the Union; his predictions were eventually published in 1603 and were enduringly popular. Thomas vanished one day, and was said to have gone back to the fairy queen.

William Thompson (1824–1907) Physicist

Irish-born William Thompson came to Glasgow as a child, entering university at 10 years and becoming professor of natural philosophy at 22. He made discoveries in thermodynamics, hydrodynamics and electricity; devised the absolute (Kelvin) temperature scale; invented the submarine telegraph cable (personally supervising its laying in the Atlantic); improved marine compasses; and invented electrical instruments (his house was the first to be lit by electricity). He was one of the leaders in pure and applied sciences of his generation, was a superb teacher and a successful businessman, making optical instruments.

Alexander 'Greek' Thomson (1817–1875) Architect

Glaswegian architect who designed buildings of all types, from churches and warehouses to great houses and tenements. His neo-classical style earned him the name 'Greek' Thomson. Among his finest work still standing is the United Presbyterian church in St Vincent St, Walmer Crescent, Moray Place (where he himself lived) and Great Western Terrace. His style was highly popular, and was copied and adapted by followers, ultimately bequeathing to Glasgow some of the world's finest Victorian architecture, as well as a sense of dignity and grandeur. Unlike Mackintosh, Thomson's work was not so revolutionary as to disconcert and upset his fellows, and his genius was acknowledged in his own lifetime.

William Wallace (c. 1270–1305) Patriot

Scotland's greatest patriot., Wallace was one of the few to emerge from the Wars of Independence with uncompromised honesty and selfless motive. He was a minor noble from Elderslie and one of the few to take on Edward I when he assumed the overlordship of Scotland. After English forces murdered his father, brother and wife, he retaliated, killing the English sheriff at Lanark in May 1297 and joining forces with Sir Andrew Murray before going on to win a great victory at Stirling Bridge. He became Guardian of Scotland in the name of John Balliol. But further successes, some in the north of England, did not draw to his cause the Scots nobles, preoccupied with in-fighting and not wanting to follow a leader of lower social status. Defeat at Falkirk began the decline; missions for support abroad distracted his efforts, and by the early 1300s he was back to waging low-scale guerrilla warfare. With a price on his head, he was betrayed in 1305 by one of his own followers outside Glasgow and handed over to be sent to London for trial. Wallace was accused of treason, a charge he refuted on the grounds that he never acknowledged Edward as king and was his enemy, not a rebel. But the trial was a formality, and on 23 August he was dragged in chains through the streets to Smithfield where before a baying crowd he was hanged, cut down before he was dead, disembowelled and quartered; his limbs were sent as a warning to Newcastle, Berwick, Stirling and Perth. Wallace was recognised as a patriotic hero in his own lifetime, and modern times have seen his name brought to the fore again by Mel Gibson's Braveheart movie.

Robert Watson-Watt (1892–1973) Pioneer of radar

A descendant of James Watt, pioneer of the steam engine, Watson Watt began his radar career in meteorology, detecting storms to warn the pilots of fragile First World War planes of their approach. He developed the already current notions of radar (radio detection and ranging), devising a system to operate simply and efficiently in wartime. A national network was in place by the time war broke out – essential to Britain's gaining and maintaining mastery of the skies throughout the war, notably in the crucial 1940 Battle of Britain.

James Watt (1736–1819) Pioneer of the steam engine

Instrument-maker who modified the steam engine – until then limited in its use – giving it a far wider range of applications; Watt's work underpinned the technology explosion that became the Industrial Revolution. Other inventions included a steam locomotive (which he did not develop) and a chemical document copier. He was first to use the term 'horsepower' and he discovered the composition of water. As an instrument-maker he also took surveying work to boost his income, and successfully surveyed many of Scotland's canals. The unit of power, the 'watt', is named after him.

Nora Wattie (1899–1994) Pioneer in social medicine

One of history's unsung heroines and heroes, whose lives profoundly affect those they touch, Nora Wattie was a doctor specialising in ante-natal and neonatal health. She worked to alleviate the suffering of women and their babies who were infected with sexually transmitted diseases by husbands returning home after the war. The maternity and child welfare service she set up and ran over three decades in Glasgow, with its ante-natal care and health-visitor system, gained national and international recognition.

John Wheatley (1869–1930) Politician

Irish-born Labour publisher and politician who was responsible for transferring the allegiances of the large Scots-Irish communities in Scotland away from concern solely with Irish affairs to support for the Labour Party, a legacy which remains largely intact today. His 1924 housing act sparked the start of government-subsidised council-house building that saw thousands of families rehomed for the first time in houses with water, sanitation and electricity.

Peter Williamson (1730–1799) Adventurer

Serial kidnap victim Peter Williamson was first stolen from the Aberdeen quayside at age 10 to be sold into American slavery, then again as an adult when a local American Indian tribe held him prisoner for months. On his return to Britain his exposé of official connivance in the kidnap trade in Aberdeen brought him banishment and a libel suit, although a counter-suit of his own won the day. More happily settled in Edinburgh, he set up a penny post scheme which was bought out by the

GPO; he published the city's first street directory; and became the proprietor of a popular coffee house.

James Young (1811–1883) Discoverer of paraffin

The successful inventor of a process of manufacturing paraffin from coal, 'Paraffin' Young became a rich man on the proceeds of his invention and business. He used his money to pay the debts on Livingstone's African trips, and endowed a chair at his alma mater, Anderson's College (now Strathclyde University).

RELIGION

• CHURCHES IN SCOTLAND •

MEMBERSHIP

GENERAL STATISTICS
(all figures are approximate)

	No.	*Percentage*
Scots claiming membership of a church	1,250,000	25% of population
Christian religions	1,190,000	95% of religious adherents
Non-Christian faiths	60,000	5% of religious adherents

CHRISTIAN CHURCH NUMBERS

Church	Est. membership	Actual attendance at service
Roman Catholic Church	720,000	240,000
Church of Scotland	710,000	200,000
Scottish Episcopal Church	50,000	16,800
Baptist	17,000	15,000
Other Christian churches	50,000	not known

• CHRISTIAN CHURCHES IN SCOTLAND •

ARCHBISHOPS AND BISHOPS OF THE CATHOLIC CHURCH SINCE THE RESTORATION OF THE HIERARCHY, 1878

The Catholic Church in Scotland operated without a recognised hierarchy for three centuries after the Reformation; when the Church reached sufficient numbers in the late 19th century, the hierarchy was restored by Rome.

Archbishops of St Andrews and Edinburgh (archdiocese created 1878)

1878-1883	John Strain (1810-1883)
1883-1885	vacant
1885-1892	William Smith (1819-1892)
1892-1900	Angus MacDonald (1844-1900)
1900-1928	James Smith (1841-1928)
1928-1929	vacant
1929-1950	Andrew McDonald (1871-1950)

Archbishops of St Andrews and Edinburgh (cont'd)
1950-1951	vacant
1951-1985	Gordon Gray (1910-1993); created Cardinal 1969; retired 1985
1985-	Keith O'Brien (1938-)

Archbishops of Glasgow (archdiocese created 1878)
1878-1902	Charles Eyre (1817-1902)
1902-1920	John Maguire (1852-1920)
1920-1922	vacant
1922-1943	Donald Mackintosh (1877-1943)
1943-1945	vacant
1945-1963	Donald Campbell (1894-1963)
1963-1964	vacant
1964-1974	James Scanlan (1899-1976); resigned 1974
1974-	Thomas Winning (1925-); created Cardinal 1994

Bishops of Aberdeen (diocese created 1878)
1878-1889	John MacDonald (1818-1889)
1889	Colin Grant (1832-1889)
1890-1898	Hugh MacDonald (1841-1898)
1899-1918	Aeneas Chisholm (1836-1918)
1918-1946	George Bennett (1875-1946)
1947-1950	John Matheson (1901-1950)
1950-1963	Frank Walsh (1901-1974); resigned 1963
1963-1965	vacant
1965-1976	Michael Foylan (1907-1976)
1977-	Mario Conti (1934-)

Bishops of Argyll and the Isles (diocese created 1878)
1878-1892	Angus MacDonald (1844-1900); created Archbishop of St Andrews and Edinburgh, 1892
1892-1918	George Smith (1840-1918)
1919-1938	Donald Martin (1873-1938)
1939-1945	Donald Campbell (1894-1963); created Archbishop of Glasgow, 1945
1946-1959	Kenneth Grant (1900-1959)
1960-1968	Stephen McGill (1912-); created Bishop of Paisley, 1968
1969-1990	Colin Macpherson (1917-1990)
1990-1996	Roderick Wright (1941-); resigned 1996
1996-1999	Ian Murray (1932 -)

Bishops of Dunkeld (diocese created 1878)
1878-1887	George Rigg (1814-1887)
1887-1890	vacant
1890-1900	James Smith (1841-1928); created Archbishop of St Andrews and Edinburgh, 1900

Bishops of Dunkeld (cont'd)

1901-1912	Angus Macfarlane (1843-1912)
1913-1914	Robert Fraser (1858-1914)1914-1949 John Toner (1882-1949)
1949-1955	James Scanlan (1899-1976); created Bishop of Motherwell, 1955
1955-1981	William Hart (1904-1992); resigned 1981
1981-	Vincent Logan (1941-)

Bishops of Galloway (diocese created 1878)

1878-1893	John McLachlan (1826-1893)
1893-1914	William Turner (1844-1914)
1914-1943	James McCarthy (1853-1943)
1943-1952	William Mellon (1877-1952)
1952-1981	Joseph McGee (1904-1983); resigned 1981
1981-	Maurice Taylor (1926-)

Bishops of Motherwell (diocese created 1948)

1948-1954	Edward Douglas (1901-1967); resigned 1954
1954-1955	vacant
1955-1964	James Scanlan (1899-1976); created Archbishop of Glasgow, 1964
1964-1982	Francis Thomson (1917-1987); resigned 1982
1982-	Joseph Devine (1937-)

Bishops of Paisley (diocese created 1948)

1948-1968	James Black (1894-1968)
1968-1988	Stephen McGill (1912-); retired 1988
1988-	John Mone (1929-)

MODERATORS OF THE GENERAL ASSEMBLY OF THE CHURCH OF SCOTLAND

The Church of Scotland was established by the Scottish Parliament in 1560 and again in 1690. In its first 140 years, the church alternated between episcopal and presbyterian government, until the presbyterian system was finally settled in 1690, and the Scottish Episcopalian Church broke away.

The Church of Scotland's ruling body is the annual General Assembly, consisting of ministers and elders (church office-holders). A new moderator presides over the assembly every year; the following list shows the office holders for the last 20 years.

Date of taking office	Name
2000	Andrew McLellan (Moderator Designate until the General Assembly in May 2000)
1999	John B. Cairns
1998	Alan Main
1997	Alexander McDonald

Moderators of the General Assembly of the Church of Scotland (cont'd)

Date of taking office	Name
1996	John H. McIndoe
1995	James Harkness
1994	James A. Simpson
1993	James L. Weatherhead
1992	Hugh Wyllie
1991	William B.R. Macmillan
1990	Robert Davidson
1989	William J.G. McDonald
1988	James A. Whyte
1987	Duncan Shaw
1986	Robert Craig
1985	David M.B.A. Smith
1984	John M.K. Paterson
1983	J. Fraser McLuskey
1982	John McIntyre
1981	Andrew B. Doig

SCOTTISH EPISCOPAL CHURCH DIOCESES AND BISHOPS: HOLDERS OF THE OFFICE OF PRIMUS AND THEIR DIOCESES

The General Synod is the governing body of the Scottish Episcopal Church, with representatives voted to it. The bishops choose a convener from among themselves – the Primus. The current primus is Richard Holloway, the Bishop of Edinburgh who is due to retire in October 2000.

Dates of office	Name	Diocese
1704-1720	Alexander Rose	Edinburgh
1720-1727	John Fullarton	Edinburgh
1727	Arthur Millar	Edinburgh
1727-1731	Andrew Lumsden	Edinburgh
1731-1738	David Freebairn	Edinburgh
1738-1743	Thomas Rattray	Dunkeld
1743-1757	Robert Keith	Caithness, Orkney & The Isles
1757-1761	Robert White	Fife
1762-1782	William Falconer	Moray/Edinburgh
1782-1788	Robert Kilgour	Aberdeen
1788-1816	John Skinner	Aberdeen
1816-1837	George Gleig	Brechin
1837-1841	James Walker	Edinburgh
1841-1857	William Skinner	Aberdeen
1857-1862	Charles Terrot	Edinburgh
1862-1886	Robert Eden	Moray, Ross & Caithness
1886-1901	Hugh Jermyn	Brechin

1901-1904	James Kelly	Moray, Ross & Caithness
1904-1907	George Wilkinson	St Andrews, Dunkeld & Dunblane
1908-1934	Walter John Forbes Robberds	Brechin
1935-1943	Arthur John Maclean	Moray, Ross & Caithness
1943-1946	Ernest Denny Logie Danson	Edinburgh
1946-1952	John Charles Halland How	Glasgow & Galloway
1952-1962	Thomas Hannay	Argyll & The Isles
1962-1973	Francis Hamilton Moncreiff	Glasgow & Galloway
1974-1977	Richard Knyvet Wimbush	Argyll & The Isles
1977-1985	Alastair Iain Macdonald Haggart	Edinburgh
1985-1990	Lawrence Edward Luscombe	Brechin
1990-1992	George Kennedy Buchanan Henderson	Argyll & The Isles
1992-2000	Richard Frederick Holloway	Edinburgh

Archbishop Holloway retires early, in October 2000

BISHOPS OF THE SCOTTISH EPISCOPAL CHURCH: 1900-PRESENT DAY

Bishops of Aberdeen and Orkney
(diocese in 1865; formerly two separate diocese)

1883-1905	Arthur Gascoigne Douglas (1827-1905)
1906-1911	Rowland Ellis (1841-1911)
1912-1917	Anthony Mitchell (1868-1917)
1917-1943	Frederic Llewellyn Deane (1868-1952)
1943-1955	Herebert William Hall (1889-1955)
1956-1973	Edward Frederick Easson (1905-1988)
1973-1977	Ian Forbes Begg (1910-1989)
1978-1992	Frederick Charles Darwent (1927-)
1992-	Andrew Bruce Cameron (1941-)

Bishops of Argyll and the Isles
(diocese created in 1847; formerly two separate diocese)

1883-1906	James Robert Alexander Chinnery-Haldane (1842-1906)
1907-1942	Kenneth Mackenzie (1863-1945)
1942-1962	Thomas Hannay (1887-1970)
1963-1977	Richard Knyvet Wimbush (1909-1994)
1977-1992	George Kennedy Buchanan Henderson (1921-1996)
1992-	Douglas Maclean Cameron (1935-)

Bishops of Brechin
(first Bishop of Brechin appointed in 1566)

1876-1903	Hugh Willoughby Jermyn (1820-1903)
1904-1934	Walter John Forbes Robberds (1848-1944)
1935-1943	Kenneth Donald Mackenzie (1878-1966)
1944-1959	Eric Graham (1888-1964)
1959-1975	John Chappell Sprott (1903-1982)
1975-1990	Lawrence Edward Luscombe (1924-)

1990-1996	Robert Taylor Halliday (1932-)
1997-	Neville Chamberlain (1939-)

Bishops of Edinburgh
(first Bishop of Edinburgh appointed in 1634)

1886-1910	John Dowden (1840-1910)
1910-1929	George Henry Somerset Walpole (1854-1929)
1929-1939	Harry Seymour Reid (d. 1945)
1939-1946	Ernest Denny Logie Danson (1880-1946)
1947-1961	Kenneth Charles Harman Warner (1891-1983)
1961-1975	Kenneth Moir Carey (1908-1979)
1975-1985	Alastair Iain Macdonald Haggart (1915-1998)
1986-2000	Richard Frederick Holloway (1933-)

Bishops of Glasgow and Galloway
(diocese created in 1837; formerly two separate diocese. Glasgow was an archdiocese between 1571 and 1724).

1888-1903	William Thomas Harrison (1837-1920)
1904-1921	Archibald Ean Campbell (1856-1921)
1921-1931	Edward Thomas Scott Reid (1871-1938)
1931-1938	John Russell Darbyshire (1880-1948)
1938-1952	John Charles Halland How (1881-1961)
1952-1973	Francis Hamilton Moncreiff (1906-1984)
1974-1980	Frederick Goldie (1914-1980)
1981-1991	Derek Alec Rawcliffe (1921-)
1991-1998	John Mitchell Taylor (1932-)
1998-	Idris Jones (1943-)

Bishops of Moray, Ross and Caithness
(diocese created in 1864; formerly three separate diocese)

1886-1904	James Butler Knill Kelly (1832-1907)
1904-1943	Arthur John Maclean (1858-1943)
1943-1952	Piers Holt Wilson (d. 1956)
1953-1970	Duncan Macinnes (d. 1970)
1970-1993	George Minshull Sessford (1928-1996)
1994-1998	Gregor Macgregor (1933-)
1999-	John Michael Crook (1940-)

Bishops of St Andrews, Dunkeld and Dunblane
(diocese created in 1837; formerly three separate diocese)

1893-1907	George Howard Wilkinson (1833–1907)
1908-1930	Charles Edward Plumb (1864-1930)
1931-1938	Edward Thomas Scott Reid (1871-1938)
1939-1949	James Lumsden Barkway (1878-1968)
1950-1955	Arnold Brian Burrowes (1891-1963)
1955-1969	John William Alexander Howe (1920-)
1969- 1994	Michael Geoffrey Hare-Duke (1925-)
1995-	Michael Hany George Henley (1938-)

• CHRISTIAN MARTYRS IN SCOTLAND •

EARLY MARTYRS

Kessog a monk and bishop resident at Luss, Dunbartonshire, was murdered c 600.

Donan a monk on the island of Eigg in the Outer Hebrides, was murdered by Picts, 618.

Blathmac a monk on the island of Iona, murdered by Viking raiders, 825.

Ebba abbess of Coldingham, killed by Vikings, c 870.

REFORMED MARTYRS

Patrick Hamilton (c.1504-1528), first martyr of the Scottish Reformation. Appointed titular abbot of Fearn, Ross-shire, in 1517. Ordained priest, 1526. Married 1527. Charged by Archbishop James Beaton of St Andrews with teaching Lutheran heresy in 1528, found guilty and burnt at the stake.

Henry Forrest (d. 1533) from Linlithgow. Executed for heresy at St Andrews.

Norman Gourlay (d. 1534) Executed for heresy at Edinburgh.

David Straiton (d. 1534) from Woodstone. Excommunicated for non-payment of the tithes. Indicted for heresy, found guilty and burnt at Edinburgh.

Thomas Forret (d. 1539). Executed for heresy at Castle Hill, Edinburgh.

Duncan Simson (d. 1539). Executed for heresy at Castle Hill, Edinburgh.

John Kyllour (d. 1539) Dominican friar and playwright. Charged with heresy, found guilty and executed at Castle Hill, Edinburgh.

John Beveridge (d. 1539) Dominican friar. Indicted for heresy and executed at Castle Hill, Edinburgh.

Robert Forster (d. 1539) Executed at Castle Hill, Edinburgh.

Jerome Russell (d. 1539). Franciscan monk charged with heresy. Executed at Glasgow.

Thomas Kennedy from Ayr. Executed at Glasgow.

George Wishart (c.1510-1546). Charged with heresy while a schoolmaster in Montrose, 1538. Lived in Germany, Switzerland and England, 1538-43. Preached the doctrines of the Reformation in Scotland, 1543-46. Charged by Cardinal David Beaton with heresy, found guilty and burnt at the stake, 1546.

Walter Milne (d. 1558). Last of the Protestant pre-Reformation martyrs. Executed 1558.

POST-REFORMATION CATHOLIC MARTYRS

Father Robeson (d. 1574) hanged at Glasgow, 1574, for saying Mass.

John Ogilvie (c 1579-1615). A convert to Catholicism, he entered the Jesuit college at Olmutz, Bohemia, in 1598. Returned to Scotland, 1613, working as a priest mainly in the north east and Edinburgh. Captured in Glasgow, 1614. Found guilty of treason and hanged at Glasgow Cross, 1615. Beatified in 1929 and canonised (recognised as a saint) in 1976.

There were also the following politico-religious Catholic martyrs, executed arguably because of their unpopular or unwise secular policies rather than their religion:

David Beaton (c.1494-1546) Politically unpopular Cardinal, assassinated at St Andrews by followers of the martyred reformer George Wishart.

John Hamilton (c.1512-1571) Marian, Lutheran-inclined Archbishop of St Andrews, executed at Stirling.

Mary, Queen of Scots (1542-1587). Queen 1542-1567. Forced to abdicate, Mary fled Scotland in 1568 seeking refuge with her cousin, Elizabeth I of England. Imprisoned in England for 19 years. Executed at Fotheringay Castle, Northamptonshire, 1587, for allegedly plotting against Elizabeth.

• RELIGIOUS HOUSES IN SCOTLAND BEFORE THE REFORMATION (1560) •

MONKS

Benedictine: Coldingham, Dunfermline, Iona, Pluscarden
Cluniac: Crossraguel, Paisley
Tiron: Arbroath, Kelso, Kilwinning, Lesmahagow, Lindores
Cistercian: Balmerino, Beauly, Coupar Angus, Culross, Deer, Dundrennan, Glenluce, Kinloss, Melrose, Newbattle, Sweetheart
Valliscaulian: Ardchattan
Carthusian: Perth

REGULAR CANONS

Augustinian: Blantyre, Cambuskenneth, Holyrood, Inchaffray, Inchcolm, Inchmahome, Jedburgh, Monymusk, Portmoak, Pittenweem, St Andrews, Scone
Premonstratensian: Dryburgh, Fearn, Holywood, Soulseat, Tongland, Whithorn
Trinitarian: Aberdeen, Dirleton, Fail, Peebles, Scotlandwell

MENDICANT FRIARS

Dominican: Aberdeen, Ayr, Dundee, Edinburgh, Elgin, Glasgow, Inverness, Montrose, Perth, St Andrews, Stirling, Wigtown
Franciscan: Aberdeen, Ayr, Dumfries, Dundee, Edinburgh, Elgin, Glasgow, Haddington, Inverkeithing, Kirkcudbright, Lanark, Perth, St Andrews, Stirling
Carmelite: Aberdeen, Banff, Edinburgh, Inverbervie, Irvine, Kingussie, Linlithgow, Luffness, Queensferry, Tullilum

NUNNERIES

Cistercian: Coldstream, Eccles, Elcho, Haddington, Manuel, North Berwick, St Bothans
Augustinian: Iona
Dominican: Sciennes
Franciscan: Aberdour, Dundee

CATHEDRALS

Secular: Aberdeen, Brechin, Dornoch, Dunblane, Dunkeld, Elgin, Fortrose, Glasgow, Kirkwall, Lismore
Monastic: St Andrews, Whithorn

Source: COWAN, I B and EASSON, D E, *Medieval Religious Houses of Scotland*, Longmans, 1976

• FEAST DAYS OF SCOTTISH SAINTS AND SAINTS ASSOCIATED WITH SCOTLAND •

January
8   St Nathalan, bishop; died c. 678.
9   St Fillan, abbot; died c. 734.
13 St Kentigern (or Mungo), bishop; died 612.

February
1   St Bride of Kildare, abbess, died c.525. Celtic saint, celebrated in Ireland and Scotland.
6   St Baldred, follower of St Kentigern or Mungo, and hermit; died c.608.
18 St Colman, Bishop of Lindisfarne; died 676.
23 St Boisil, abbot of Melrose; died 664.

March
1   St Ennoc, monk; died 625.
    St Monan, missionary; lived in the 7th century.
8   St John Ogilvie, priest and martyr; 1579–1615
    St Duthac, Bishop of Ross; died 1065.
    St Kessoc, bishop; died 560. Kessoc was Scotland's patron saint before Andrew.
17 St Patrick, bishop, Apostle of Ireland; died c. 463. Patrick was believed to have been born at Dumbarton.
20 St Cuthbert, Bishop of Lindisfarne; died 687.
30 St Regulus, missionary; lived in the 4th century.

April
1   St Gilbert, Bishop of Caithness; died 1245.
16 St Magnus Erlendsson; died 1117.
17 St Donan; died 616.

May
12 St Comgall of Bangor and Tiree, monk; died 603.
16 St Brendan the Voyager, sailor and missionary; lived c. 484—577.

June
9   St Columba, abbot and missionary; 521–597. Columba evangelised across the north of Scotland
12 St Ternan, bishop; lived in the 5th century.
25 St Molic (or Moluag), missionary; lived in the 6th century. Molic was a pupil of St Brendan's.

July
1   St Serf, monk; lived in the 6th century. He was tutor to St Kentigern or Mungo.
11 St Drostan, monk; lived in the 7th century.
18 St Thenew, daughter of Loth, King of Lothian, and mother of St Kentigern, later given the nickname Mungo; lived in the 6th century.

August
11 St Blane, bishop; lived in the 6th century.

18 St Inan, missionary; lived in the 9th century.

25 St Ebba the Elder, abbess of Coldingham; died 683.

26 St Ninian, Scotland's first Christian missionary; lived c.400. Ninian was sent out from Rome to convert Scotland, and founded his church and community at Whithorn. From this base he evangelised across the south of Scotland.

27 St Maol Rubha; lived around 640–722.

30 St Fiacre, monk and missionary; lived in the sixth century. A follower of Columba who preached in France; Fiacre is the patron saint of gardeners.

September
1 St Giles, missionary; lived sometime between the 6th and 8th centuries. He went from his native Greece to preach in France; Giles is the patron saint of beggars and blacksmiths, and of the towns of Elgin and Edinburgh.

15 St Mirren, Abbot of Bangor; lived in the 7th century. Mirren is the patron saint of Paisley.

23 St Adamnan, monk and biographer of Columba; c. 624–c. 704.

25 St Barr, Bishop of Cork and missionary; lived in the 6th century. The island of Barra is named after him.

October
7 St Syth, priest or monk; dates unknown.

13 St Comgan, monk; lived in the 8th century.

November
6 St Leonard, Frankish monk; died 560. With St Andrew, he is patron saint of St Andrews.

12 St Machar, monk and missionary; lived in the 6th century. Machar is patron saint of Aberdeen.

13 St Devenick, missionary; lived in the 5th century.

16 St Margaret of Scotland, wife of Malcolm III; c. 1046–1093. Margaret is the secondary patron saint of Scotland.

18 St Fergus, missionary; lived in the 6th century.

30 St Andrew, apostle and martyr; died c. 60. Andrew is the principal patron saint of Scotland. He was crucified for his missionary work on an X-shaped cross that has traditionally formed the Scottish flag. St Regulus brought Andrew's remains out of Constantinople for safe keeping, landing at St Andrews. Andrew was credited with bringing victory in battle to Scots armies. His X-symbol first appeared on the great seal of Scotland in 1286 during the period of uncertainty after Alexander III's death.

December
14 St Drostan, monk; lived in the 6th–7th centuries.

• SECESSIONS FROM AND DISRUPTION OF THE CHURCH OF SCOTLAND •

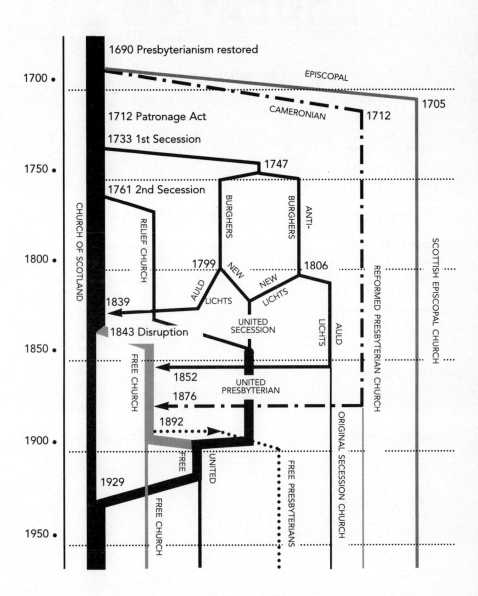

Based on a diagram in JHS Burleigh, *A Church History of Scotland*, 1960

HIGHER EDUCATION

• UNIVERSITIES •

University of Aberdeen
Founded: 1495
Full-time students: approx. 11,000

University of Abertay Dundee
Founded: 1994
Full-time students: approx. 4,000

University of Dundee
Founded: 1967
Full-time students: approx. *8,500*

University of Edinburgh
Founded: 1583
Full-time students: approx. 18,000

University of Glasgow
Founded: 1451
Full-time students: approx. 20,000

Glasgow Caledonian University
Founded: 1993
Full-time students: approx. 8,500

Heriot-Watt University
Founded: 1966
Full-time students: approx. 15,000

Napier University
Founded: 1992
Full-time students: approx. 11,512

University of Paisley
Founded: 1992
Full-time students: approx. 8,500

Robert Gordon University
Founded: 1992
Full-time students: approx. 7 500

The University of St Andrews
Founded: 1411
Full-time students: approx. 6,000

University of Stirling
Founded: 1967
Full-time students: approx. 6,000

University of Strathclyde
Founded: 1964
Full-time students: approx. 16,500

• TERM DAYS •

Candlemas	28 February	Martinmas	28 November
Whitsunday	28 May	Removal Terms	28 May, 28 November
Lammas	28 August		

• UNIVERSITY RECTORS•

UNIVERSITY OF GLASGOW

1965 Lord Reith
1966 Lord MacLeod of Fuinary
1971 Jimmy Reid
1974 Arthur Montford
1977 John Bell
1980 Reginald Bosanquet
1984 Michael Kelly

1987 Winnie Mandela
1990 Pat Kane
1993 Johnny Ball
1996 Richard Wilson
1999 Ross Kemp

UNIVERSITY OF EDINBURGH

1963 James Robertson Justice
1966 Malcolm Muggeridge
1968 Kenneth Allsop
1971 Jonathan Wills
1972 Gordon Brown
1975 Magnus Magnusson
1979 Anthony Ross

1982 David Steel
1985 Archie MacPherson
1988 Muriel Gray
1991 Donnie Munro
1994 Malcolm Macleod
1997 John Colquhoun

UNIVERSITY OF ABERDEEN

1963 Lord Hunt
1966 Frank George Thomson
1969 Jo Grimond
1972 Michael Fieldhouse Barratt
1975 Iain Cuthbertson
1978 Henderson Alexander Gall
1981 Robert John Perryment

1984 Hamish Watt
1987 Willis Pickard
1989 Colin Bell
1992 Ian Hamilton
1997 Allan Macartney
1999 Clarissa Dickson Wright

UNIVERSITY OF DUNDEE

1968 Peter Ustinov
1974 Clement Freud
1980 Rt Hon Lord Mackie of Benshee
1983 Gordon Wilson
1986 Malcolm Bruce

1989 Paul Scott
1992 Stephen Fry
1998 Tony Slattery

UNIVERSITY OF ST ANDREWS

1970 John Cleese
1973 Alan Coren
1976 Frank Muir
1979 Tim Brooke-Taylor
1982 Katharine Whitehorn

1985 Stanley Adams
1988 Nichaolas Parsons
1991 Nicky Campbell
1994 Donald Findlay
1999 Andrew Neil

SPORT

• FOOTBALL •

SCOTTISH LEAGUE CHAMPIONS

1891	Dumbarton/ Rangers	1924	Rangers	1958	Hearts
1892	Dumbarton	1925	Rangers	1959	Rangers
1893	Celtic	1926	Celtic	1960	Hearts
1894	Celtic	1927	Rangers	1961	Rangers
1895	Hearts	1928	Rangers	1962	Dundee
1896	Celtic	1929	Rangers	1963	Rangers
1897	Hearts	1930	Rangers	1964	Rangers
1898	Celtic	1931	Rangers	1965	Kilmarnock
1899	Rangers	1932	Motherwell	1966	Celtic
1900	Rangers	1933	Rangers	1967	Celtic
1901	Rangers	1934	Rangers	1968	Celtic
1902	Rangers	1935	Rangers	1969	Celtic
1903	Hibernian	1936	Celtic	1970	Celtic
1904	Third Lanark	1937	Rangers	1971	Celtic
1905	Celtic	1938	Celtic	1972	Celtic
1906	Celtic	1939	Rangers	1973	Celtic
1907	Celtic	1940	–	1974	Celtic
1908	Celtic	1941	–	1975	Rangers
1909	Celtic	1942	–	1976	Rangers
1910	Celtic	1943	–	1977	Celtic
1911	Rangers	1944	–	1978	Rangers
1912	Rangers	1945	–	1979	Celtic
1913	Rangers	1946	–	1980	Aberdeen
1914	Celtic	1947	Rangers	1981	Celtic
1915	Celtic	1948	Hibernian	1982	Celtic
1916	Celtic	1949	Rangers	1983	Dundee Utd
1917	Celtic	1950	Rangers	1984	Aberdeen
1918	Rangers	1951	Hibernian	1985	Aberdeen
1919	Celtic	1952	Hibernian	1986	Celtic
1920	Rangers	1953	Rangers	1987	Rangers
1921	Rangers	1954	Celtic	1988	Celtic
1922	Celtic	1955	Aberdeen	1989	Rangers
1923	Rangers	1956	Rangers	1990	Rangers
		1957	Rangers	1991	Rangers

1992	Rangers	1996	Rangers	2000	Rangers
1993	Rangers	1997	Rangers	2001	
1994	Rangers	1998	Celtic	2002	
1995	Rangers	1999	Rangers	2003	

SCOTTISH CUP WINNERS

1874	Queen's Park	between	followers of	1946	–
1875	Queen's Park	Celtic	and Rangers	1947	Aberdeen
1876	Queen's Park	1910	Dundee	1948	Rangers
1877	Vale of Leven	1911	Celtic	1949	Rangers
1878	Vale of Leven	1912	Celtic	1950	Rangers
1879	Vale of Leven	1913	Falkirk	1951	Celtic
1880	Queen's Park	1914	Celtic	1952	Motherwell
1881	Queen's Park	1915	–	1953	Rangers
1882	Queen's Park	1916	–	1954	Celtic
1883	Dumbarton	1917	–	1955	Clyde
1884	Queen's Park	1918	–	1956	Hearts
1885	Renton	1919	–	1957	Falkirk
1886	Queen's Park	1920	Kilmarnock	1958	Clyde
1887	Hibernian	1921	Partick Thistle	1959	St Mirren
1888	Renton	1922	Morton	1960	Rangers
1889	Third Lanark	1923	Celtic	1961	Dunfermline
1890	Queen's Park	1924	Airdrie	1962	Rangers
1891	Hearts	1925	Celtic	1963	Rangers
1892	Celtic	1926	St Mirren	1964	Rangers
1893	Queen's Park	1927	Celtic	1965	Celtic
1894	Rangers	1928	Rangers	1966	Rangers
1895	Saint Bernard's	1929	Kilmarnock	1967	Celtic
1896	Hearts	1930	Rangers	1968	Dunfermline
1897	Rangers	1931	Celtic	1969	Celtic
1898	Rangers	1932	Rangers	1970	Aberdeen
1899	Celtic	1933	Celtic	1971	Celtic
		1934	Rangers	1972	Celtic
1900	Celtic	1935	Rangers	1973	Rangers
1901	Hearts	1936	Rangers	1974	Celtic
1902	Hibernian	1937	Celtic	1975	Celtic
1903	Rangers	1938	East Fife	1976	Rangers
1904	Celtic	1939	Clyde	1977	Celtic
1905	Third Lanark	1940	–	1978	Rangers
1906	Hearts	1941	–	1979	Rangers
1907	Celtic	1942	–	1980	Celtic
1908	Celtic	1943	–	1981	Rangers
1909: Cup was with-		1944	–	1982	Aberdeen
held following riots		1945	–	1983	Aberdeen

1984	Aberdeen	1991	Motherwell	1998	Hearts
1985	Celtic	1992	Rangers	1999	Rangers
1986	Aberdeen	1993	Rangers	2000	
1987	St Mirren	1994	Dundee Utd	2001	
1988	Celtic	1995	Celtic	2002	
1989	Celtic	1996	Rangers	2003	
1990	Aberdeen	1997	Kilmarnock	2004	

SENIOR CLUBS

Club	Aberdeen
Nickname	The Dons
Venue	Pittodrie
Largest home crowd	45,061 (v Hearts, 1954)
Trophies	European Cup Winners Cup 1983
	4 championships, 7 Scottish Cups,
	5 League Cups

Club	Airdrie
Nickname	The Diamonds
Venue	Shyberry Excelsior
Largest home crowd	8,762 (v Celtic, 1998)
Trophies	1 Scottish Cup

Club	Albion Rovers
Nickname	The Rovers
Venue	Cliftonhill Stadium
Largest home crowd	27,381 (v Rangers, 1936)

Club	Alloa
Nickname	The Wasps
Venue	Recreation Park
Largest home crowd	13,000 (v Dunfermline, 1939)

Club	Arbroath
Nickname	The Red Lichties
Venue	Gayfield Park
Largest home crowd	13,510 (v Rangers, 1952)

Club	Ayr United
Nickname	The Honest Men
Venue	Somerset Park
Largest home crowd	25,225 (v Rangers, 1969)

Club	Berwick Rangers
Nickname	The Borderers

Venue	Shielfield Park
Largest home crowd	13,365 (v Rangers, 1967)
Club	Brechin City
Nickname	The City
Venue	Glebe Park
Largest home crowd	8,122 (v Aberdeen, 1973)
Club	Celtic
Nickname	The Bhoys
Venue	Celtic Park
Largest home crowd	92,000 (v Rangers, 1954)
Trophies	European Cup Winners 1967
	36 championships, 30 Scottish Cups
	10 League Cups
Club	Clyde
Nickname	The Bully Wee
Venue	Broadwood Stadium
Largest home crowd	52, 000 (v Rangers at Shawfield, 1908)
Trophies	3 Scottish Cups
Club	Clydebank
Nickname	The Bankies
Venue	Share at Boghead
Largest home crowd	14,900 (v Hibs, 1965)
Club	Cowdenbeath
Nickname	The Blue Brazil
Venue	Central Park
Largest home crowd	25,586 (v Rangers, 1949)
Club	Dumbarton
Nickname	The Sons
Venue	Boghead Pak
Largest home crowd	18,000 (v Raith Rovers, 1957)
Trophies	2 championships, 1 Scottish Cup
Club	Dundee
Nickname	The Dark Blues
Venue	Dens Park
Largest home crowd	43,024 (v Rangers, 1953)
Trophies	1 championship, 1 Scottish Cup,
	3 League Cups
Club	Dundee Utd
Nickname	The Arabs
Venue	Tannadice
Largest home crowd	28,000 (v Barcelona, 1966)
Trophies	1 championship, 1 Scottish Cup, 2 League Cups

Club	Dunfermline
Nickname	The Pars
Venue	East End Park
Largest home crowd	27,816 (v Celtic, 1968)
Trophies	2 Scottish Cups

Club	East Fife
Nickname	The Fifers
Venue	New Bayview Park
Largest home crowd	22,515 (v Raith Rovers, 1950)
Trophies	1 Scottish Cup, 3 League Cups

Club	East Stirlingshire
Nickname	The Shire
Venue	Firs Park
Largest home crowd	12,000 (v Partick Thistle, 1921)

Club	Falkirk
Nickname	The Bairns
Venue	Brockville Park
Largest home crowd	23,100 (v Celtic, 1953)
Trophies	2 Scottish Cups

Club	Forfar Athletic
Nickname	The Loons
Venue	Station Park
Largest home crowd	10,780 (v Rangers, 1970)

Club	Hamilton Academicals
Nickname	The Accies
Venue	Share at Firhill
Largest home crowd	28,690 (v Hearts at Douglas Park, 1937)

Club	Heart of Midlothian
Nickname	The Jam Tarts
Venue	Tynecastle
Largest home crowd	53,396 (v Rangers, 1932)
Trophies	4 championships, 6 Scottish Cups 4 League Cups

Club	Hibernian
Nickname	The Hibees
Venue	Easter Road
Largest home crowd	65,860 (v Hearts, 1950)
Trophies	4 championships, 2 Scottish Cups 2 League Cups

Club	Inverness Caledonian Thistle
Nickname	Caley
Venue	Caledonian Stadium

Largest home crowd	5,821 (v Dundee, 1998)
Club	Kilmarnock
Nickname	Killie
Venue	Rugby Park
Largest home crowd	35,995 (v Rangers, 1962)
Trophies	1 championship, 3 Scottish Cups
Club	Livingston
Nickname	Livvy
Venue	Almondvale Stadium
Largest home crowd	4,100 (v East Stirling, 1996)
Club	Montrose
Nickname	The Gables Endies
Venue	Links Park
Largest home crowd	8,983 (v Dundee, 1973)
Club	Morton
Nickname	The Ton
Venue	Cappielow Park
Largest home crowd	23,500 (v Celtic, 1922)
Trophies	1 Scottish Cup
Club	Motherwell
Nickname	The Well
Venue	Fir Park
Largest home crowd	35,632 (v Rangers, 1952)
Trophies	1 championship, 2 Scottish Cups, 1 League Cup
Club	Partick Thistle
Nickname	The Jags
Venue	Firhill Park
Largest home crowd	49,838 (v Rangers, 1922)
Trophies	1 Scottish Cup, 1 League Cup
Club	Queen of the South
Nickname	The Doonhamers
Venue	Palmerston Park
Largest home crowd	24,500 (v Hearts, 1952)
Club	Queen's Park
Nickname	The Spiders
Venue	Hampden Park
Largest home crowd	95,772 (v Rangers, 1930)
Trophies	10 Scottish Cups
Club	Raith Rovers
Nickname	The Rovers
Venue	Stark's Park

Largest home crowd	31,306 (v Hearts, 1953)
Trophies	1 League Cup
Club	Rangers
Nickname	The Gers
Venue	Ibrox Stadium
Largest home crowd	118,567 (v Celtic, 1939)
Trophies	European Cup Winners Cup 1972
	48 championships, 28 Scottish Cups
	21 League Cups
Club	Ross County
Nickname	The County
Venue	Victoria Park
Largest home crowd	8,000 (v Rangers, 1966)
Club	St Johnstone
Nickname	The Saints
Venue	McDiarmid Park
Largest home crowd	10,504 (v Rangers, 1990)
Club	St Mirren
Nickname	The Buddies
Venue	St Mirren Park (Love Street)
Largest home crowd	47,438 (v Celtic, 1925)
Trophies	3 Scottish Cups
Club	Stenhousemuir
Nickname	The Warriors
Venue	Ochilview Park
Largest home crowd	12,500 (v East Fife, 1950)
ClubClub	Stirling Albion
Nickname	The Beanos
Venue	Forthbank Stadium
Largest home crowd	26,400 (v Celtic at Annfield, 1959)
Club	Stranraer
Nickname	The Blue
Venue	Stair Park
Largest home crowd	6,500 (v Rangers, 1948)

WORLD CUP CAMPAIGNS

1958 Sweden

Group 2

	Pld	W	D	L	F	A	Pts
France	3	2	0	1	11	7	4
Yugoslavia	3	1	2	0	7	6	4
Paraguay	3	1	1	1	9	12	3
Scotland	3	0	1	2	4	6	1

8th June 1958, Västeras
Scotland (0) 1 Yugoslavia (1) 1   Scorers: *Murray 47; Petakovic 6*

11th June 1958, Norrköping
Paraguay 3 (2) Scotland 2 (1)   Scorers: *Aguero 3, Re 44, Parodi 74; Mudie 32, Collins 76*

15th June 1958, Örebro
France 2 (2) Scotland 1 (0)   Scorers: *Kopa 22, Fontaine 45; Baird 65*

Scotland and Paraguay were eliminated from the competition.
Brazil won the 1958 World Cup, beating the Sweden 5-2 in the final.

1974 West Germany
Coach: Willie Ormond

Group 2

	Pld	W	D	L	F	A	Pts
Yugoslavia	3	1	2	0	10	1	4
Brazil	3	1	2	0	3	0	4
Scotland	3	1	2	0	3	1	4
Zaïre	3	0	0	3	0	14	0

14th June 1974, Westfalen Stadion, Dortmund
Scotland 2 (0) Zaïre 0 (0)   Scorers: *Lorimer 26, Jordan 33*

18th June 1974, Wald Stadion, Frankfurt
Brazill 0 (0) Scotland 0 (0)

22nd June 1974, Wald Stadion, Frankfurt
Scotland 1 (0) Yugoslavia 1 (0)   Scorers: *Jordan 90; Karasi 81*

Scotland and Zaïre were eliminated from the competition.
West Gemany won the 1974 World Cup, beating the Netherlands 2-1 in the final.

1978 Argentina
Coach: Ally McLeod

Group 4

	Pld	W	D	L	F	A	Pts
Peru	3	2	1	0	7	2	5
Netherlands	3	1	1	1	5	3	3
Scotland	3	1	1	1	5	6	3
Iran	3	0	1	2	2	8	1

3rd June 1978, Estadio Cordoba, Cordoba

Peru 3 (1) Scotland 1 (1)   Scorers: *Cueto 42, Cubillas 70, 76; Jordan 15*

7th June 1978, Estadio Cordoba, Cordoba

Iran 1 (0) Scotland 1 (1)   Scorers: *Danaifar 77; Eskandarian (og) 43*

11th June 1978, Estadio Mendoza, Mendoza

Scotland 3 (1) Netherlands 2 (1)   Scorers: *Dalglish 43, Gemmill (pen) 46, 67;*
Rensenbrink (pen) 34, Rep 71

Scotland and Iran were eliminated from the competition.

Argentina won the 1978 World Cup, beating the Netherlands 3-1 in the final.

1982 Spain
Coach: Jock Stein

Group 6

	Pld	W	D	L	F	A	Pts
Brazil	3	3	0	0	10	2	6
USSR	3	1	1	1	6	4	3
Scotland	3	1	1	1	8	8	3
New Zealand	3	0	0	3	2	12	0

15th June 1982, Estadio La Rosaleda, Malaga

IScotland 5 (3) New Zealand 2 (0)   Scorers: *Dalglish 18, Wark 29, 32, Robertson 73*
Archibald 80; Sumner 55, Wooddin 65

18th June 1982, Estadio Benito Villamarin, Seville

Brazil 4 (1) Scotland 1 (1) Scorers: *Zico 33, Oscar 48, Eder 64, Falcao 86; Narey 18*

22nd June 1982, Estadio La Rosaleda, Malaga

Scotland 2 (1) USSR 2 (0) Scorers: *Jordan 15, Souness 87; Chivadze 60, Shengelia 84*

Scotland and New Zealand were eliminated from the competition.

Italy won the 1982 World Cup, beating West Germany 3-1 in the final.

1986 Mexico
Coach: Alex Ferguson

Group E

	Pld	W	D	L	F	A	Pts
Denmark	3	3	0	0	9	1	6
West Germany	3	1	1	1	3	4	3
Uruguay	3	0	2	1	2	7	2
Scotland	3	0	1	2	1	3	1

4th June 1986, Estadio Neza '86, Nezahualcoyotl
Denmark 1 (0) Scotland 0 (0)   Scorers: *Elkjær-Larsen 58*

8th June 1986, Estadio La Corregidora, Queretaro
West Germany 2 (1) Scotland 1 (1) Scorers: *Völler 22, Allofs 50; Strachan 17*

13th June 1986, Estadio Neza '86, Nezahualcoyotl
Scotland 0 (0) Uruguay 0 (0)

Uruguay joined Denmark and West Germany in the next round as one of the four best third place teams. Scotland were eliminated from the competition.
Argentina won the 1986 World Cup, beating West Germany 3-2 in the final..

1990 Italy
Coach: Andy Roxburgh

Group C

	Pld	W	D	L	F	A	Pts
Brazil	3	3	0	0	4	1	6
Costa Rica	3	2	0	1	3	2	4
Scotland	3	1	0	2	2	3	2
Sweden	3	0	0	3	3	6	0

11th June 1990, Stadio Luigi Ferraris, Genoa
Costa Rica 1 (0) Scotland 0 (0)   Scorers: *Cayasso 50*

16th June 1990, Stadio Luigi Ferraris, Genoa
Scotland 2 (1) Sweden 1 (0) Scorers: *McCall 10, Johnston (pen) 83; Strömberg 85*

20th June 1990, Stadio Delle Alpi, Turin
Brazil 1 (0) Scotland 0 (0)   Scorer: *Müller 82*

Scotland and Sweden were eliminated from the competition.
West Germany won the 1990 World Cup, beating Argentina 1-0 in the final.

1998 France
Coach: Craig Brown

Group A

	Pld	W	D	L	F	A	Pts
Brazil	3	2	0	1	6	3	6
Norway	3	1	2	0	5	4	5
Morocco	3	1	1	1	5	5	4
Scotland	3	0	1	2	2	6	

10th June 1998, Stade de France, St Denis
Brazil 2 (1) Scotland 1 (1)   Scorers: *Sampaio 4, Boyd (og) 73; Collins (pen) 38*

16th June 1998, Stade Lescure, Bordeaux
Scotland 1 (0) Norway 1 (0) Scorers: *Burley 66; H Flo 46*

23rd June 1998, Stade Geoffroy Guichard, Saint-Etienne
Morocco 3 (1) Scotland 0 (0)   Scorer: *Bassir 22, 85, Hadda 47*

Morocco and Scotland were eliminated from the competition.
France won the 1998 World Cup, beating Brazil 3-0 in the final.

• GOLF •

BRITISH OPEN CHAMPIONSHIP COURSES IN SCOTLAND

Course	*Year*
Carnoustie	1931, 1937, 1953, 1968, 1975, 1999
Muirfield	1892, 1896, 1901, 1906, 1912, 1929, 1935, 1948, 1959, 1966, 1972, 1980, 1987, 1992
Musselburgh	1874, 1877, 1880, 1883, 1886, 1889
Prestwick	1860-72, 1875, 1878, 1881, 1884, 1887, 1890, 1893, 1898. 1903, 1908, 1914, 1925
St Andrews	1873, 1876, 1879, 1882, 1885, 1888, 1891, 1895, 1900, 1905, 1910, 1921, 1927, 1933, 1939, 1946, 1955, 1957, 1960, 1964, 1978, 1984, 1995, 2000
Troon	1923, 1950, 1962, 1970, 1973, 1982, 1989, 1990, 1997
Turnberry	1977, 1986, 1994

• HORSE RACING •

SCOTTISH GRAND NATIONAL WINNERS AND VENUES SINCE 1900

1900 Dorothy Vane at Bogside	1940 No race
1901 Big Busbie at Bogside	-46
1902 Canter Home at Bogside	1947 Rowland Roy at Bogside
1903 Chit Chat at Bogside	1948 Magnetic Fin at Bogside
1904 Innismacsaint at Bogside	1949 Wot No Sun at Bogside
1905 Theodocian at Bogside	1950 Sanvina at Bogside
1906 Creolin at Bogside	1951 Court Painter at Bogside
1907 Barney III at Bogside	1952 Flagrant Mac at Bogside
1908 Atrato at Bogside	1953 Queen's Taste at Bogside
1909 Mount Prospect's Fortune	1954 Queen's Taste at Bogside
at Bogside	1955 Bar Point at Bogside
1910 The Duffrey at Bogside	1956 Queen's Taste at Bogside
1911 Couvrefeu II at Bogside	1957 Bremontier at Bogside
1912 Couvrefeu II at Bogside	1958 Game Field at Bogside
1913 Couvrefeu II at Bogside	1959 Merryman II at Bogside
1914 Scarabec at Bogside	1960 Fincham at Bogside
1915 Templedowney at Bogside	1961 Kinmont Wullie at Bogside
1916 No race	1962 Sham Fight at Bogside
1917 No race	1963 Pappageno's Cottage at
1918 No race	Bogside
1919 The Turk at Bogside	1964 Popham Down at Bogside
1920 Music Hall at Bogside	1965 Brasher at Bogside
1921 Race abandoned	1966 African Patrol at Ayr
1922 Sergeant Murphy at Bogside	1967 The Fossa at Ayr
1923 Harrismith at Bogside	1968 Arcturus at Ayr
1924 Royal Chancellor at Bogside	1969 Playlord at Ayr
1925 Gerald L at Bogside	1970 The Spaniard at Ayr
1926 Estuna at Bogside	1971 Young Ash Leaf at Ayr
1927 Estuna at Bogside	1972 Quick Replay at Ayr
1928 Aedeen at Bogside	1973 Esban at Ayr
1929 Donzelon at Bogside	1974 Red Rum at Ayr
1930 Drintyre at Bogside	1975 Barona at Ayr
1931 Annandale at Bogside	1976 Barona at Ayr
1932 Clydesdale at Bogside	1977 Sebastian V at Ayr
1933 Libourg at Bogside	1978 King Con at Ayr
1934 Southern Hero at Bogside	1979 Fighting Fit at Ayr
1935 Kellsboro' Jack at Bogside	1980 Salkeld at Ayr
1936 Southern Hero at Bogside	1981 Astral Charmer at Ayr
1937 Right'un at Bogside	1982 Cockle Strand at Ayr
1938 Young Mischief at Bogside	1983 Canton at Ayr
1939 Southern Hero at Bogside	1984 Androma at Ayr

1985 Androma at Ayr
1986 Hardy Lad at Ayr
1987 Little Polveir at Ayr
1988 Mighty Mark at Ayr
1989 Roll-a-Joint at Ayr
1990 Four Trix at Ayr
1991 Killone Abbey at Ayr
1992 Captain Dibble at Ayr
1993 Run For Free at Ayr
1994 Earth Summit at Ayr

1995 Willsford at Ayr
1996 Moorcroft Boy at Ayr
1997 Belmont King at Ayr
1998 Baronet at Ayr
1999 Young Kenny at Ayr
2000

• RUGBY •

The Five Nations Championship

The International Championship, later known as the "Five Nations", began in 1882. Scotland, England, Ireland and Wales were joined by France between 1910 and 1937, the French rejoining in 1947. Civil unrest in Ireland in 1972 prevented the completion of the championship. The "Five Nations" became the "Six Nations" in 2000, with the entry of Italy to the competition.

The Calcutta Cup

Points were introduced in 1890. Winners of Scotland v England prior to 1890 are underlined.

The Grand Slam

Wales completed the first Grand Slam in 1908, defeating all opponents in the competition. Scotland's first Grand Slam was in 1925.

1871
Raeburn Place
Sco: 1 Goal 1 Try, Eng: 1 Try

1872
Kennington Oval
Eng: 1 Goal 1 Dropped Goal, 2 Tries, Sco: 1 Dropped Goal

1873
Hamilton Crescent – no scoring

1874
Kennington Oval
Eng: 1 Dropped Goal, Sco: 1 Try

1875
Raeburn Place – no scoring

1876
Kennington Oval
Eng: 1 Goal 1 Try, Sco: 0

1877
Raeburn Place
Sco: 1 Dropped Goal, Eng: 0

1878
Kennington Oval – no scoring

1879
Raeburn Place – draw
Sco: 1 Dropped Goal, Eng: 1 Goal

1880
Manchester
Eng: 2 Goals 3 Tries, Sco: 1 Goal

1881
Raeburn Plac – draw
Sco: 1 Goal 1 Try
Eng: 1 Dropped Goal 1 Try

1882
Manchester
Eng: 0, Sco: 2 Tries
Five Nations: England

1883
Raeburn Place
Sco: 1 Try, Eng: 2 Tries
Five Nations: England

1884
Blackheath
Eng: 1 Goal, Sco: 1 Try
Five Nations: none

1885
no match
Five Nations: none

1886
Raeburn Place – no scoring
Five Nations: Scotland

1887
Manchester – draw
Eng: 1 Try, Sco: 1 Try
Five Nations: Scotland

1888
no match
Five Nations: none

1889
no match
Five Nations: none

1890
Raeburn Place
Sco: 0, Eng: 1 Goal 1 Try (6 points)
Five Nations: England/Scotland

1891
Richmond
Eng 4, Sco 11
Five Nations: Scotland

1892
Raeburn Place
Sco 0, Eng 5
Five Nations: England

1893
Headingley
Eng 0, Sco 8
Five Nations: Wales

1894
Raeburn Place
Sco 6, Eng 0
Five Nations: Ireland

1895
Richmond
Eng 3, Sco 6
Five Nations: Scotland

1896
Hampden Park
Sco 11, Eng 0
Five Nations: Ireland

1897
Manchester
Eng 12, Sco 3
Five Nations: none

1898
Edinburgh
Sco 3, Eng 3
Five Nations: none

1899
Blackheath
Eng 0, Sco 5
Five Nations: Ireland

1900
Inverleith
Sco 0, Eng 0
Five Nations: Wales

1901
Blackheath
Eng 3, Sco 18
Five Nations: Scotland

1902
Inverleith
Sco 3, Eng 6
Five Nations: Wales

1903
Richmond
Eng 6, Sco 10
Five Nations: Scotland

1904
Inverleith
Sco 6, Eng 3
Five Nations: Scotland

1905
Richmond
Eng 0, Sco 8
Five Nations: Wales

1906
Inverleith
Scot 3, Eng 9
Five Nations: Ireland/Wales

1907
Blackheath
Eng 3, Sco 8
Five Nations: Scotland

1908
Inverleith
Sco 16, Eng 10
Five Nations: Wales – Grand Slam

1909
Richmond
Eng 8, Sco 18
Five Nations: Wales – Grand Slam

1910
Inverleith
Sco 5, Eng 14
Five Nations: England

1911
Twickenham
Eng 13, Sco 8
Five Nations: Wales – Grand Slam

1912
Inverleith
Sco 8, Eng 3
Five Nations: England/Ireland

1913
Twickenham
Eng 3, Sco 0
Five Nations: England – Grand Slam

1914
Inverleith
Sco 15, Eng 16
Five Nations: England – Grand Slam

1915
no game
Five Nations: none

1916
no game
Five Nations: none

1917
no game
Five Nations: none

1918
no game
Five Nations: none

1919
no game
Five Nations: none

1920
Twickenham
Eng 13, Sco 4
Five Nations: England/Scotland/Wales

1921
Inverleith
Sco 0, Eng 18
Five Nations: England – Grand Slam

1922
Twickenham
Eng 11, Sco 5
Five Nations: Wales

1923
Inverleith
Sco 6, Eng 8
Five Nations: England – Grand Slam

1924
Twickenham
Eng 19, Sco 0
Five Nations: England – Grand Slam

1925
Murrayfield
Sco 14, Eng 11
Five Nations: Scotland – Grand Slam

1926
Twickenham
Eng 9, Sco 17
Five Nations: Ireland/Scotland

1927
Murrayfield
Sco 21, Eng 13
Five Nations: Ireland/Scotland

1928
Twickenham
Eng 6, Sco 0
Five Nations: England – Grand Slam

1929
Murrayfield
Sco 12, Eng 6
Five Nations: Scotland

1930
Twickenham
Eng 0, Sco 0
Five Nations: England

1931
Murrayfield
Scot 28, Eng 19
Five Nations: Wales

1932
Twickenham
Eng 16, Sco 3
Five Nations: England/Ireland/Wales

1933
Murrayfield
Sco 3 Eng 0
Five Nations: Scotland

1934
Twickenham
Eng 6, Sco 3
Five Nations: England

1935
Murrayfield
Sco 10, Eng 7
Five Nations: Ireland

1936
Twickenham
Eng 9, Sco 8
Five Nations: Wales

1937
Murrayfield
Sco 3, Eng 6
Five Nations: England

1938
Twickenham
Eng 16, Sco 21
Five Nations: Scotland

1939
Murrayfield
Sco 6, Eng 9
Five Nations: England/Ireland/Wales

1940
no game
Five Nations: none

1941
no game
Five Nations: none

1942
no game
Five Nations: none

1943
no game
Five Nations: none

1944
no game
Five Nations: none

1945
no game
Five Nations: none

1946
no game
Five Nations: none

1947
Twickenham
Eng 24, Sco 5
Five Nations: England/Wales

1948
Murrayfield
Scot 6, Eng 3
Five Nations: Ireland – Grand Slam

1949
Twickenham
Eng 19, Sco 3
Five Nations: Ireland

1950
Murrayfield
Scot 13, Eng 11
Five Nations: Wales – Grand Slam

1951
Twickenham
Eng 5, Sco 3
Five Nations: Ireland

1952
Murrayfield
Sco 3, Eng 19
Five Nations: Wales – Grand Slam

1953
Twickenham
Eng 26, Sco 8
Five Nations: England

1954
Murrayfield
Sco 3, Eng 13
Five Nations: England/France/Wales

1955
Twickenham
Sco 6, Eng 9
Five Nations: France/Wales

1956
Murrayfield
Scot 6, Eng 11
Five Nations: Wales

1957
Twickenham
Eng 16, Sco 3
Five Nations: England – Grand Slam

1958
Murrayfield
Sco 3, Eng 3
Five Nations: England

1959
Twickenham
Eng 3, Sco 3
Five Nations: France

1960
Murrayfield
Sco 12, Eng 21
Five Nations: England/France

1961
Twickenham
Eng 6, Sco 0
Five Nations: France

1962
Murrayfield
Sco 3 Eng 3
Five Nations: France

1963
Twickenham
Eng 10, Sco 8
Five Nations: England

1964
Murrayfield
Sco 15, Eng 6
Five Nations: Scotland/Wales

1965
Twickenham
Eng 3, Sco 3
Five Nations: Wales

1966
Murrayfield
Scot 6, Eng 3
Five Nations: Wales

1967
Twickenham
Eng 27, Sco 14
Five Nations: France

1968
Murrayfield
Sco 6, Eng 8
Five Nations: France – Grand Slam

1969
Twickenham
Eng 8, Sco 3
Five Nations: Wales

1970
Murrayfield
Sco 14, Eng 5
Five Nations: France/Wales

1971
Twickenham
Eng 15, Sco 16
Murrayfield
Sco 26, Eng 6
Five Nations: Wales – Grand Slam

1972
Murrayfield
Sco 23, Eng 9
Five Nations: none

1973
Twickenham
Eng 20, Sco 13
Five Nations: Engl/Fra/Ire/Sco/Wal

1974
Murrayfield
Sco 16, Eng 14
Five Nations: Ireland

1975
Twickenham
Eng 7, Sco 6
Five Nations: Wales

1976
Murrayfield
Eng 12, Sco 22
Five Nations: Wales – Grand Slam

1977
Twickenham
Eng 26, Sco 6
Five Nations: France – Grand Slam

1978
Murrayfield
Sco 0, Eng 15
Five Nations: Wales – Grand Slam

1979
Twickenham
Eng 7, Sco 7
Five Nations: Wales

1980
Murrayfield
Sco 18, Eng 30
Five Nations: England – Grand Slam

1981
Twickenham
Eng 23, Sco 17
Five Nations: France – Grand Slam

1982
Murrayfield
Sco 9, Eng 9
Five Nations: Ireland

1983
Twickenham
Eng 12, Sco 22
Five Nations: France/Ireland

1984
Murrayfield
Sco 18, Eng 6
Five Nations: Scotland – Grand Slam

1985
Twickenham
Eng 10, Sco 7
Five Nations: Ireland

1986
Murrayfield
Sco 33, Eng 6
Five Nations: France/Scotland

1987
Twickenham
Eng 21, Sco 12
Five Nations: France – Grand Slam

1988
Murrayfield
Sco 6, Eng 9
Five Nations: France/Wales

1989
Twickenham
Eng 12, Sco 12
Five Nations: France

1990
Murrayfield
Sco 13, Eng 7
Five Nations: Scotland – Grand Slam

1991
Twickenham
Eng 21, Sco 12
Murrayfield (World Cup)
Sco 6, Eng 9
Five Nations: England – Grand Slam

1992
Murrayfield
Sco 7, Eng 25
Five Nations: England – Grand Slam

1993
Twickenham
Eng 26, Sco 12
Five Nations: France

1994
Murrayfield
Sco 14, Eng 15
Five Nations: Wales

1995
Twickenham
Eng 24, Sco 12
Five Nations: England – Grand Slam

1996
Murrayfield
Sco 9, Eng 18
Five Nations: England

1997
Twickenham
Eng 41, Sco 13
Five Nations: France – Grand Slam

1998
Murrayfield
Sco 20, Eng 34
Five Nations: France – Grand Slam

1999
Twickenham
Eng 24, Sco 21
Five Nations: Scotland

2000
Twickenham

• SHINTY •

1896	Kingussie	1933	Oban	1970	Newtonmore
1897	Beauly	1934	Caberfeidh	1971	Newtonmore
1898	Beauly	1935	Kyles Athletic	1972	Newtonmore
1899	Ballachulish	1936	Newtonmore	1973	Glasgow Mid
1900	Kingussie	1937	Oban Celtic		Argyll
1901	Ballachulish	1938	Oban at Oban	1974	Kyles Athletic
1902	Kingussie	1939	Caberfeidh	1975	Newtonmore
1903	Kingussie	1940	-	1976	Kyles Athletic
1904	Kyles Athletic	1941	-	1977	Newtonmore
1905	Kyles Athletic	1942	-	1978	Newtonmore
1906	Kyles Athletic	1943	-	1979	Newtonmore
1907	Newtonmore	1944	-	1980	Kyles Athletic
1908	Newtonmore	1945	-	1981	Newtonmore
1909	Newtonmore	1946	-	1982	Newtonmore
1910	Newtonmore	1947	Newtonmore	1983	Kyles Athletic
1911	Ballachulish	1948	Newtonmore	1984	Kingussie
1912	Ballachulish	1949	Oban Celtic	1985	Newtonmore
1913	Beauly	1950	Newtonmore	1986	Newtonmore
1914	Kingussie	1951	Newtonmore	1987	Kingussie
1915	-	1952	Inverness	1988	Kingussie
1916	-	1953	Lovat	1989	Kingussie
1917	-	1954	Oban Celtic	1990	Skye
1918	-	1955	Newtonmore	1991	Kingussie
1919	-	1956	Kyles Athletic	1992	Fort William
1920	Kyles Athletic	1957	Newtonmore	1993	Kingussie
1921	Kingussie	1958	Newtonmore	1994	Fort William
1922	Kyles Athletic	1959	Newtonmore	1995	Kingussie
1923	Furnace	1960	Oban Celtic	1996	Kingussie
1924	Kyles	1961	Kingussie	1997	Kingussie
1925	Inverary	1962	Kyles Athletic	1998	Kingussie
1926	Inverary	1963	Oban Celtic	1999	Kingussie
1927	Kyles Athletic	1964	Kilmallie	2000	
1928	Kyles Athletic	1965	Kyles Athletic	2001	
1929	Newtonmore	1966	Kyles Athletic	2002	
1930	Inverary	1967	Newtonmore	2003	
1931	Newtonmore	1968	Kyles Athletic	2004	
1932	Newtonmore	1969	Kyles Athletic	2005	

• COMMONWEALTH GAMES •

SCOTTISH GOLD MEDAL WINNERS

Athletics

	Venue	Winner	Event
1930	Hamilton, Canada	Duncan Wright	Marathon
1934	London	Alan Hunter	440 yds hurdles
1950	Auckland	Duncan Clark	Hammer
1954	Vancouver	Joseph McGhee	Marathon
1966	Kingston, Jamaica	Jim Alder	Marathon
1970	Edinburgh	Rosemary Payne	Discus
1970	Edinburgh	Ian Stewart	5,000 m
1970	Edinburgh	Lachie Stewart	10,000 m
1970	Edinburgh	Rosemary Stirling	800 m
1978	Edmonton	Scotland team	4 x 100 m relay
1978	Edmonton	Allan Wells	200 m
1982	Brisbane	Margaret Ritchie	Discus
1982	Brisbane	Allan Wells	100 m
1982	Brisbane	Allan Wells	200 m
1986	Edinburgh	Liz Lynch	10,000 m
1990	Auckland	Liz McColgan	10,000 m
1994	Victoria, Canada	Yvonne Murray	10,000 m

Badminton

	Venue	Winner	Event
1986	Edinburgh	Billy Gilliland & Dan Travers	Men's doubles

Bowls

	Venue	Winner	Event
1934	London	Robert Sprot	Men's singles
1974	Christchurch, NZ	John Christie & Alex McIntosh	Men's doubles
1982	Brisbane	John Watson & David Gourlay	Men's doubles
1982	Brisbane	William Wood	Men's singles
1986	Edinburgh	George Adrain & Grant Knox	Men's doubles
1990	Auckland	Scotland	Men's fours
1994	Victoria, Canada	Richard Corsie	Men's singles
1994	Victoria, Canada	Sarah Gourlay & Frances White	Women's doubles
1998	Kuala Lumpur	Joyce Lindores & Margaret Letham	Women's doubles

Boxing

	Venue	Winner	Event
1930	Hamilton, Canada	James Rolland	Lightweight (60 kg)
1950	Auckland	Henry Gilliland	Featherweight (57 kg)
1950	Auckland	Hugh Riley	Flyweight (51 kg)
1954	Vancouver	Richard Currie	Flyweight (51 kg)
1954	Vancouver	John Smillie	Bantamweight (54 kg)
1958	Cardiff	Jackie Brown	Flyweight (51 kg)
1958	Cardiff	Dick McTaggart	Lightweight (60 kg)
1962	Perth, Australia	Robert Mallon	Flyweight (51 kg)
1962	Perth, Australia	John McDermott	Featherweight (57 kg)
1970	Edinburgh	Tom Imrie	Light-Middleweight (71 kg)
1990	Auckland	Charlie Kane	Light-Welterweight (63.5 kg)
1994	Victoria, Canada	Paul Shepherd	Flyweight (51 kg)
1998	Kuala Lumpur	Alex Arthur	Featherweight (57 kg)

Fencing

	Venue	Winner	Event
1962	Perth, Australia	Alexander Leckie	Men's foil
1970	Edinburgh	Alexander Leckie	Men's sabre

Judo

	Venue	Winner	Event
1990	Auckland	Loretta Cusack	Women – 56 kg

Shooting

	Venue	Winner	Event
1978	Edmonton	Alister Allan	Small bore rifle
1982	Brisbane	Alister Allan	Small bore rifle – 3 positions
1982	Brisbane	Alister Allan & Bill McNeil	Air rifle – pairs

Shooting

	Venue	Winner	Event
1982	Brisbane	Arthur Clarke	Full bore rifle
1990	Auckland	Ian Marsden & James Dunlop	Open skeet – pairs
1994	Victoria, Canada	Shirley McIntosh	Women: small bore rifle, prone

Squash

	Venue	Winner	Event
1998	Kuala Lumpur	Peter Nicol	Men's singles

Swimming and Diving

	Venue	Winner	Event
1934	London	Norman Hamilton	200 yds breaststroke
1934	London	Willie Francis	100 yds backstroke
1950	Auckland	Elenor Gordon	220 yds breaststroke
1950	Auckland	Peter Heatly	Highboard diving
1954	Vancouver	Elenor Gordon	220 yds breaststroke
1954	Vancouver	Peter Heatly	Springboard diving
1954	Vancouver	Scotland team	3 x 110 yds medley relay
1958	Cardiff	Ian Black	220 yds butterfly
1958	Cardiff	Peter Heatly	Highboard diving
1974	Christchurch, NZ	David Wilkie	200 m breaststroke
1974	Christchurch, NZ	David Wilkie	200 m individual medley

Wrestling

	Venue	Winner	Event
1934	London	Edward Melrose	Bantamweight 57 kg

EVENTS AND FESTIVALS

• TRADITIONAL SCOTTISH FESTIVALS •

A CALENDAR

JANUARY

1 January
New Year's Day, or Ne'erday Long-celebrated and increasingly popular festival. It traditionally involved first footing: visiting neighbours, family and friends – preferably as soon as possible after the 'bells' at midnight.

Orkney Ba' Games Old-style, uninhibited football games held in Kirkwall, Orkney, between the Uppies and the Doonies, depending what part of the town someone comes from.

First Monday in January
Handsel Monday Traditionally when handsel (usually a gift of money) was given to servants by employers.

5/6 January
Auld Yule & Uphalieday Traditional celebrations of Twelfth Night and the Epiphany. Celebrations varied around the country, from burning evergreen leaves to eating special celebration cakes.

11 January
Burning of the Clavie One of the traditional Celtic winter fire festivals and a throwback to ancient Pictish celebrations; at Burghead in Moray.

Last Tuesday in January
Up-helly-Aa Another traditional fire-festival, this time of Norse origin, celebrating Shetland's Nordic heritage. Lerwick hosts masquerades, guising and a full-dress torchlit procession, culminating in the burning of a Viking galley.

25 January
Burns Night Celebration of the birth of the national bard Robert Burns. Burns Suppers usually feature haggis with whisky, and recitations of his poetry.

FEBRUARY

2 February
Candlemas Day Like the Romans, the Celts regarded February as the start of spring. Candlemas Day was originally a Roman festival, then the feast of the Purification of the Virgin, celebrated with pageants and religious plays. Now it is one of the legal

'Quarter Days', when rents and other duties must be paid. Schoolchildren also traditionally gave their teachers gifts on this day.

14 February
St Valentine's Day Celebrated in Scotland as all over Europe. Young unmarried people drew names written on pieces of paper to see who their sweetheart would be for the coming year.

MARCH

1 March
Whuppity Scoorie A traditional springtime festival said to chase away evil spirits, it mainly involved running fights between the young men of Lanark and David Dale's New Lanark village.

Tuesday before Ash Wednesday
Fastern's E'en Scots Mardi Gras, or Shrove Tuesday, when all the meat, butter and fat in the house were used up before the fasting of Lent.

APRIL

1 April
Hunt the Gowk Traditional April Fool's practical jokes and pranks were played, usually involving sending someone on a false, or fool's errand. A gowk was a cuckoo, a bird associated with foolery.

2 April
Tailie Day or Preen-tail Day The practical jokes continued as paper tails were attached to unsuspecting victims.

Easter An ancient pagan festival of the spring equinox was superceded by the Christian celebration. The recognisable Easter customs – painted egg-rolling, making hot-cross buns – were also celebrated in Scotland; they have now been joined by the more recent arrivals of chocolate eggs and the Easter Bunny.

MAY

1 May
Beltane Another ancient pagan fire festival, this time celebrating May Day and the approach of summer. Bonfires were lit on hilltops all across Scotland.

15 May
Whitsunday Seventh Sunday after Easter, this was the second of the Scottish 'Quarter Days'. It always falls on the same day, unlike Whit Sunday, or Pentecost, on the seventh Sunday after Easter.

25 May
Flitting Day Most Scots rented their houses by annual lease, and this was the day the leases expired.

JUNE

Riding the Marches The traditional Borders riding festivals, dating from the time when the border needed policing to prevent encroachment, start in June and carry on during the summer. Most Borders towns have their own.

Highland Games These also traditionally begin in June, with many towns having their events throughout the summer (see p. 204). Scottish Highland Games normally include piping, traditional dancing, tossing the caber and throwing the hammer, or some other weight.

Mid June

Guid Nychburris Celebrating the town of Dumfries and intended to encourage neighbourliness among its inhabitants. The week-long festival features the crowning of the Queen of the South.

17 June

Lanimer Day Traditional festival held in Lanark sees houses bedecked in greenery, and a fair in the town centre.

JULY

Last two weeks

Glasgow Fair Most Scots towns have a summer fortnight traditionally regarded as a local-holiday period, but Glasgow's is the oldest – dating from the 12th century – and still the most popular.

AUGUST

1 August

Lammas Third of the 'Quarter Days'. It marked the start of autumn and the harvest season, and festivals and fairs were held across the country. It was also known by the name 'Loaf Mass', recognising the baking of the first of the new grain into bread.

Early August

The Burryman Traditional and still-observed ceremony in South Queensferry. The Burryman, a native of the town, is covered in burrs over his body and head, and is led through the town by attendants. The procession goes on for several hours. The ceremony apparently dates back to the 14th century.

Horse and Boys Ploughing Match At St Margaret's Hope in South Ronaldsay, this very old pre-harvest ritual sees elaborately dressed local youngsters mimicking horses and ploughmen as they 'plough' furrows on the beach.

Mid August

Edinburgh International Festival & Fringe High point of the Scots cultural year and an important event on the international arts calendar. The Edinburgh Festival has been running for over 50 years. The theatre, music, dance, revues, talks and exhibitions of the Festival and Fringe have been supplemented by the Television, Book and Film Festivals in recent years.

15 August
Marymas Bannocks were baked and eaten in honour of the Virgin Mary.

SEPTEMBER

First Saturday in September
Braemar Gathering Reputedly dating back to the 11th century, it was Queen Victoria who ensured the success of the highland games at Braemar by her attendance at them in 1848. The Royal family has been a feature of them ever since.

29th September
Michaelmas As patron saint of the sea and sailors, the feast of St Michael was enthusiastically celebrated, particularly in the west of Scotland. Several harvest celebrations coincided with St Michael's Day, often involving the baking of cakes made from newly harvested cereals.

OCTOBER

18th October
St Luke's Day or Sour Cakes Day A celebration linked to the Royal Burgh of Rutherglen, where cakes were baked and eaten with sour cream.

31st October
Halloween The evening of All Hallows' (or All Saints') Day and the last day of the year in the old Celtic calendar. Halloween was an early Christian festival grafted onto the Celtic festival of Samhain, which was both a feast of thanksgiving and of the dead. It is a night when ghosts, witches and all manner of evils are abroad and many of the Celtic rites associated with the day evolved into the trappings of Halloween, particularly 'guising' where children dressed up and went round neighbouring houses with 'tattie bogles' or 'neep lanterns' (candles inside hollowed-out turnips with ferocious carved faces). The old traditions of Halloween in Scotland have been swamped recently by the growth of the more sanitised and commercialised customs of the Americans' 'trick-or-treat'.

5th November
Guy Fawkes Night Commemorating the abortive Gunpowder Plot of Guido (Guy) Fawkes to blow up the Houses of Parliament in1605, the event is celebrated with fireworks and bonfires. In the days preceding it, the cry of 'penny for the guy' can often be heard (as children plead for money from passers-by in the street with an effigy of Fawkes). This is not a specifically Scottish festival although it is often overlooked that one of main reasons for Fawkes' attempted regicide was to 'blow the Scots back again into Scotland', i.e. the removal of the recently crowned James VI as joint ruler of both countries, along with his followers.

11th November
Martinmas The feast of St Martin, tutor to St Ninian, was the last Scottish quarter-day of the year when rents and contracts fell due. With fodder becoming scarce by this time of the tear, cattle were often killed at this time and salted meats and puddings prepared for the coming winter months.

30th November

St Andrew's Day The feast of Scotland's patron saint used to be widely celebrated but the day is not a public holiday in Scotland and St Andrew's Night is now celebrated more by expatriate Scots around the world than native Scots at home.

DECEMBER

24th December

Sowans Nicht This Christmas Eve tradition in some parts of Scotland derived from the eating of 'sowans', a dish made from oat husks and fine meal steeped in water.

25th December

Christmas Day Traditionally celebrated in medieval Scotland. But this stopped in the 16th century – the kill-joy fundamentalists of post-Reformation Scotland frowned on celebrations, and Christ's birth was no exception. Christmas was a working day in Scotland until the mid-20th century and has only recently re-emerged, this time on the back of international business and commercial practices.

26th December

The Mason's Walk Boxing Day is the feast of St John the Apostle and Evangelist and a source of Masonic celebration across Scotland. In Melrose, masons parade by torchlight around the market square before walking to the abbey to conduct a service.

31th December

Hogmanay Long treated as a more important festival in Scotland than Christmas, Hogmanay was seen as a time of preparation: houses were cleaned and business was concluded to let the new year start afresh. While in recent years, the growing commercialisation of Christmas has overshadowed Hogmanay, there has been a recent revival in its celebration with mass street parties, particularly in Edinburgh.

• HIGHLAND GAMES AND CELTIC FESTIVALS •

SCOTLAND

Location	Event	Usually Held
Aberdeen	Aberdeen Highland Games	July
Aberfeldy	Atholl & Breadalbane Highland Gathering	August
Aberlour	Aberlour-Blairmore Highland Games	August
Aboyne	Aboyne Highland Games	August
Airth	Airth Highland Games	July
Alexandria	Balloch & Loch Lomond Highland Games	July
Arbroath	Arbroath Highland Games	August
Ardrossan	Ardrossan Highland Games	June
Arisaig	Arisaig Highland Games	July
Auchinblae	Drumtochty Highland Games	June
Ballater	Ballater Highland Games	August
Bathgate	Bathgate & West Lothian Highland Games	May
Bearsden	Bearsden & Milngavie Highland Games	June

Location	Event	Usually Held
Beauly	Beauly Highland Games	June
Birnam	Birnam Highland Games	August
Blackford	Blackford Highland Games	May
Blair Atholl	Blair Atholl Highland Gathering	May
Blairgowrie	Blairgowrie Highland Games	September
Bonar Bridge	Invercharron Highland Games	September
Braemar	Braemar Royal Highland Gathering	September
Bridge of Allan	Bridge of Allan Highland Games	August
Brodick	Brodick Highland Games	August
Burntisland	Burntisland Highland Games	July
Bute	Isle of Bute Highland Games	August
Callander	Callander World Highland Games	July
Campbeltown	Southend Highland Games	July
Crieff	Penny's Crieff Highland Gathering	August
Cupar	Cupar Highland Games	July
Dingwall	Dingwall Highland Gathering	July
Dornoch	Dornoch Highland Gathering	August
Drumnadrochit	Glenurquhart Highland Gathering	August
Dufftown	Dufftown Highland Games	July
Dunbar	Dunbar Highland Games	May
Dunbeath	Dunbeath Highland Games	August
Dundee	Dundee Highland Games	July
Dunoon	Cowal Highland Gathering	August
Durness	Durness Highland Gathering	July
Edinburgh	Edinburgh Highland Games	July
Fochabers	Elgin Highland Games	July
Forfar	Forfar Highland Games	June
Forres	Forres Highland Games	July
Fort William	Lochaber Highland Games	July
Glenfinnan	Glenfinnan Gathering & Highland Games	August
Glenrothes	Glenrothes Highland Games	July
Grantown-on-Spey	Grantown-on-Spey Highland Games	June
Halkirk	Halkirk Highland Games	July
Helensburgh	Rosneath & Clynder Highland Games	July
Helmsdale	Helmsdale & District Highland Games	August
Inverary	Inverary Highland Games	July
Invergarry	Glengarry Highland Games	July
Invergordon	Invergordon Highland Gathering	August
Inverkeithing	Inverkeithing Highland Games	August
John o' Groats	Caithness Highland Gathering	August
Kenmore	Kenmore Highland Games	July
Killin	Killin Highland Games	July
Kilmore	Kilmore & Kilbride Highland Games	June
Lochaline	Morvern Highland Games	July
Lochcarron	Lochcarron Highland Games	July

Location	Event	Usually Held
Lochearnhead	Balquhidder, Lochearnhead & Strathyre Highland Games	July
Lochinver	Assynt Highland Games	August
Luss	Luss Highland Gathering	July
Mallaig	Mallaig & Morar Highland Games	August
Markinch	Markinch Highland Games	June
Montrose	Montrose Highland Games	August
Nairn	Nairn Highland Games	August
Nethy Bridge	Abernethy Highland Games	August
Newburgh	Newburgh Highland Games	June
Newtonmore	Newtonmore Highland Games	August
North Uist	North Uist Highland Games	July
Oban	Argyll Highland Games	August
Oldmeldrum	Oldmeldrum Sport & Highland Games	June
Peebles	Peebles Highland Games	September
Perth	Perth Highland Games	August
Pitlochry	Pitlochry Highland Games	September
Portree	Skye Highland Games	August
Shotts	Shotts Highland Games	June
South Uist	South Uist Highland Games	July
St Andrew's	St Andrew's Highland Games	July
Stirling	Stirling Highland Games	July
Stonehaven	Stonehaven Highland Games	July
Stornoway	Lewis Highland Games	July
Strathardle	Strathardle Highland Gathering	August
Strathdon	Lonach Gathering	August
Strathmiglo	Strathmiglo Highland Games	June
Strathpeffer	Strathpeffer Highland Gathering	August
Tain	Glenmorangie Tain Highland Gathering	August
Taynuilt	Taynuilt Highland Games	July
Thornton	Thornton Highland Games	July
Tobermory	Mull Highland Games	July
Tomintoul	Tomintoul Highland Games	July

AUSTRALIA

Location	Event	Usually Held
Berwick, Victoria	Berwick Highland Gathering	February
Bundanoon, NSW	Bundanoon Highland Games	March
Daylesford, Victoria	Daylesford Highland Gathering	December
Geelong, Victoria	Geelong Highland Gathering	March
Kapunda, S. Aust.	Kapunda Celtic Festival	April
Maclean, NSW	Maclean Highland Gathering	March
Newtown, NSW	Gaelic Day	August

Location	Event	Usually Held
Nunawading, Victoria	Nunawading Highland Gathering	March
Penrith, NSW	A Celtic Celebration	October
Ringwood, Victoria	Ringwood Highland Gathering	March
Ross, Tasmania	Ross Highland Games	March
Sydney, NSW	Celtic Australia Day Festival	January
Sydney, NSW	Sydney Highland Games	January

BARBADOS

Location	Event	Usually Held
Bridgetown & other sites	Barbados Celtic Festival & Highland Games	May

CANADA

Location	Event	Usually Held
Almonte, Ontario	North Lanark Highland Games	August
Ancaster, Ontario	Hamilton Tartan Games	May
Antigonish, Nova Scotia	Antigonish Highland Games	July
Antigonish, Nova Scotia	Atlantic Provinces Piping & Drumming Indoor Meet	July
Barrie, Ontario	Barrie Highland Games	July
Barrie, Ontario	Molson Highland Games	July
Bartibogue, NB	Miramichi Highland Gathering	July
Bedford, Nova Scotia	Metro Scottish Festival & Highland Games	July
Calgary, Alberta	Calgary Highland Games	September
Cambridge, Ontario	Cambridge Highland Games	July
Canmore, Alberta	Canmore Highland Games	September
Cape Breton, Nova Scotia	Celtic Colours International Festival	October
Chatham, Ontario	Chatham-Kent Supreme Highland Games	July
Coburg, Ontario	Coburg Highland Games	June
Cochrane, Alberta	Dancing in the Rockies Celtic Festival	October
Comox Valley, BC	Comox Valley Highland Games	May
Coquitlam, BC	Vancouver United Scottish Highland Games	June
Dutton, Ontario	Dutton Highland Games	June
Edmonton, Alberta	Edmonton Highland Games	July
Edmonton, Alberta	Northern Canadian Highland Dance Championships	July
Embro, Ontario	Zorra Caledonian Highland Games	June
Etobicoke, Ontario	CeltFest	April
Fergus, Ontario	Fergus Scottish Festival & Highland Games	August

Location	Event	Usually Held
Fort Edmonton, Alberta	Fort Edmonton Games	July
Fort Erie, Ontario	Loch Sloy Highland Games	June
Fredericton, NB	New Brunswick Highland Games	July
Georgetown, Ontario	Georgetown Highland Games	June
Grand Prairie, Alberta	Grand Prairie Highland Games	June
Haliburton, Ontario	Haliburton Highland Games	June
Halifax, Nova Scotia	Fiddles of the World	July
Halifax, Nova Scotia	Halifax Scottish Games	July
Halifax, Nova Scotia	Nova Scotia International Gathering of the Clans	June–July
Halifax, Nova Scotia	Nova Scotia International Tattoo	June
Keswick, Ontario	Georgina Highland Games	June
Kingston, Ontario	Kingston Celtic Festival	September
Maxville, Ontario	Glengarry Highland Games	July
Middleton, Nova Scotia	Annapolis Valley Highland Games	August
Montreal, Quebec	Montreal Highland Games	August
New Glasgow, Nova Scotia	Festival of the Tartans	July
Orillia, Ontario	Orillia Scottish Festival	July
Pictou, Nova Scotia	The Spirt Is Highland	September
Pugwash, Nova Scotia	Pugwash Gathering of the Clans	June
Red Deer, Alberta	Red Deer Highland Games	June
Sarnia, Ontario	Sarnia Highland Games	August
Saskatoon, Saskatchewan	Saskatoon Highland Games	May
Selkirk, Manitoba	Manitoba Highland Gathering	July
Sertoma, Ontario	Sertoma Highland Games	May
St Ann's, Nova Scotia	St Ann's Gaelic Mod	August
Summerside, PEI	Celtic Festival of Summerside	July
Uxbridge, Ontario	Highlands of Durham Games & Celtic Festival	July
Vancouver, BC	Sons of Scotland Highland Games	May
Victoria, BC	Victoria Highland Games	May
Winnipeg, Manitoba	Winnipeg Scottish Heritage Festival	June

FINLAND

Location	Event	Usually Held
Oulu	Highland Heavy Events World Championships	July

FRANCE

Location	Event	Usually Held
Lorient, Brittany	Festival Interceltique de Lorient	August
Lesneven, Brittany	Lesneven Celtic Gathering	April-May

JAPAN

Location	Event	Usually Held
Tokyo	Celtic Festival of Japan	October

NEW ZEALAND

Location	Event	Usually Held
Dunedin	Dunedin International Scottish Gathering	November
Dunedin	Scottish Week	March
Fairlie	Hamilton Highland Games	December
Havelock North	Hastings Highland Games	April
Hawkes Bay	Hawkes Bay Easter Highland Games	April
Palmerston North	NZ Pipe Band Championships	March
Remura, Auckland	Auckland Highland Games & Gathering	November
Tauranga	Tauranga Highland Games	March
Temuka	Temuka Caledonian Games	January
Turakina, Rangitikei	Turakina Highland Games	January
Waipu	Waipu Caledonian Society Highland Games	January

SOUTH AFRICA

Location	Event	Usually Held
Amanzimtoti	Natal South Coast Gathering	May
Durban	Natal Scottish Gathering	April
Johannesburg	Northern Johannesburg Caledonian Society Gathering	May
Johannesburg	Royual Scottish Gathering	September
Port Elizabeth	Eastern Cape Gathering	April
Pretoria	Pretoria Caledonian Society Gathering	June
Rosettenville	Southern Johannesburg Caledonian Society Gathering	June

UNITED STATES

Location	Event	Usually Held
Eagle River, AK	Alaska Scottish Highland Games	June
Jasper, AL	Jasper Highland Games & Irish Festival	April
Huntsville, AL	North Alabama Scottish Festival	June
Montgomery, AL	Alabama Highland Games	September
Batesville, AR	Ozark Scottish Festival	April
Hot Springs, AR	Mid-American Celtic Festival & Scottish Highland Games	Nov

Location	Event	Usually Held
Maumelle, AR	Festival of the Scots	October
Flagstaff, AZ	Arizona Highland Celtic Festival	July
Mesa, AZ	Arizona Scottish Gathering & Highland Games	February
Tucson, AZ	Tucson Celtic Festival & Scottish Highland Games	November
Bakersfield, CA	Kern County Annual Scottish Gathering & Games	April
Ben Lomond, CA	Loch Lomond Highland Games	October
Campbell, CA	Campbell Highland Games & Celtic Gathering	June
Chino, CA	Pacific Highland Gathering & Games	October
Corte Madera, CA	Marin County Highland Gathring	May
Costa Mesa, CA	United Scottish Society of S California Scottish Festival	May
Long Beach, CA	Queen Mary Scottish Festival	February
Madera, CA	Fresno Highland Games & Gathering	September
Mariposa, CA	Mariposa Highland Games & Celtic Festival	May
Modesto, CA	Modesto Highland Games	June
Monterey, CA	Monterey Scottish Festival Highland Games	May
Oakland, CA	Oakland Scottish Highland Games	July
Pleasanton, CA	Scottish Games & Gathering	September
San Francisco, CA	Caledonian Club of San Francisco Scottish Gathering & Games	June
San Luis Obispo, CA	Central Coast Gathering & Games	May
Vista, CA	San Diego Scottish Highland Games	June
Woodland, CA	Sacramento Valley Scottish Games & Gathering	April
Colorado Springs, CO	Pikes Peak Highland Games & Celtic Festival	July
Estes Park, CO	Long's Peak Scottish Highland Festival	September
Grand Junction, CO	Celtic Festival & Highland Games	September
Highlands Ranch, CO	Colorado Scottish Festival & Rocky Mountain Highland Games	Aug
Kiowa, CO	Kiowa Highland Games	May
Sheridan, CO	Colorado Scottish Clan Highland Games	June
Casselberry, FL	Central Florida Scottish Highland Games	January
Dunedin, FL	Dunedin Highland Games & Festival	April
Fort Lauderdale, FL	Southeast Florida Scottish Festival & Games	March
Jacksonville, FL	Jacksonville Scottish Highland Games	February
Tallahassee, FL	Tallahassee Scottish Highland Games & Celtic Festival	October
Culloden, GA	Culloden Highland Games & Scottish Festival	April
Savannah, GA	Savannah Scottish Games & Highland Gathering	May
Shellman, GA	Shellman Georgia Highland Games	November
Stone Mountain, GA	Stone Mountain Highland Games	October
Garden City, ID	Treasure Valley Celtic Festival & Highland Games	October
Oak Brook, IL	Illinois St Andrew's Highland Games	June
Rockford, IL	Rockford Scottish Highland Games	July
Springfield, IL	Springfield Highland Games & Celtic Festival	May
Columbus, IN	Columbus Scottish Festival	July

Location	Event	Usually Held
Fort Wayne, IN	Indiana Highland Games	July
McPherson, KS	McPherson Scottish Festival & Highland Games	September
Lucas, KY	Glasgow Highland Games	June
Jackson, LA	Highland Games of Louisiana	November
Brunswick, ME	Maine Highland Games	August
Fair Hill, MD	Colonial Highland Gathering	May
Brimfield, MA	Western Massachusetts Highland Games & Celtic Festival	June
Alma, MI	Alma Highland Festival & Games	May
Livonia, MI	St Andrew's Society of Detroit Highland Games	August
Jackson, MS	Scottish Highland Games of Mississippi	August
Kansas City, MO	Kansas City Scottish Highland Games	June
Glasgow, MT	Glasgow Montana Highland Games	September
Missoula, MT	Missoula Highland Games & Gathering of the Clans	August
Lincoln, NH	New Hampshire Highland Games	September
Albuquerque, NM	Rio Grande Valley Celtic Festival & Highland Games	May
Amherst, NY	Amherst Museum Scottish Festival & Highland Games	August
Altamont, NY	Capital District Scottish Games	September
Liverpool, NY	Central New York Scottish Games	August
Old Westbury, NY	Long Island Scottish Games	August
Archdale, NC	Triad Highland Games	August
Huntersville, NC	Loch Norman Highland Games	April
Linville, NC	Grandfather Mountain Highland Games	July
Red Springs, NC	Flora MacDonald Highland Games	October
Oberlin, OH	Ohio Scottish Games Weekend	June
Midwest City, OK	USCO Scottish Heritage Festival	March
Tulsa, OK	Oklahoma Scottish Games & Gathering	September
Gresham, OR	Portland Scottish Highland Games	July
Bethlehem, PA	Celtic Classic Highland Games & Festival	October
Carlisle, PA	McLain Highland Festival	September
Devon, PA	Delco Scottish Games	June
Ligonier, PA	Ligonier Highland Games	September
Mount Pleasant, SC	Charleston Scottish Games & Highland Gathering	September
Gatlinburg, TN	Gatlinburg Scottish Festival & Games	May
Amarillo, TX	League of Celtic Nations Festival	August
San Antonio, TX	San Antonio Highland Games	April
Salt Lake City, UT	Utah Scottish Festival & Highland Games	June
Alexandria, VA	Virginia Scottish Games & Gathering of the Clans	July
Chesapeake, VA	Hampton Roads Highland Games	June
Fredericksburg, VA	Fredericksburg Intl. Scottish Highland Games & Irish Festival	June

Location	Event	Usually Held
Richmond, VA	Richmond Highland Games & Celtic Festival	October
Ferndale, WA	Bellingham & Whatcom County Highland Games	June
Enumclaw, WA	Pacific Northwest Scottish Highland Games	July
Graham, WA	Tacoma-Pierce County Highland Games	June
Kelso, WA	Kelso Highlander Festival	September
Mount Vernon, WA	Skagit Valley Highland Games & Scottish Faire	July
Glendale, WI	MIlwaukee Highland Games & Scottish Festivals	June

FOOD AND DRINK

• TRADITIONAL SCOTS FOODS •

A GLOSSARY

Arbroath smokies Smoke-cured fish, unlike Finnan haddock they need no more cooking. They are gutted with the heads removed, though kept closed, and are smoked in pairs

Bannock Cake or bread baked from barley flour or oatmeal; formerly cooked with no raising agent

Bashed Mashed

Bawd Hare

Black Bun Spiced cake wrapped in a short pastry dough

Bree Soup

Bridie Pastry casing for meat filling, traditionally flavoured with beef dripping

Brose Oatmeal or barley cooked with milk or water from the vegetables or meat

Chappit tatties Mashed potatoes

Clabbie dubhs Derived from the Gaelic, this shellfish's name translates as 'big black mouth'. Otherwise known as horse mussels.

Clapshot Potatoes and turnips

Clootie dumpling A fruit dumpling boiled in a cloth ('cloot'), often made with oatmeal instead of breadcrumbs

Cock-a-leekie Chicken and leek soup

Collops Thin slices of meat, usually from the leg

Cranachan Whisky, heather honey, toasted oatmeal and soft-fruit pudding

Crappit heids Haddock heads stuffed with fish intestines and boiled in fish stock

Crowdie Cottage cheese

Cullen skink Soup of Finnan haddie with milk and potatoes

Dundee cake Whisky-flavoured fruit cake studded with almonds

Edinburgh rock Pastel-coloured, crumbly candy sticks

Finnan haddie Smoke-cured haddock with no added dye; the fish are gutted, heads removed and split open

Haggis The classic haggis recipe was given in *The Simpsons* by Willie the Groundskeeper as follows: 'Chopped heart and lungs, boiled in a wee sheep's stomach! Tastes as good as it sounds!'

Heid (as in Potted heid) Head, usually of a sheep

Hough Shin of beef

Mealy pudding Black or white puddings made from animal intestines

Neep Turnip (swede or rutabaga)

Partan Crab

Porridge Oatmeal boiled in water
Potted Moulded, set and jellied
Rumbledethumps Mixed potatoes, onion and cabbage, topped with cheese and
  grilled
Selkirk bannock Rich, fruit, yeasted bannock
Shortbread Baked plain short biscuit made of flour, butter and sugar in 6-4-2 pro-
  portions
Skink A soup of vegetables boiled in a beef stock
Skirlie Onion and oatmeal fried with dripping
Sloke Laverbread
Spoots Razor fish
Stovies Potatoes cooked au gratin
Sugar-ally Liquorice
Tablet Candy made of condensed milk, butter and sugar; harder than fudge but
  crumblier than toffee

• MALT WHISKY •

A REGIONAL GUIDE

Malt whiskies are categorised by region of origin – different regions, with
their different geographical and geological attributes, as well as their different
climates, are recognised to produce whiskies whose tastes are recognisably
distinct. The lists below show the main categories.

Campbeltown
Glen Scotia
Longrow
Springbank

Highland
Aberfeldy
Balbalir
Banff
Ben Nevis
Blair Athol
Clynelish
The Dalmore
Dalwhinnie
Deanston
The Edradour
Glen Albyn
Glencadam
Glen Deveron
Glen Garioch

Highland (cont'd)
Glengoyne
Glenlochy
Glen Mhor
Glenmorangie
Glen Ord
The Glenturret
Glenugie
Inchmurrin
Lochside
Millburn
North Port
Oban
Old Fettercairn
Old Pulteney
Royal Brackla
Royal Lochangar
Teaninich
Tomatin
Tullibardine

Speyside*
Aberlour
An Cnoc
Ardmore
Aultmore
Balmenach
The Balvenie
Benriach
Benrinnes
Benromach
Caperdonich
Cardhu
Coleburn
Convalmore
Cragganmore
Craigellachie
Dailuaine
Dufftown
Glenburgie
Glendronach
Glendullan
Glenfarclas
Glenfiddich
Glen Grant
Glen Keith
The Glenlivet
Glenlossie
Glen Moray
The Glen Rothes
Glentauchers
Imperial
Inchgower
Knockando
Linkwood
Longmorn
The Macallan

Speyside (cont'd)
Miltonduff
Mortlach
Pittyvaich
The Singleton of Auchroisk
Speyburn
Strathisla
Tamdhu
Tamnavulin
Tomintoul
Tormore

Islands
Highland Park
Isle of Jura
Ledaig
Scapa
Talisker
Tobermory

Islay
Ardbeg
Bowmore
Bruichladdich
Bunnahabhain
Caol Ila
Lagavulin
Laphroaig
Port Ellen

Lowlands
Auchentoshan
Bladnoch
Glenkinchie
Inverleven
Littlemill
Rosebank
St Magdalene

* Although Speyside is in the Highlands, it is treated as a sub-category as its whiskies are quite distinctive

• MALT WHISKY •

A PRONUNCIATION GUIDE

Many of the famous whiskies listed above have names whose pronunciation baffles not just non-Scots, but even many natives, with their intimidating combinations of 'b's, 'd's and 'h's. The guide below gives pointers on how to ask for what you want without embarrassment.

Remember that 'ch' is, generally speaking, not pronounced at the front of the mouth (as in 'chips') but at the back, as in German pronunciation. Underlinings indicate where the emphasis falls

Whisky name	Pronunciation	Whisky name	Pronunciation
Aberlour	Aber-lower (as in 'flower')	Glen Mhor	Glen Voar
		Glenmorangie	Glen-moranjee
Auchentoshan	Ochen-toshan	Glentauchers	Glen-tochers
Auchroisk (Singleton of)	Othrusk	Islay	Eye-la
Balmenach	Bal-mey-nach	Laphroaig	La-froyg
Bruichladdich	Brew-ich-laddie	Ledaig	Led-chig
Bunnahabhain	Boon-a-haavun	Old Pulteney	Old Pult-nay
Caol Ila	Kaal-eea	Pittyvaich	Pitt-ee-vay-ich
Cardhu	Kar-doo	St Magdalene	St Magdaleen
Clynelish	Kline-leesh	Strathisla	Strath-eye-la
Craigellachie	Krai-gellachy	Tamdhu	Tam-doo
Dailuaine	Dall-you-an	Tamnavulin	Tamna-voo-lin
Edradour	Edra-dower (as in 'flower')	Teaninich	Tee-an-inich
		Tomintoul	Tomin-towel
Glen Garioch	Glen Gee-ree	Tullibardine	Tully-bard-eyn

• WHISKY DISTILLERIES •

A VISITOR'S GUIDE

The distilleries in the list that follows can be visited at present, although visitor facilities vary greatly: some are open by appointment only while others have full-scale visitor centres. Intending visitors should always call ahead.

Aberfeldy Distillery, Aberfeldy, Perthshire; Tel: 01887-822000
Ardbeg Distillery, Port Ellen, Islay; Tel: 01496-302244
Ardmore Distillery, Kennethmont, Aberdeenshire; Tel: 01464-3213
Auchroisk Distillery, Mulben, Banffshire; Tel: 01542-8606333
Aultmore Distillery, Aultmore, Keith, Banffshire; Tel: 01542-882762

Ben Nevis Distillery, Lochy Bridge, Fort William; Tel: 01397-700200

Benrinnes Distillery, Aberlour, Banffshire; Tel: 01340-871215

Blair Athol Distillery, Pitlochry, Perthshire; Tel: 01796-482003

Bowmore Distillery, Bowmore, Islay; Tel: 01496-810441

Bunnahabhain Distillery, Port Askaig, Islay; Tel: 01496-840646

Caol Ila Distillery, Port Askaig, Islay; Tel: 01496-302760

Cardhu Distillery, Knockando, Moray; Tel: 01340-810204

Clynelish Distillery, Brora, Sutherland; Tel: 01408-623000

Coleburn Distillery, Longmorn, Elgin, Moray; Tel: 01398-700200

Dallas Dhu Historic Distillery, Mannachie Road, Forres, Morayshire; Tel: 01309-676548

Dalmore Distillery, Alness, Ross-shire; Tel: 01349-882362

Dalwhinnie Distillery, Dalwhinnie, Inverness-shire; Tel: 01528 522208

Dufftown Distillery, Dufftown, Keith, Banffshire; Tel: 01340-820224

Edradour Distillery, Pitlochry, Perthshire; Tel: 01796-472095

Fettercairn Distillery, Laurencekirk, Kincardineshire; Tel: 01561-340205

The Glenburgie-Glenlivet Distillery, Forres, Moray; Tel: 01343-850258

Glen Grant Distillery, Rothes, Morayshire; Tel: 01542 783 318

Glen Keith Distillery, Keith, Banffshire; Tel: 01542-783042

Glen Moray Distillery, Elgin, Moray; Tel: 01343-542577

Glen Ord Distillery, Muir of Ord, Ross-shire; Tel: 01463 872004

Glencadam Distillery, Brechin, Angus; Tel: 01356 622 217

Glendronach Distillery, Forgue, By Huntly, Aberdeenshire; Tel: 01466-730202

Glendullan Distillery, Dufftown, Keith, Banffshire; Tel: 01340-820250

Glenfarclas Distillery, Ballindalloch, Speyside; Tel: 01807-500245/500209

Glenfiddich Distillery, Dufftown, Banffshire; Tel: 01340-820373

Glengoyne Distillery, Dumgoyne, Near Killearn, Stirlingshire; Tel: 01360-550254;
    website: www.glengoyne.com

Glenkinchie Distillery, Pencaitland, East Lothian; Tel: 01875-342004

The Glenlivet Distillery, Glenlivet; Tel: 01542-783220

Glenlossie-Glenlivet Distillery, Birnie, Elgin, Moray; Tel: 01343-86331

Glenmorangie Distillery, Tain, Ross-shire; Tel: 01862-892477

Glentauchers Distillery, Mulben, Banffshire; Tel: 01542-860272

Glenturret Distillery, The Hosh, Crieff, Perthshire; Tel: 01764-657008;
    website: www.glenturret.com

Highland Park Distillery, Kirkwall, Orkney; Tel: 01856-820619

Inchgower Distillery, Buchan, Banffshire; Tel: 01542-831161

Isle of Arran Distillery, Lochranza, Arran; Tel: 01770-830264

Isle of Jura Distillery, Craighouse, Jura; Tel: 01496-820240

Knockando Distillery, Knockando, Aberlour, Banffshire; Tel: 01340-6205

Lagavulin Distillery, Port Ellen, Islay; Tel: 01496-302400

Laphroaig Distillery, Port Ellen, Islay; Tel: 01496-302418

Linkwood Distillery, Elgin, Moray; Tel: 01343-547004

Macallan Distillery, Craigellachie, Banffshire; Tel: 01340-871471

Macduff Distillery (Glendeveron), Banff, Banffshire; Tel: 01261-812612

Miltonduff-Glenlivet Distillery, Elgin, Moray; Tel: 01343-547433

Mortlach Distillery, Dufftown, Keith, Banffshire; Tel: 01340-820318

Oban Distillery, Oban, Argyllshire; Tel: 01631-572004

Royal Brackla Distillery, Cawdor, Nairnshire; Tel: 016677-404280

Royal Lochnagar Distillery, Crathie, Ballater, Aberdeenshire; Tel: 01339-742273

Scapa Distillery, Kirkwall, Orkney; Tel: 01856-872071

Springbank Distillery, Campbeltown, Argyll; Tel: 01586-552085

Strathisla Distillery, Keith, Banffshire; Tel: 01542-783044

Talisker Distillery, Carbost, Skye; Tel: 01478-640314

Teaninich Distillery, Alness, Ross-shire; Tel: 01349-882461

Tobermory Distillery, Tobermory, Mull; Tel: 01688 302645

Tomatin Distillery, Tomatin, Inverness-shire; Tel: 01808-511444

Tormore Distillery, Advie, Grantown-on-Spey, Moray; Tel: 01807-510244

Tullibardine Distillery, Blackford, Perthshire; Tel: 01764 682 252

SCOTS MEASURES, WEIGHTS & MONEY

The charts below show equivalent measures and amounts across all three columns. Scots measures and weights varied according to the area standards used; those given here are typical.

• SCOTS MEASURES (1707) •

LIQUID MEASURE

Scots	Equivalent Imperial	Equivalent Metric
1 gill	0.749 gill	0.053 l
4 gills = 1 mutchkin	2.996 gills	0.212 l
2 mutchkins = 1 chopin	1 pint 1.992 gills	0.848 l
2 chopins = 1 pint*	2 pints 3.984 gills	1.696 l
8 pints = 1 gallon	3 gallons 0.25 gills	13.638 l
*1 pint = 104.2034 cub ins	1 pint = 34.659 cub ins	1 litre = 61.027 cub ins

DRY MEASURE (FOR WHEAT, PEAS, BEANS & MEAL)

Scots	Equivalent Imperial	Equivalent Metric
1 lippie (or forpet)	0.499 gallons	2.268 l
4 lippies = I peck	1.996 gallons	9.072 l
4 pecks = 1 firlot*	3 pecks 1.986 galls	36.286 l
4 firlots = 1 boll	3 bushels 3 pecks 1.944 galls	145.145 l
16 bolls = 1 chalder	7 quarters 7 bushels 3 pecks	2322.324 l
*1 firlot = 2214.322 cub ins	1 gallon = 277.274 cub ins	1 litre = 61.027 cub ins

DRY MEASURE (FOR BARLEY, OATS & MALT)

Scots	Equivalent Imperial	Equivalent Metric
1 lippie (or forpet)	0.728 galls	3.037 l
4 lippies = 1 peck	1 peck 0.912 galls	13.229 l
4 pecks = 1 firlot*	1 bushel 1 peck 1.65 galls	52.916 l
4 flrlots = 1 boll	5 bushels 3 pecks 0.6 galls	211.664 l
16 bolls = 1 chalder	11 quarters 5 bushels 1.615 galls	3386.624 l
*1 firlot = 3230.305 cub ins		

Linear & Square Measures, Weights and Money continue on p. 222

• SCOTTISH BANKS •

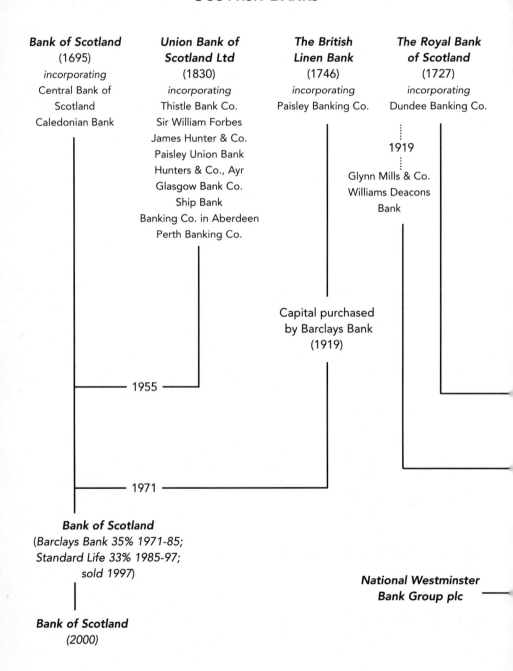

Bank of Scotland
(1695)
incorporating
Central Bank of
Scotland
Caledonian Bank

**Union Bank of
Scotland Ltd**
(1830)
incorporating
Thistle Bank Co.
Sir William Forbes
James Hunter & Co.
Paisley Union Bank
Hunters & Co., Ayr
Glasgow Bank Co.
Ship Bank
Banking Co. in Aberdeen
Perth Banking Co.

**The British
Linen Bank**
(1746)
incorporating
Paisley Banking Co.

**The Royal Bank
of Scotland**
(1727)
incorporating
Dundee Banking Co.

1919

Glynn Mills & Co.
Williams Deacons
Bank

Capital purchased
by Barclays Bank
(1919)

1955

1971

Bank of Scotland
*(Barclays Bank 35% 1971-85;
Standard Life 33% 1985-97;
sold 1997)*

Bank of Scotland
(2000)

**National Westminster
Bank Group plc**

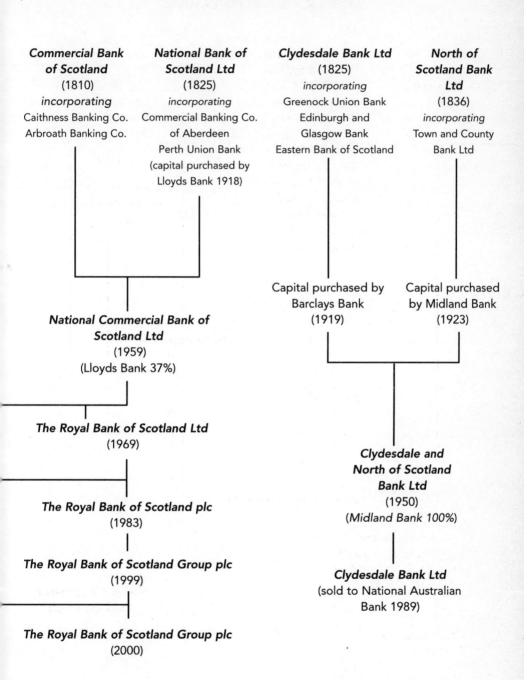

Commercial Bank of Scotland
(1810)
incorporating
Caithness Banking Co.
Arbroath Banking Co.

National Bank of Scotland Ltd
(1825)
incorporating
Commercial Banking Co.
of Aberdeen
Perth Union Bank
(capital purchased by
Lloyds Bank 1918)

Clydesdale Bank Ltd
(1825)
incorporating
Greenock Union Bank
Edinburgh and
Glasgow Bank
Eastern Bank of Scotland

North of Scotland Bank Ltd
(1836)
incorporating
Town and County
Bank Ltd

National Commercial Bank of Scotland Ltd
(1959)
(Lloyds Bank 37%)

Capital purchased by
Barclays Bank
(1919)

Capital purchased
by Midland Bank
(1923)

The Royal Bank of Scotland Ltd
(1969)

The Royal Bank of Scotland plc
(1983)

Clydesdale and North of Scotland Bank Ltd
(1950)
(*Midland Bank 100%*)

The Royal Bank of Scotland Group plc
(1999)

Clydesdale Bank Ltd
(sold to National Australian
Bank 1989)

The Royal Bank of Scotland Group plc
(2000)

LINEAR & SQUARE MEASURES

Scots	Equivalent Imperial	Equivalent Metric
1 inch	1.0016 in	2.54 cm
8.88 in = 1 Scots link	8.8942 in	22.55 cm
12 in = 1 foot	12.0192 in	30.5287 cm
$3^1/_{12}$ feet = 1 ell	37.0598 in ($1^1/_{37}$ yards)	94.1318 cm
6 ells = 1 fall (fa)	6.1766 yards (1.123 poles)	5.6479 m
4 falls = 1 chain	24.7064 yrd (1.123 chains)	22.5916 m
10 chains = 1 furlong	247.064 yrd (1.123 furlongs)	225.916 m
8 furlongs = 1 mile	1976.522 yrd (1.123 miles)	1.8073 km

• SCOTS WEIGHTS (1707) •

Scots	Equivalent Avoirdupois	Equivalent Metric
1 drop	1.093 drains	1.921 g
16 drops = 1 ounce	1 oz 1.5 drains	31 g
16 ounces = 1 pound	1 lb 1 oz 8 drains	496 g
16 pounds = I stone	17 lb 8 oz	7.936 kg

• SCOTS MONEY (1707) •

Scots	Equivalent Sterling
1 penny	$1/_{12}$ penny
2 pennies = 1 bodle	$1/_6$ penny
2 bodles = 1 plack	$1/_3$ penny
3 bodles = 1 bawbee	$1/_2$ penny
2 bawbees = 1 shilling	1 penny
13 shillings 4 pence = 1 merk	1 shilling $1^1/_2$ pennies
20 shillings = 1 pound	1 shilling 8 pennies